CHINESE RAILWAYS AND BRITISH INTERESTS

1898–1911

CHINESE RAILWAYS AND BRITISH INTERESTS 1898-1911

by E-tu Zen Sun

KING'S CROWN PRESS
COLUMBIA UNIVERSITY, NEW YORK, 1954

KING'S CROWN PRESS
is an imprint established by Columbia University Press for the purpose of making certain scholarly material available at minimum cost. Toward that end, the publishers have used standardized formats incorporating every reasonable economy that does not interfere with legibility. The author has assumed responsibility for editorial style and for proofreading.

PUBLISHED IN GREAT BRITAIN, CANADA, INDIA, AND PAKISTAN
BY GEOFFREY CUMBERLEGE, OXFORD UNVERSITY PRESS
LONDON, TORONTO, BOMBAY, AND KARACHI

MANUFACTURED IN THE UNITED STATES OF AMERICA

LIBRARY OF CONGRESS CATALOG CARD NUMBER: 54-12129

To My Parents

Foreword

THE QUESTION of China's adjustment to the modern world involves two aspects of her national life. On the one hand the essential factor is how the various elements in China reacted to the situation of change, and how the forces of modernization were affected by the traditional, pre-industrial society. On the other hand the role played by the great powers, and the process and methods by which they sought to establish and maintain their interests in China, are a necessary part of the picture.

The following chapters attempt to discern the interrelationship of these factors through a detailed examination of a specific phase of Sino-Western intercourse: the railway movement in China during the last years of the Ch'ing dynasty, and its relations with Britain, the leading commercial and financial power in East Asia. It is hoped that the material contained in this volume will give some idea as to how the more articulate Chinese policy makers dealt with the problems of their times. The writings and papers of persons who were directly involved in the railway question, as well as the collections of official documents, have yielded much useful information. The railway problem was only one single aspect of the complex process that marked China's evolution during the past half century, yet it is a highly significant aspect; others in the politico-economic history of modern China still await investigation.

The division of the material into geographic units is deliberate but, I trust, not arbitrary. It is done chiefly because of two considerations. First, local conditions differed in the various parts of China, and each set of conditions left its own effects on railway development in the particular region concerned, such as, for example, the different degrees of gentry interest in south and north China. Secondly, within the framework of the contemporary "spheres of interest" power politics, geographic delimitation was an important factor that contributed to the final results. The present plan has been adopted, therefore, to facilitate the narrative and to highlight the specific problems that were encountered in the negotiations with regard to individual railways.

It is my privilege to express here my gratitude to Professors David E. Owen and John K. Fairbank of Harvard University, from whom I received much valuable advice and encouragement during the first phase of the present study when it was being carried out as a doctoral dissertation. I am indebted to Professor Knight Biggerstaff of Cornell University for reading the manuscript and giving me his criticisms and comments, and to Professor Sidney Painter of the Johns Hopkins University, who has given me many helpful suggestions from the point of view of a Western historian. Further, I wish to thank the following for the help and cooperation they have extended to me: Dr. A. K. Chiu and staff of the Library of the Harvard-Yenching Institute, who were always ready to make available to me the facilities of the Chinese collection; the Director of the Houghton Library, Harvard University, who has given me permission to use in the present volume material gathered from the manuscript collections there; and the editors of the *Far Eastern Quarterly,* who have kindly permitted me to incorporate in Chapter III some material from an article of mine published in that journal. Thanks are due my friend Mrs. Richard G. King, who skillfully and patiently prepared the manuscript. Finally, I am grateful to Shiou-Chuan Sun, my husband, whose sympathetic understanding made possible the completion of this volume.

E-TU ZEN SUN

State College, Pennsylvania
1953

Contents

Maps

CHINESE RAILWAYS AND BRITISH INTERESTS 1898–1911

Introduction

THE STUDY of railway enterprise in modern China can be undertaken from several points of view. It may be treated as a problem of finance, wherein the predominant concern would be loans, interest payments and the administration of revenues. Again, railway enterprise may be analyzed as a phase of the advance in technological civilization in China. In this context the gradually growing number of miles of tracks and their increasing penetration into the various parts of the country, the training of personnel and the utilization of domestic and foreign materials, would be the chief points of interest. Still another approach, however, touches on more fundamental issues. From this point of view the railway figures not only as the means of rapid modern communication, but also as a steel prop with which a nation tried to bolster the dilapidated structure of an old politico-economic system, and as such it became an integral part of the structure. Since the objectives of the railway were so far-reaching, and since the relation between China and the Great Powers existed on an unequal basis, it was inevitable that foreign manufacturers of this prop should enter the scene, and put in a claim to share in the benefits resulting from the house-repairing. This last approach is the one that will be followed in the present study: on the one hand, the railway is considered in the context of China's efforts at modernization, and on the other hand its role in China's foreign relations will be investigated.

The development of Chinese railways had, from their earliest days in the 1870's, been closely entangled with foreign interests. Of these, the British predominated, owing to

Britain's leading position in Chinese foreign trade and to long British contact with China. When considered against the background of British economy as a whole, railway investments in China could be seen to fall into their place in the over-all picture of capital movements and to assume a pertinent role. For British investments abroad were increasing in large proportions, so that by the turn of the century they amounted to approximately half of the current savings in Britain. These were handled by many banks which dealt specially with foreign areas, but which had directing boards that met in London. The Hongkong and Shanghai Banking Corporation, for instance, was one such institution, and it was the most important financial agent representing British railway interests in China. Railways constituted a large share of the total amount of British investments abroad. In addition to the high interest returns that accrued from all investments in foreign lands, railway investments also had the immediate result of bringing substantial orders for construction material, rolling stock, and so on, to British manufacturers. Indeed, it was judged that "in the Railway Age, the development of foreign and colonial railway systems abroad out of British capital, when British materials, British savings, and British engineering enterprise were opening up the world for the supply of food and raw materials, was greatly in the interest of this country as well as of the world." [1]

Beyond economic considerations, railway concessions in China were also matters of grave political concern to the British. The British Empire was undergoing basic changes in both its internal policy and external relations. These changes were, in part, inspired and intensified by the competition offered by the rise of other industrial and imperialist powers in the 1880's and '90's with the result that the British mercantile community and the London government began to feel anxious for Britain's position in China. In this con-

BRITISH-FINANCED CHINESE RAILWAYS IN 1911

text, then, an investigation of British interest in Chinese railways must deal with the problem not only as a branch of British investments abroad, but more especially as a manifestation of Britain's world interest. The importance of her stake in the railways was often beyond the measure of shillings and pence; it was not merely a question of her relation with China. The railway was a major issue in the relations of the Great Powers in China. This will be the basis upon which British activities regarding Chinese railways are examined in the following chapters.

The choice of the years 1898–1911 as the period for special study is based on several considerations. Foreign acquisition of railway rights in China reached a climax in 1898, and concessions for six of the railroads discussed here were obtained by Britain in that year. The making of the preliminary agreements is therefore a necessary part of the story. Then followed a decade (1902–1911) of Chinese and foreign efforts at control of the railway system. This was when certain elements in China asserted a positive voice in railway matters, when the Ch'ing dynasty in its last years was making an effort at modernization, and when new international balances were defined in the Far East. The railway came to be the meeting point of Chinese national aspirations and the politics of international equilibrium.

In tracing the course of Anglo-Chinese railway loan negotiations in our period, more than merely the specific loan terms are uncovered. A striking revelation is the kind of problems that a nonindustrial society had to face when confronted with the task of major modern undertakings, such as a main rail line. The questions of the raising of necessary funds, of the allocation of executive power, of interrelations with the various parts of the country and with various industries feeding the railway—all these would have presented difficulties to be solved. Add to this the financial domination of the British, and the situation then affected both the internal and external relationships of Chinese society. However, for the British investors themselves the question was no less complex. Not only did they have to contend with a growing Chinese interest in the railways, but they also had to be alert to changes in the over-all needs of the British Empire, and be ready to adjust their financial policy in China in accordance with the pattern of world diplomacy.

THE BRITISH SHARE

Among the British mercantile and colonial community, a belief prevailed through the nineteenth and into the twentieth century, that China was a field specially reserved for the comfortable expansion of British interest and British influence, because, it was argued, the world owed the opening of China to "English treasure and blood."[2] That belief was the result of Britain's unchallenged commercial hegemony during the nineteenth century. But in the late 1890's, the onrush of imperialist competition caused the British merchants to shudder at the vision of a fall from their high position. At the same time the huge potential value of the Chinese market figured importantly in British calculations. For instance, the foreign trade of China, though small in volume, was steadily increasing, in 1899 reaching a new high level with an increase of 25 per cent over the previous year; the British share in both the direct trade and the carrying trade also steadily and proportionately increased.[3] Besides being the period of great export of capital from Britain, it was a time, also, when British industry was beginning to depend more heavily on the nonindustrialized countries for some items of staple export, such as cotton goods.[4] But now the prospect of an ever expanding China interest, and the creation of a "Yangtse Protectorate" was threatened by foreign competition, and both the British merchant community and the London Foreign Office became alarmed. If an "almost panicky feeling" was seizing the European Powers at that time, and if the Continental economists "regarded the question of expansion as nothing less than a question of life and death," [5] the British had reason to feel more desperate not only for what they might or might not gain, but also for fear of what they might lose to the other powers.

In this atmosphere the "battle for concessions" was conducted. The political preponderance of Russia and, to a lesser extent, of Germany at Peking was deeply resented by the British, a sentiment well demonstrated by the bitter tone employed by the British minister at Peking, Sir Claude MacDonald.[6] Thus it was that when the Peking-Hankow Railway concession was granted to a Belgian syndicate some six months after the British had obtained the Yangtse non-alienation assurance from the Tsungli Yamen (the office in charge of foreign affairs in the Peking government), the British retaliated and obtained a series of railway and mining concessions.[7] Judging from the correspondence between London and the British Legation in Peking in those days, it could hardly be maintained that Whitehall was negligent in the matter of its Chinese interests. For both economic and political reasons MacDonald was instructed to press demands for various concessions on the Peking government, in order that Britain might have a more material basis for challenging the preponderance of other European nations in the Far Eastern balance of power.

British railway acquisitions in 1898 included projected lines that traversed the territories of ten provinces, from Honan and Shantung on the North China Plain, to Kiangsu and Chekiang on the Lower Yangtse, and Kwangtung and Yunnan in the south and southwest.[8] Geographically they constituted a group of widely scattered holdings that threatened the interests of other powers in various parts of China.

The British firms active in the field of concession hunting were few in number, and in form they were all private concerns. Foremost among them were the Hongkong and Shanghai Banking Corporation, and Jardine, Matheson and Company, leading financial and shipping houses in the Orient. In 1898 they combined forces to form the British and Chinese Corporation, Ltd., in order to compete more effectively with the German financial group in China, especially in railway matters.[9] This was the agency that obtained most of the British railway concessions that year—the Shanghai-Nanking, Canton-Kowloon, Soochow-Hangchow-Ningpo, and Pukou-Sinyang lines, and part interest in the Tientsin-Chinkiang Railway; it became the "chosen instrument" of the British government in China.[10] The other firm of importance in 1898 was the Peking Syndicate, an English company founded in London in 1897, initiated by an Italian named Luzatti. This Syndicate obtained the Honan and Shansi mining rights and the right to construct a railway for the transportation of mineral products to the Yangtse. From January 1904 to the middle of 1905, a new concern called the Chinese Central Railways, Ltd. came into being through the combination of forces of the Peking Syndicate, the British and Chinese Corporation, and a French financial and railway group which included the Banque de l'Indo-Chine. It was established in an effort to eliminate (1) the clash of interests between the English concerns over railway undertakings north of the Yangtse River, and (2) the rivalry between British and French interests for railways in central and south China. But in this new company the British partner was by far the dominant factor.[11]

As the British firms led the other powers in the number of concessions and in mileage in 1898, so they also led in the total amount of loans made to the Chinese government. According to one estimate, between 1898 and 1912 the British railway loans secured on Chinese government guarantees were fourteen in number with a total of over £18,660,000 in principal. This was in contrast to Germany's £9,500,000, the £5,000,000 or £6,000,000 each of France and Belgium, and the £2,000,000 of Japan.[12] The usual advantages that accompanied the loans were the management of fiscal and general affairs of the railway for the duration of the loan, and the right of first mortgage over the property of the railway, or the hypothecation of a part of China's internal revenue as security for payment of the debt.

But if the whole picture of foreign railway interests in China were examined, it will become evident that the above figures do not tell the complete story. First, while Britain took the lead in loans for Chinese government railways, she had constructed less mileage than the other powers in building directly under foreign control.[13] With the construction rights of this type of railway usually went jurisdiction rights over certain areas along the railway, together with the right to exploit the natural resources and to establish telegraphic communications within ten miles of each side of the railway. Such were the cases of the Russian-controlled Chinese Eastern Railway and the Japanese South Manchurian Railway in Manchuria, and of the German lines in Shantung. To the British businessmen, their control through the medium of the loan appeared mild and inefficient when compared with such practices as these.

Second, as has been pointed out above, British concessions were distributed over different and distant parts of China. But those of Russia, Germany, and France were neatly centered in regions that each power had marked out as its own sphere of influence. Consequently it was a comparatively easy matter for the other powers to consolidate their respective interests and fortify their positions, while for Britain it became a matter of not offending the established interests of other powers in their "spheres." This situation pointed to the necessity of the formulation of a clear-cut British policy in China.

THE INTERNATIONAL BALANCE

What really disturbed the British merchant in China was not so much the appearance of foreign competitors, as the fact that the latter were forging ahead with formal state support. He realized that such a method in the end would make his foreign rivals the dominating factors of Western expansion in China, and that he must rechart his course to meet the novel situation. In July, 1898, for instance, before the series of railway concessions had been obtained, the Chairman of the China Association, R. S. Gundry, addressed a letter to Lord Salisbury. In it he emphasized the "political importance" of the Peking-Hankow Railway, and proposed that a policy of British state-finance in China be inaugurated to oppose Russian state-finance.[14] A further comment on the changing aspect of international business competition was made two years later, when J. W. Jamieson, the Commercial Attaché in Peking, said, apropos of railway concessions, "the [China] Association should devote attention to getting permission for capitalists to construct railways in China as limited companies, instead of by means only of loans." [15]

This question of economic practice involved two aspects of British policy which were not easily resolved. For one thing, although it was basically not possible to separate the activities of government and finance, and the British government had intervened vigorously through the use of diplomatic pressure in behalf of British concession seekers, the time-hallowed nineteenth century principle of laissez faire would have to be scrapped if the London Foreign Office was to follow the example of the Continental Powers in the matter of enterprises in China. But the English nation was not yet prepared for so drastic a change in economic policy.[16] Furthermore, since the problem of railway development concerned the Chinese body politic, the question of foreign finance of the railways was therefore a political problem. The China Association, though considered to be voicing the interests of the commercial community, was no less conscious of the need for political remedies for the situation in China. In a letter in 1898 the Association proposed two ways of abating the risk of other foreign powers' using their railways to make territorial claims on China: "China may be encouraged and helped to assert her sovereignty, or spheres of national interest . . . may be defined." [17] But as events turned out, it appeared that the British government was not able to choose either one of the alternatives suggested by the Association which would have affected with far-reaching repercussions the internal structure as well as the international status of China. The policy which evolved was one that integrated Britain's economic undertakings in China—especially railway activities—completely into the framework of Britain's imperial diplomacy.

Under the growing pressure of imperialist competition, British business circles began to agitate for the adjustment of British policy in China to world politics. In 1900 a split in the China Association was followed by the founding of the China League, composed of the advocates of a more aggressive British policy in China.[18] In the early days of the Russo-Japanese War, when a Russian victory was expected by observers of the international scene, this League urged that some means be devised by which British interest would be guarded against the possibility of an upsetting of the Far Eastern status quo, in which British commercial activities still predominated. In March, 1904, A. R. Burkill, Honorary Secretary of the League, wrote an interesting letter to Lord Lansdowne. It showed that this body was ready to seek cooperation with foreign nations—particularly with the United States—as a means of preserving "the political and commercial supremacy" of Great Britain in China, against a Continental Bloc much feared by the British at that time.[19] The League also directly approached W. W. Rockhill, then serving in the United States State Department, with regard to Anglo-American cooperation in China. From a memorandum addressed to Rockhill by the League, we learn that the latter's first aim was to popularize Chinese affairs, and in Parliament to encourage the government to adopt a clear and consistent line of policy. Then it continued to explain the nature of that policy:

It would aim, in the first place, at the maintenance of all existing rights throughout the whole of the territories of the Chinese Empire, and the furtherance of British interests by all legitimate means. Secondly, it would endeavour to support, in cooperation with other Powers, a Progressive Government in China, which by moderate and steady reform would secure the tranquility, prosperity, and independence of that Empire. Thirdly, *and in any case,* its object would be to see that there shall be no such disturbance of the balance of power in the Far East as would endanger our Imperial position or affect the safety of our Indian Empire.[20]

An interesting parallel to the above opinion was expressed by the British Minister at Peking, Sir Ernest Satow, on a proposed arrangement with regard to China to be carried out at the end of the Russo-Japanese War. Voicing a fear of "certain Powers" because of their control of railways in China, Satow announced himself in favor of a guarantee of China's integrity, and suggested a "condominion" of the powers for the reform of the Chinese government. "This seems a huge task, pregnant with international difficulties, but not, I think, insuperable if America, England, and Japan can work together." [21] In fact, the similarity is so striking between the opinion of the China League and the thoughts of Sir Ernest Satow that one is led to infer that the latter had been inspired by the former, and cleared through the Foreign Office. In sounding out the United States about the formation of a Far Eastern entente, the London government indicated that it was entertaining ideas of a more positive policy toward the problem of China; it was considering using political pressure to prevent her partition by the Continental Powers. But since the Russian victory never occurred, no more was heard, for the time being, of such a comprehensive plan.

The emphasis placed on the necessity of preserving the political equilibrium in the Chinese Empire, and on the importance of some sort of cooperation between Britain and other powers, was in keeping with the general diplomatic developments of that decade. On the one hand, Britain took fresh interest in China as a field for her investments at the close of the Russo-Japanese War; [22] on the other hand, the foremost Far Eastern problem that confronted British policy-makers was still the general security of the British Empire in a world where the balance of power —both economical and political—was fast changing. The problem could not be regarded as an isolated issue, but must be dealt with and solved, in the larger context of the rising Anglo-German tension and the formation of the Triple Entente. Meanwhile, a new power had entered the Pacific hemisphere in a quest to spread its national interests and influence—the United States. It was to become actively engaged in Chinese railway politics in the latter part of our period, and there were some who thought that an Anglo-American combination against other powers in China was possible in this field.

However, aside from the weighty considerations of empire politics, railway concessions in China were still matters to be treated with care by the British government. Support was given to the business concessionaire outright whenever necessary, if the concession involved no conflict with other powers. Otherwise, if the concessions involved the dangers of an imbroglio with any power, the methods then would be modified in order the better to suit Britain's interests in China to her position in the diplomatic world. Her relation to such pacts as the United States–Japanese convention of 1908, the Russo-Japanese convention of 1910, and the renewal of the Anglo-Japanese alliance in 1911, became more defined. Where they were left to choose, neither the British financiers nor the Foreign Office wished to abandon material acquisitions in China. But in certain regions—for instance, Manchuria—the London authorities thought it better policy to concede the predominance to other powers. In yet other parts of the country, the active rivalry of the powers was resolved in the creation of an international consortium. In so doing, the risk of completely losing the economic advantages was avoided through the combination of western financial forces, while international conflict in China became lessened, so that it would not add weight to the already taut threads of European diplomatic relations.

THE CHINESE SCENE

Turning now to the Chinese side of the railway problem, we observe a situation no less complex and changeable than the international scene. An essential factor in the outburst of railway activities in the decade before 1911 was the Chinese effort at modernization, in which the building of railways played a conspicuous role. Modernization was generally regarded as a panacea for the weaknesses of the Chinese nation; on it depended the economic, political, and diplomatic future of China. It was reflected in many areas of the national life, and a number of theories sprang up regarding the best way to achieve modernization.[28] In railway matters it involved the interplay of government policy, popular sentiment, foreign and local interests. It is in this context that the significance of the railway question to the Chinese is to be considered and understood.

The need for railroads in China was first actively advocated by certain officials after the war with France. In 1889 Chang Chih-tung, an advocate of reform who was then Governor-General of Kwangtung and Kwangsi, memorialized the Throne on the military, political, and economic values of a railway which would run from the vicinity of Peking to Hankow. This was the first time when a railway of such length and importance was so definitely proposed in China.[24] However, the Court remained passive, and the Chinese people in general were still indifferent to these technological innovations. Then in 1898 a large number of concessions were obtained by the powers, while the government of China seemed more than ever to be utterly incapable of controlling the economic and political fortunes of the country. But in the long run the battle for concessions itself proved to be a stimulant to the nation. After the further shock of the Boxer upheaval, and the invasion by the Allied Expeditionary Force, the situation in the empire assumed a changed aspect. After 1901 the spread of technological knowledge was considered a necessity,[25] and at the same time the interest in railways became positive. In government circles it became a concept that was taken for granted. In 1905, for instance, such a sentence as "Railways are the key to national reform" could be tossed into a memorial as an uncontestable maxim by Sheng Hsüan-huai.[26] Sheng, an industrialist who was vitally interested in such things as the telegraph, steam navigation, and modern mining, as well as the railway, was appointed Director-General of the Imperial Railway Administration in 1892 through the recommendation of Chang Chih-tung and others. But it was only after 1900 that his role was played out in its full significance and multiple ramifications.

The background for the new show of energy in railway matters lay in the general dissatisfaction of the Chinese people with a ruling regime that for over half a century had been unable to cope with the problems arising out of a changed state of foreign relations. In this unrest were blended desire for political change, and eagerness for economic advance, particularly for the widespread introduction of technological improvements as a means of strengthening the country. Politically the new situation found expression in two ways. In the educated people two groups took shape, the constitutional reformists and the revolutionists, each advocating in its own way basic changes in the Chinese political structure.[27] At Court the desire to save the dynasty was strong, and it led to the promulgation of an elaborate series of decrees from 1905. These dealt with governmental reorganization, and with the adoption of western procedures in the fields of education, finance, and law.[28] The establishment of a constitutional government especially became an issue of the times. However, the reform measures also served another end of the Throne: it was attempting to utilize them as a means of concentrating political power in the central government, especially in the hands of Manchus, thereby strengthening the moribund dynasty.[29] That policy aroused conflicting opinions between Peking and the provinces, and added to the difficulties and complexities of carrying out modernizing programs for the nation.

In the field of industrial and technical development, interest was expressed from more than one quarter. The concern of the government over railways was manifested chiefly in administrative reorganizations. The need for a more specialized government agency to administer railway affairs was increasingly felt, and in that respect four changes took place between 1896 and 1907. The Imperial Chinese Railway Administration was first established, with Sheng Hsüan-huai serving as Director-General. Originally it was associated with the Board of Naval Affairs, but in 1896 was transferred to the Bureau of Railways and Mines, and in 1903 to the Board of Commerce. In 1906, after the abolition of the old Railway Administration, the Board of Posts and Communications was organized, with a department specially assigned to manage railway matters; under its jurisdiction a new Railway Administration was formed in 1907, to supervise the general administration of railways and their relation with foreign concessionaires.[30] At the same time, railway personnel was being trained at various schools.[31] Ways were also devised for better coordination, information, and control by the central authorities over the various lines through a system of periodic inspection by Railway Councillors.[32] And in 1907 all imports of railway material from abroad were declared exempt from duty, so that railroad building could be further encouraged in the nation.[33]

At the policy forming level in the Peking government, designs for a national railway system began to take shape. There was anxious desire to link up the different parts of China into one organic unit through modern communication, and there were frequent official discussions of the railway question. Suggestions to make the railway serve political and military, as well as economic, ends appeared.

The Board of Commerce in 1906 made the proposal that this Board should draw up an over-all railway time chart for the entire empire, according to which the future building of railways in the provinces would be scheduled. This idea met with imperial approval.[34] A year later, in the summer of 1907, the Board of Posts and Communications presented to the Throne a plan of national trunk lines and railway systems, which was based on the suggestions made by Governor-General Ch'ing Ch'un-hsüan of Kwangtung and Kwangsi.[35] Taking Peking as the focal point, the plan would create an integrated railway net radiating from the capital and consisting of four major systems. The main lines

THE FOUR SYSTEMS OF THE RAILWAY PLAN OF THE BOARD OF POSTS AND COMMUNICATIONS, 1907

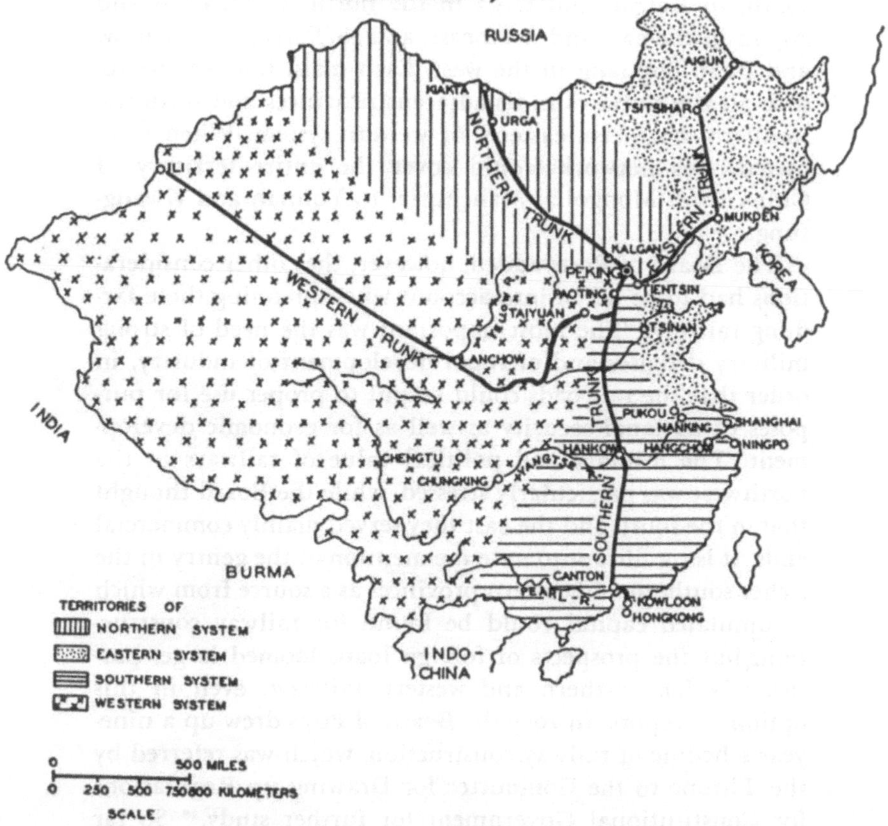

were to run from Peking to Hankow and Canton in the south, to Kalgan and Urga in the north, to Mukden and Aigun in the east and northeast, and to Taiyuan, Lanchow, and Ili in Sinkiang in the west. Each main line was to absorb all the railways in its adjacent provinces and form the southern, northern, eastern, or western system. When completed, this network would cover the entire territory of China from Mongolia, Manchuria, to Yunnan and Kwangtung.

The Board of Posts added, however, that other considerations had to be taken into account when planning these far-flung railways. The most important was the need of strong military defenses and of rapid development of industry, in order that the railroads could be put to proper use for purposes of national security as well as for economic development. The military and political value of railways in the northwest was particularly stressed, while the Board thought that in the south and the east they served mainly commercial ends. It is significant to note the mention of the gentry in the richer southern and eastern provinces as a source from which accumulated capital could be found for railway construction, but the prospects of foreign loans loomed large, particularly for northern and western railways, even in this optimistic report. In 1909 the Board of Posts drew up a nine-year schedule of railway construction, which was referred by the Throne to the Committee for Drawing up Regulations for Constitutional Government for further study.[36] So far as paper-planning was concerned, the railway was made a part of the central government's business.

The striking feature in these government plans was the way in which they sidestepped the question of capital. With what were the railroads to be financed? There was a general indication that in certain cases the moneyed gentry of the provinces would furnish the necessary amounts. And if these were not available, foreign loans could always be found.

How did this attitude accord with the opinion of that part of the Chinese population interested in the modernization of China?

In considering popular efforts in that direction after the turn of the century, one is inevitably confronted with the movement for the "redemption" of foreign-controlled railways. This redemption movement was a part of the general assertion of Chinese national rights. Its supporters included all segments of the articulate public: government officials, gentry capitalists, and students who had been deeply stirred by the recent rise of Japan. One of the points on which the government and the people were able to reach a superficial accord—briefly at any rate—was the exclusion of foreign capital from all Chinese industrial enterprises, including mining and railway construction.[37] The dynastic government however was often, under foreign pressure, unable to carry out those grand resolutions, and in the end the gentry became the most active element in agitating for all-Chinese railways.

That the gentry-merchants in the provinces should become the most articulate spokesmen against foreign railway concessions was no accident; it was a phenomenon having its roots in the nature of Chinese society. The gentry, in fact, were the only group in the Chinese economic structure who possessed adequate material means and general knowledge to become actively interested in the new industrial developments. To their class belonged both political influence—at least local—and accumulated wealth acquired chiefly through land rents. They furnished the largest percentage of industrial leadership toward the end of the nineteenth century.[38]

When railway building became an important issue in the land, the gentry in the more developed provinces realized that it was a chance to enter a new field of investment. Therefore it was they who figured so prominently in the movement for redemption of several railway concessions; it was they who organized railway companies, and disputed the right of construction with the British concessionaire in the case of the Shanghai-Hangchow-Ningpo Railway loan. They became the rivals of the foreign concessionaires, for their own as well as the country's interest, and were noted for their anti-foreign attitudes. The contemporary movement for constitutional government further added to the weight of the gentry in public affairs, since they were the class that the established orders of Chinese society recognized as fit for positions of public dignity.[39] However, since their purposes and activities often contradicted with those of the dynasty, the problems awaiting solution became increasingly complex.

The major railway lines in all parts of China were built with foreign loans and supervision. From the point of view of the British, such loans were made chiefly by private British financial firms, with no direct governmental control involved. On the surface of things, all these activities were justifiable in the name of commercial expansion and the investment of capital.[40] But the Chinese could see a further element in the situation: that behind the financier always stood a strong foreign government, ready to lend its support; that the concessionaire's economic controls meant the loss by the Chinese of specific rights over the nation's railways, such as the authority of management, purchase, and appointment. Financial regulation was largely taken out of the hands of the Chinese, because of the hypothecation of railway revenues for the service of the loan. Consider also the fact that after 1901, when the Boxer indemnity had been settled upon, China's foreign debt had become extremely high, with a considerable portion of the Imperial Maritime Customs and internal revenues hypothecated for the repayment of loans and debts.[41] Under these circumstances, the Chinese regarded the further pledging of railway property and revenue as evils to be avoided and prevented.

By 1905 all these factors helped to produce the movement for the redemption or the cancellation of railway loans. Henceforth, it was proclaimed, the railways were to be built with Chinese funds under Chinese supervision. Few new concessions were made in that decade, and where cancellation was not possible the final loan terms for the concessions granted in 1898 were, in many cases, modified to be more favorable to China than the preliminary agreements. One British writer remarked that the Chinese seemed to desire "to secure wherever possible at least a theoretical control regardless of cost." [42] Not only were such railways as the Hankow-Canton, the Shanghai-Hangchow-Ningpo, and the Peking-Hankow lines, running through the political heartland of China, the objects of plans of redemption, but railways in the border provinces were also subject to the movement. The gentry and officials of Szechuan and Yunnan, for instance, were anxiously concerned over the railway rights in their provinces. Kwangtung, Fukien, and Kiangsi undertook railway construction of their own.[43]

This anti-foreign aspect of the national concern for railways was watched with apprehension by the Great Powers. As the power possessing the largest trading interest in China and occupying the most influential position in the Far East, England became vitally concerned with the new trends. In 1906 the situation as it affected the future of British railway concessions in China was brought to the attention of the House of Commons,[44] while a United States State Department official wrote to the American Minister at Peking:

> I am very much taken with your designation used in despatches of the new party in China as the "rights recovery" party. . . . Confidential communications which have reached me from London indicate that British interests are much more alarmed than the press would seem to indicate.[45]

The desire of the Chinese to regain control of their railways was, then, a factor to be contended with. The point to be observed is the extent to which Britain was able to press her claims in face of this nascent nationalism.

A word must be said here of the characteristics of the Chinese economy which rendered difficult the effective execution of extensive government railway plans or the construction of major lines entirely by the Chinese. Because of the decentralized, rural nature of the traditional economic structure, the foremost difficulty encountered in railway enterprise was the lack of large capital accumulations sufficient to underwrite the building of railways of any great length. The central government itself possessed no means of translating its plans into action. Since the empire's fiscal system was operated not on a modern budget but on fixed minimum returns from individual provinces,[46] the Government Treasury was in no position to undertake sizable projects. In the provinces it was difficult also to raise the necessary amounts, because the moneyed classes were hesitant about participating in this new type of long-range investment; they were especially reluctant when the projects involved official control of the railways.

An additional difficulty lay in the fact that the type of financial management required by the operation of railways was something entirely alien to the traditional social structure of China. While it was comparatively easy to bring Western material innovations into the country, the intangible principles on which they operated were more difficult to grasp, and nineteenth-century Western economic thought, sparsely introduced by a few interested individuals, had found in China no congenial environment in which to flourish during the last years of the Ch'ing Dynasty.[47] To cite only a few examples: when the Peking-Hankow Railway was proposed in 1898, the Throne ordered the line to be divided into a northern and a southern section, and a different director was appointed to take charge of each section.[48] That line, however, was eventually built under unified supervision of the Belgian concessionaire. In the case of the Hankow-Canton line after its redemption in 1905, the competition among the three provinces for material benefits of the road was for a while unbelievably fierce.[49] The situation was repeated with added force when the Hankow-Szechuan line came up for discussion. This road was treated not as a single trunk line connecting two important areas of the country, but rather as partly a Hupeh line and partly a Szechuan line, and much bad temper was stirred up among the natives of the provinces as to the demarcation of their respective railway interests. A man like Chang Chih-tung was able to take a broader view of the matter than many of his contemporaries. Yet he was not always able to exclude provincialism from his policy. For example, partly out of expediency, but partly also out of conviction, he objected strenuously to the taking over of Hupeh railways by the Board of Posts and Communications.[50] The railway as an institution that transcended the territorial jurisdiction of provincial authorities and that required a system of centralized finance was not understood by the enthusiasts of the time.

At the same time, fervent though the gentry had been in their demands for the exclusion of foreign capital in the construction of the railways, when their abilities were put to the test, weaknesses very often appeared. The bankruptcy of the Szechuan Railway Company, for instance, seemed to have been caused by the trustees' eagerness to reap immediate profits from the investments. Nearly $2,000,000 were lost through embezzlement, waste, and speculation before any construction had been started.[51]

Whatever the strength or the weakness of the gentry capitalists and their enterprises may have been, the fact was not changed that the relation between the provincial railway companies and the government was an important factor in the situation. The government played a leading role in railway development, and in its relation with the private companies was reflected the reaction of the gentry on official policy. Several modes of control had been tried—"merchant" or "private" enterprise, government enterprise, and "merchant enterprise under government supervision," the last being especially favored by Chang Chih-tung.[52] But at every turn they were so intricately interrelated with the problem of foreign loans, especially British loans, that the success or failure of each method must be observed within the framework of the railway loan negotiations.

The major elements in the railway complex in our period, in so far as the British were concerned, were twofold: on the one hand, Britain, possessor of the largest number of concessions, wanted to maintain her superior position in China amid increasing Chinese and international obstacles. On the other hand, China on her own volition was eager to push forward railway projects but lacked the means to do so. The tangible results of that situation was a number of British loans contracted for the purpose of building Chinese government railways. The following pages will be an investigation of the history of the individual loans.

I

The Making of the Preliminary Agreements

THE MAJORITY of railways dealt with in the present work had their origin in the battle for concessions that reached its climax in 1898. This "battle" consisted of the demands and counterdemands from St. Petersburg, Berlin, Paris, and London; the signing away, bit by bit by the rulers of China, of her resources into the hands of the Great Powers; the rivalry and high-handed methods of the imperialist nations. To all practical purposes, the part played by China in this phenomenon of Western expansion amounted only to a negative role.

It then may be questioned whether it is worthwhile to re-tread the grounds of the battle for concessions, since the activities of the powers have already been made known through a number of scholarly works. In other words, is anything to be gained by examining the Chinese material relating to the events of 1895–1898?

It goes without saying that the historical importance of the battle for concessions lay in the political as well as the economic implications of the foreign acquisitions in China. In this context, Chinese reaction to the onrush of foreign encroachment was a necessary factor in the entire picture of Sino-Western relations. Were the Chinese officials entirely passive? Had there been evidences of the formulation of any consistent policy vis-à-vis the foreign demands? Such questions could not be readily answered if the events were viewed entirely from the side of the Great Powers.

Furthermore, the railways were a part of concession politics. Because with each railway concession went the opportunity to control that line of communication and to consolidate special foreign interests in that region, it was always regarded by the Chinese not as merely an undertaking in transportation, but as a matter to be deliberated in view of its political and international repercussions. The attitude displayed by the ruling authorities with regard to a particular power, therefore, would be reflected in the state of affairs concerning that power's railway interests. The position of Britain in the battle for concessions served, in this sense, as background for her railway interests in China. To this end, then, it is useful to study the process that led to the conclusion of preliminary railway loan agreements in 1898 between British syndicates and Chinese administrators.

The outcome of the Sino-Japanese War left China not only in military and financial ruin, but also at a loss as to the path that should be followed in the international labyrinth. It is well known that the Franco-German-Russian intervention for Japan's retrocession of Liaotung Peninsula had swung the Chinese government—especially Li Hung-Chang whose authority was greatly injured by the shattering outcome of the war—into the Russian orbit. The treaty of 1896, granting to Russia, among other things, exclusive railway privileges in Manchuria, was the widely acclaimed evidence of a Russophile policy under the direction of Li. While the menace of Japan penetrated all consciousness, a diplomatic support among the powers was sought by all, but it was questionable whether many had thought of devising a long-range national policy on the basis of Russo-Chinese affinity. The concern now was primarily a matter of finding a practical and immediate solution for the emergency. As one metropolitan official put it, previously China should have been allied with Britain to check Russia, but now she should line up with Russia against Japan; he thought Britain and Japan had become associates, while Russia had helped to bring about the retrocession.[1] It is interesting further to note that concrete proposals were offered by Chang Chih-tung, then Acting Governor-General of Liangkiang, for a secret alliance with the Tsar's government in order to borrow the strength of the latter's navy for China's defense. Russia might be granted, he suggested, more lenient commercial regulations, better boundary delimitation, the use of Chinese harbors for coaling, and the right of troop transit—all this in return for Russian aid to China in time of future "disturbances." Chang thought the Tsungli Yamen should start the negotiations, but that in no case must Sir Robert Hart, the British Inspector-General of the Imperial Chinese Maritime Customs since 1863, be informed of this matter for fear that he would obstruct it. Bearing in mind Anglo-Russian rivalries in the Far East, he felt confident that Russia would accede to those proposals.[2] Another high official, Liu K'un-i, entertained similar notions in 1895.[3]

But two and a half years later, as the Kiaochow and Port Arthur crisis arose, both Chang and Liu completely reversed their stands; they then stood for an alliance with Russia's antagonist Britain. This tendency toward what seemed to be power politics, however, must not be regarded as an aspiration toward a Bismarckian system, because it was not a planned system, and its initiators were still not quite able to free themselves from the bounds of tradition.[4] Rather than a European-style international scheme of alliances and alignments, the motive behind the efforts was perhaps still the idea that China as "the middle kingdom" could sway the balance of the outside world by a little shifting of her weight. But the officials did not seem to realize that in the world of competing imperialist powers, such maneuvers were actually signs of dependence on external support, and would help to encourage further aggression from all directions. The railway advantages ceded to Russia in the Treaty of 1896, for example, were much more than what the Peking government had been willing to grant in 1895; and the ambitions of the British mercantile community, stimulated by French and Russian activities in China, were laid out in a vigorous letter to the Foreign Office in November, 1896, which became the basis of British demands pressed on the Chinese government in the next two years.[5]

INDICATIONS OF BRITISH POLICY

Contrary to the general impression, the London government had not remained lethargic regarding its French and Russian rivals in China. Suspicion of the French, in fact, emerged soon after the latter's annexation of Annam in 1885, particularly as a result of the reduction of duties across the land frontier of China. The policy of counterpoise showed itself, also, early in this quarter, when the British Minister O'Conor asked that the West River be opened to foreign trade—which the British believed they could dominate from their down-river bastions of Canton and Hongkong—as compensation.[6] The renewed advance of France in southwestern China after the intervention of 1895 caused a recurrence of alarm. While the English Chambers of Commerce and the China merchants were pressing for a Burma-Yunnan Railway,[7] the Foreign Office was quietly conducting its own negotiations with the Chinese government. The Franco-Chinese agreement of June, 1895, touched upon some border territory that the British claimed lay within the jurisdiction of Burma, and demanded for compensation at another point, Yeh-jen-shan. Negotiations followed in the latter part of 1895.

A report from Minister Kung Chao-yuan at London, after a confidential interview with Salisbury, indicated that the Prime Minister was seeking to kill two birds with one stone, and assuming the attitude of being at once firm in what he desired but not intransigent, so that a bargain might be struck. Salisbury intimated that once the West River was opened, a compromise might be reached on the boundary issue; and Kung's opinion was that either one or the other of those two demands would have to be granted to Britain if a peaceful settlement was desired.[8] Sir Nicholas O'Conor also mentioned the possibility of reaching a more lenient boundary decision in exchange for the opening of West River to Nanning; but as the Tsungli Yamen refused to open the waterway far enough to satisfy the British, no agreement could be arrived at.[9] Additional demands were subsequently presented by the new British Minister Sir Claude MacDonald—such as establishing more British consulates in Yunnan, and the extension of a Burmese railway into Yunnan. The final result, the Anglo-Chinese agreement of February 4, 1897, was therefore the fruit of over two years of negotiations. It adjusted the Sino-Burmese frontier territory, provided for the possible connection of a Chinese railway with the Burmese at the boundary, and declared the West River open to foreign trade up to Wuchow.[10]

Britain's rivalry with Russia was marked by their intense competition for a loan to the Chinese government for the third payment of the Japanese indemnities, while the German occupation of Kiaochow and Russian activities at Port Arthur were beginning to stir up profound apprehension among the mercantile circle. Later when the Peking government dropped the loan negotiations with both countries, it was out of fear and dislike for the terms offered by both the British and Russian governments, although it is interesting to note that the Chinese Minister to London informed Salisbury that the loan had to be refused due to Russian menace.[11] But the "compensations" that China had to grant to the British were of far greater importance to Britain's Far Eastern interest than the loan itself. In the end, an Anglo-German loan was secured, while age-long aspirations of the British mercantile interests were also realized, such as the Chinese government's Yangtse nonalienation assurance, and the question of a British Inspector-General for the Imperial Maritime Customs. Well might the Old China Hands congratulate themselves on the auspicious beginning for 1898.[12]

The significance of the tenacious and shrewd bargaining of the British government was not lost upon the Chinese officials, who were then being particularly watchful of the behavior of the foremost commercial power in the Far East. The successful maneuvers of her diplomats in the above two instances undoubtedly contributed to produce a situation in 1898, in which not only did the British government further pursue the policy of counter-concessions, but was also abetted by the position assumed by many Chinese high officials in their quest for an effective check against the encroachments of Germany and Russia at the height of the Kiaochow and Port Arthur crisis.

NEW TREND IN CHINESE POLICY REGARDING BRITAIN

Two motivating forces seemed to have prompted a new appraisal of Anglo-Chinese relations in the early days of 1898. First, in the words of Hukuang Governor-General Chang Chih-tung, it was felt that "The situation being what it is, it seems necessary to come to some sort of arrangement with England thereby assuring her good behaviour. Otherwise disaster will be due from this quarter." [13] The root of this contention was fear of British demands for similar territorial rights as those demanded by Russia and Germany. Being unable to reject the latter, it was feared that China would have given the international balance a heavy tip to one side, causing a wild scramble by all powers. To redress the situation an entente with England was suggested, with Japan thrown into the bargain. Chang advocated a direct approach to the London government, and at the same time to try to hold Russia in check by reminding St. Petersburg of Britain's predilection for counterdemands should Russia occupy Port Arthur.

Secondly, Britain was regarded by some as the logical choice of a power for mediation in the Kiaochow affair. If international mediation was to be the best way of solving this problem, then Britain was the only power that could take the lead, owing to her widespread world interests and lack of sympathy with Germany.[14]

In other words, while British counterdemands were feared, it was also hoped that the British government would put its weight behind China and help the latter ward off foreign aggressors. That Britain might demand recompense for such aid—if forthcoming, that a scramble for concessions was already taking place with Britain included among the contending members—these facts did not seem to have entered into the calculations of the overwhelmed Chinese officials. Russia and Germany were clearly recognized to be the strongest competitors against Britain's power and interest in China, and their antagonism was considered sufficient reason for Britain to become partial to China's cause.

An outright alliance between Britain and China seemed the logical conclusion to such trends of thought. It is notable that the desirability of England's alliance with Japan or China had been mentioned by Lord Loch more than once during the China Association political debate in December, 1897, as a counter-poise against the Dreibund.[15] Three months later, MacDonald reported from Peking that

> The idea of an alliance between Great Britain, Japan, and China, with regard to which I was privately sounded by the Privy Council, seems to have originated with the Hukuang Viceroy, Chang Chih-tung. It has met with much favour, the fact that China contributes nothing to the strength of the alliance being left out of account.[16]

Chang's proposal of an Anglo-Chinese-Japanese alliance against the Continental Powers was in fact communicated to Peking several weeks before. He attributed its origin not to himself but to an officer of the Japanese general staff who had visited Chang in Wuchang and claimed to be making the proposal under "secret Governmental orders." But Peking hesitated at its anti-Russian implications, and, for fear of disastrous repercussions, the Throne ordered Chang not to give assent to this plan.[17] Two weeks later, however, upon the repeated urging of not only Chang Chih-tung but also the latter's subordinate, Hunan Governor Chen Pao-chen, the Throne ordered the matter be deliberated by the Tsungli Yamen.[18] It apparently had travelled far enough in the official channels subsequently to be turned down by the British Minister, as noted above.

These manifestations of the alliance idea were probably not connected, and in the consummation of the Anglo-Japanese alliance four years later China was too weak to be counted as a partner. But it was a certainty that in the hectic days of 1897–1898 the desire arose among several quarters, to achieve some sort of power equilibrium over the vast expanses of Chinese territory, and that the battle for concessions itself was seized by some leading Chinese policy-makers as a means to this end.

By the end of January, 1898, events became more crystallized. Terms demanded by London for the third Japanese indemnity loan proved that the British were out to get what material advantages they could.[19] A British loan on those terms—including inland steam navigation, *likin* (inland transit dues) reforms, a Yangtse nonalienation promise—was strenuously opposed by the two powerful governor-generals of the Yangtse valley, Chang Chih-tung and Liu K'un-i. They held that it would be better to arrange for a postponement of payments with the Japanese government for the time being, than to let the administration of *likin* revenue fall under Sir Robert Hart's control. Britain, bitterly resentful of Germany's gains in Kiaochow, would surely not agree to a loan on easy terms. In his communication to the Tsungli Yamen, Chang Chih-tung expressed their forebodings in these terms:

My previous suggestions for an alliance with England aimed only at controlling her action and preventing her from unreasonable acts and forceful occupations. They were not due to any belief that she is reliable. I beg that for the sake of our national welfare you base your deliberations on long-range calculations, and do not submit to her threats launched amid our present extremity.[20]

But the pressure of the contending powers in those winter months made it impossible for the Chinese government to assume a positive role, to engineer a sheer political alliance with Britain, or categorically to reject British demands. Under MacDonald's persistent urging, the Tsungli Yamen proclaimed the nonalienability of the Yangste region on February 11, 1898, and two days later it gave the assurance regarding a British head of the Customs Inspectorate-General.[21] Henceforth Chinese policy planning became more and more clearly an effort on the one hand to parry the mounting foreign demands, and on the other hand to rationalize the government's yielding under duress into an attempt at creating an equilibrium of powers.

In proportion to China's uneasiness regarding Russian intransigence at Port Arthur and Talienwan rose her officials' estimation of the importance of Britain. On February 17, 1898, Chang Chih-tung gave an analysis of the situation to the Tsungli Yamen, and predicted that Britain was about to launch large-scale demands for concessions. Should the Tsungli Yamen be unable to reject these demands, he suggested that they be bought off at the price of concessions along these lines: first, China was to let Britain guide and participate in the training of her navy; second, discerning the British anxiety over north China concessions, he proposed that railway rights in Honan and Shansi provinces be granted to the British on a loan basis; third, mines in Yunnan could also be opened with British financial and technical aid.[22]

Within the same month the question of Wei-hai Wei entered the field of Anglo-Chinese diplomacy. Negotiations for its lease were done with comparative dispatch, and the agreement for the lease reflected such ideas as were expressed by Chang Chih-tung. One of the difficulties raised by the Chinese government, MacDonald reported, was that China would be left without a suitable harbor for her naval ships recently launched in England and Germany. MacDonald suggested the problem be solved by an agreement for the use of Wei-hai Wei harbor by Chinese warships. This provision was incorporated into the final agreement for the lease. "Yamen showed," said the British Minister, "what is now prevailing feeling here, great desire for England's friendship and support against Russia, and if we could hold out any encouragement it would prevent the change of feeling which will be produced if we have to gain our end by force." [23]

This was indeed an ironic commentary to Chang Chih-tung's program mentioned before. While the Chinese officials thought that they would be able to offset the powers one against another through the politics of concessions, their purpose became immediately obvious to the British who in turn utilized this tendency in Chinese policy for the advancement of British interest in China. This interweaving of the British and Chinese motives resulted in the preponderance of British concessions granted in the year 1898–1899.

BRITISH RAILWAY CONCESSIONS

Sir Claude MacDonald's classic remark, "we do not seem to have come out second best," referred to railway rights that had been obtained by British syndicates with his help. Not that he ever resorted to such uncouth tactics as an ultimatum. He said, however, "the fact that the fleet was concentrating was of course known to them [Peking officials]." [24] Of an estimated 6,420 miles of railroads, financial and construction rights of 2,800 went to the British, with the London Foreign Office standing generally behind demands initiated by the British mercantile circles.[25] However, with the exception of the Imperial Railways of North China loan, made for the construction of the line between Shanhaikuan and Newchuang, all the agreements concluded in 1898 were of a preliminary nature.

The North China Railways were originally built in 1877 for transportation of the products of the Kaiping coal mine, and were extended to Peking only in 1894. Lack of Chinese funds for construction of the line beyond the Great Wall after the Japanese War resulted in the British loan of 1898. It was the first loan agreement of its kind, setting down the general framework of terms for later loans in regard to such matters as the security for the loan, and disposition of railway revenues.[26] The loan, to be taken up by the British and Chinese Corporation, was for £2,300,000. It elicited strong protests from the Russian government, but the London Foreign Office was also equally concerned, and did all it could to counteract Russian efforts. Late in July MacDonald was instructed to persuade the Tsungli Yamen with promise of England's support of China against any power that committed act of aggression on China, in return for China's granting a British subject to build or support any railway—or similar public work. This was when rumours of pending Russian invasion of Ili in Sinkiang were flying high as a result of the Shanhaikuan railway conflict. The Tsungli Yamen, however, refused the offer, possibly because it was unwilling to snub Russia in such a direct fashion. But Lord Salisbury kept up the pressure and, in the next month, told the Chinese Minister at London "I strongly advise China to pay no regard to her [Russian] objection."[27]

The result was a compromise. The British got the loan with the attendant powers of financial control, and the Russians were pacified by a declaration from the Tsungli Yamen that the railway would perpetually remain the property of the Chinese government, and that the Chinese administrator of this railway should maintain legal control of the line so long as payments were regularly made. With this, the final loan agreement was signed in October and duly ratified by the Throne. The loan was to be issued at the price of 90 to the Railway Administration with a 5 per cent interest, and the entire property and revenue of the railway were pledged as security. The duration of the loan was increased from the originally contemplated twenty-five years to forty-five years. Regarding this last point, Railway Administrator Hu Yü-fen held that the change was much to the better for China: not only could she now pay back the debt by easier stages, but the longer duration would also serve more effectively as a balance of influence against "strong neighbours."[28] But whether it could be as effective a check on Russian ambitions was a matter largely to be decided by Russia and Britain. All this time London was trying unsuccessfully to come to a general agreement with St. Petersburg regarding the "open door" in China, while indications of Russian preference for a delimitation of spheres were impressed on Salisbury.[29] In actual fact, the British firm and London government were themselves practising the doctrine of "spheres." The agreement made it plain that British financial control could be exercised at any moment over this government railway through loan terms.

The first preliminary agreement concluded in 1898 was that of the Shanghai-Nanking Railway loan. Because of the absence of a strong foreign rival in this area, the control of the line was more apparently vested in the hands of the British creditor; and this preliminary agreement, designated to be model for other British railway loans, contained provisions that were considered the most disadvantageous by the Chinese.

That the Shanghai-Nanking line should lead the others in the crop of new concessions was no accident. Linking the largest commercial port in the Far East with an administrative center, and guarding the approaches to the Yangtse valley, this railway was early noted down by the British in their preoccupation with that region. Rowland MacDonald Stephenson, an English engineer, who, after a career in promoting railways in India, attempted to draw up a scheme of railways for the Chinese government in 1863, included the Shanghai-Nanking line in his "Yangtse System"; and in 1898 the London Foreign Office directly helped the British and Chinese Corporation to obtain a concession over this line.[30] The early Chinese advocates of railways also regarded it as one of the important lines that ought to be built as speedily as possible. Directly after the Sino-Japanese War, when Chang Chih-tung was Acting Governor-General of Liangkiang, there was talk for several months of the surveying and construction of this railroad by the provincial gentry under government auspices.[31] But nothing seemed to have been materialized from these efforts in 1895–1896.

German interest was added to the Shanghai-Nanking railway as the concession hunting of the powers intensified early in 1898, and an attempt was made by British and German banks to make this a joint enterprise. Chang Chih-tung then advanced the suggestion that Germany be permitted to construct this railway, on condition that she withdrew her demands for railway and mining rights in Shantung. Clinging to the notion of creating a power equilibrium, he thought the interest of all the great powers in Shanghai would serve to block unwarranted increase of German influence. Chang's belief in the wisdom of such a course was deepened when the German Minister Von Heyking showed him the draft contract covering an Anglo-German undertaking respecting this rail line. Borrowing from two sources at once, said Chang, would give China a good deal more freedom for controlling the situation than borrowing from one.[32]

From the same premise, but especially because of Britain's anxiety regarding the Yangtse region, Chang Chih-tung was opposed to granting the concession to the British alone. But when the Anglo-German combination broke up in the beginning of April,[33] the choice lay between a German or a British contract—to stave off both contending parties the Chinese authorities were not capable of doing. After a few weeks of negotiations, Chang expressed his misgivings to Sheng Hsüan-huai, Director-General of the Imperial Railway Administration:

> Foreigners have often likened the tracks of a railway to a pair of scissors, and said that wherever the railway extends the country is cut open. Nowadays the foreigners are too ruthless. In the region around Soochow, Shanghai, and, along the Yangtze, the interests of England are already extremely heavy, therefore we should not by any means let the British undertake the Shanghai-Nanking Railway single-handed.[34]

Instead of a British concession, Chang said, he would rather have the line made into an Anglo-German joint enterprise. Or better still, the Belgians might be persuaded to undertake this railway, with the Americans replacing the Belgians on the Peking-Hankow line. In this way German and English predominance on the lower Yangtse, and French and Russian influence over the Peking-Hankow Railway, would all be avoided at one stroke.[35]

These ingenious plans are valuable to the student of history only because they so unmistakably revealed a prevalent Chinese attitude regarding foreign concession seekers. Actually it was not easy to shake each of the powers off its area of concentration of interest. Between the Railway Director-General Sheng Hsüan-huai, and the Tsungli Yamen which was hard pressed by MacDonald, it was decided that the British should be granted the rights of the Shanghai-Nanking Railway. It is illuminating to see that in his argument justifying this decision Sheng also relied on the argument that it would improve Anglo-Chinese relations, and therefore would erect a buffer against aggressive Russian and German designs.[36]

The preliminary agreement was concluded in Peking on May 13, 1898, between Sheng and the British and Chinese Corporation, the latter represented by Jardine's agent. The document was precipitatedly signed, the Tsungli Yamen wishing to face with a *fait accompli* possible German agitation through the touring Prince Henry.[37] Since there was not sufficient time for full consultation with provincial authorities before the signature took place, the way was left open for changes at the time when the final agreement was to be drawn.[38] We shall look at the provisions later in the book. Suffice it to say here that the terms for this loan were highly satisfactory to the British and Chinese Corporation, and that the degree of its control over the railway was by no means diminished by what modifications were introduced at a later date.

By midyear in 1898, foreign railway expansions seemed to have reached a stage of saturated calm. To ward off British and French control of the line, and to add a balance against the enormous loads of concessions of all the European powers, the right to build the Hankow-Canton Railway on a loan basis was granted to an American firm, the American China Development Co.; [39] the Peking-Hankow contract was about to be consummated with the Belgian syndicate, and British engineers had begun to survey the Shanghai-Nanking route. It must be remembered that the lines remained the legal property of the Chinese government. It was believed then that the powers would be content with their acquisitions and relative positions, and that the semblance of an equilibrium of their interests in China would offer the country a chance to have these railways built without further obligations to the powers. Sheng Hsüan-huai's report to the Throne, made in response to an inquiry after the existing state of railways, reflected that atmosphere of hopeful lull:

> Given the conditions of China today, it is, needless to say, difficult to borrow from other countries on a strictly business basis, without substantial guarantees. After more than a twelvemonth's tortuous negotiations the loan for the three said railways [Peking-Hankow, Hankow-Canton, and Shanghai-Nanking] have been finally settled upon, and construction of these lines can be expected to be rapidly brought about. . . .
>
> These three lines will be built with loans from three different Powers. With strict terms and a lenient time period, with one contract constantly compared with another, it is believed that the completion of one line will mean the simultaneous completion of the others.[40]

But the largest number of British railway concessions were yet to be demanded and obtained and with them was revealed strikingly the diplomatic tactics of the Chinese officials amid a hostile world. The final conclusion of the Belgian railway loan—carried through in Peking, it was said, mainly on the strength of Franco-Russian support—was supposed to have been the fuse that led to the burst of British demands for compensation in August and September. However, it seemed possible that the situation was similar to that at the beginning of the year,[41] in which the "compensations" were really of more concern to the British than the cause for which they were pressed at Peking. On September 6 the Tsungli Yamen acceded to all the railway demands, confirming some of the concessions for which negotiations had already begun, and granting new ones. They included the Peking Syndicate's right to construct railways from their Shansi and Honan mining area to the Yangtse. Also included were the right to finance and build the Canton-Kowloon, Pukou-Sinyang, and Soochow-Hangchow-Ningpo railways by the British and Chinese Corporation; and a partial concession on the vital Tientsin-Chinkiang line.[42] Add to these the newly acquired increase in the leased territory to the rear of Kowloon, as well as the engagement for rail links between Yunnan and Burma, and Britain's railway interests in China were rounded out and strategically placed over practically the entire country.

What were the peculiarities of the situation that made possible this rich range and wide distribution of British acquisitions? The first factor that comes to mind is the actual economic value of the concessions. While railways were considered as instruments of commercial expansion, the mines of Shansi and Honan were believed to contain endless wealth for their exploiters. Contemporary estimates of European geographers regarding China's mineral resources further bolstered the British Minister's conviction that the concessions obtained by Britain far outweighed those of other powers in economic value.[43] Secondly, the aim of the British government to checkmate the growth of foreign preponderances in China was a very real one, although at that time London was much belabored by the mercantile interests for following a policy not sufficiently aggressive for them. There were doubts as to whether the government would adopt a vigorous policy of spheres, or to continue the age-long pursuit of placing China under the commercial supremacy of Britain and open up the whole country through better trade regulations, or to follow both policies simultaneously, such as suggested by the Liverpool Chamber of Commerce.[44] The outcome was never clearly defined in any official statement, but as it developed it assumed an aspect resembling the combination of these alternatives:

extract from China a large number of concessions in widely separated parts of the empire, but at the same time make them all connectable with some special area primarily of concern to Britain. The major railway demands were linked either with the Yangtse region or with some British-administered territory. The Foreign Office urged MacDonald to obtain a British concession of the East China trunk line, the Tientsin-Chinkiang Railway, before the mercantile circle had expressed any enthusiasm for the venture. MacDonald's pressure also succeeded in making the Tsungli Yamen grant the mining and railway concessions to the Peking Syndicate with such speed that they were obtained long before the Syndicate could be placed on an operating basis.[45] These incidents indicated that, from the British point of view, the concessions had to be acquired, not only because of their economic value, but also for the political weight they might add to Britain's side in her competition with other powers in China.

And finally, the large number and wide distribution of British concessions were greatly facilitated by the semi-willingness on the part of the Peking government. British demands seldom met with serious objections from the officials. Chang Chih-tung, for example, stood in favor of granting the Shansi-Honan mining and railway rights to the British, so that by the retention of British interest in North China, Russian influence might be diluted. "The bear, the tiger, and the wolf have different names, but they are all man-eaters."[46] The argument being that, since it was impossible to reject the British railway demands, China must try to utilize them for her own purposes, while at the same time she should be wary of all foreign concession seekers alike. It also has been observed above that the Shanghai-Nanking Railway loan was awarded to the British and Chinese Corporation with the complete approval of the Director-General of the Railway Administration, supported by the contention that it would promote friendly relations with Britain. Similarly, the Soochow-Hangchow-Ningpo Railway was decided in favor of the same corporation without too much reluctance, after the dissolution of the short-lived Anglo-German partnership in April. This, the Chinese officials calculated, would serve as another balance against German inroads in Eastern China.[47]

There seemed to have been another motive for the Chinese accession to British railway demands. It was the formally non-governmental nature of the concessions. Placed in the hands of private firms, the loans and control of the rail lines were regarded with less apprehension by the Chinese officials than were the railway enterprises directly under forign government auspices, such as the French and Russian lines. When objections were raised, for instance, against the building of the Canton-Kowloon Railway for fear that it would destroy the value of coastal defenses of South China, Sheng Hsüan-huai was adamant against any idea of the cancellation of the preliminary agreement. He contended that this agreement, concluded with Jardine's, marked the successful transference of a diplomatic demand to the field of business contract; its cancellation would inevitably bring forth the matter for diplomatic negotiations, and it was feared that the results therefrom would prove to be even more unfavorable to China.[48] Under existing conditions, the railways were at least Chinese government property, and their administration rested nominally within the framework of provincial jurisdiction. And since those were preliminary agreements, there was hope that the terms might be somewhat modified when it came to writing the final agreements.

This does not mean, of course, that the Chinese government would have voluntarily offered the railway concessions as gifts to the British syndicates. Those schemes of alignment, which ostensibly aimed at the creation of a power-equilibrium in China, in the last analysis were largely but mental exercises of officials who sought to alleviate the humiliation of their inability to stand up against foreign encroachments by trying to make the most of an intolerable situation. The fist-pounding foreign representatives—of whom not the least bellicose was Sir Claude MacDonald who enjoyed the support of London and the Royal Navy,[49]—filled the officials with a grievious sense of helplessness, and probably inspired many of them to try their hands at a sort of power politics. But the truth was that they lacked the means and the determination seriously to resist the demands made by the British Minister.

How narrow the bridge was that the Chinese government trod among the powers, and the wariness with which each power was watched, could be illustrated by an Imperial order issued in the winter of 1898. Lord Charles Beresford was then making his tour of China, gathering information about British trade, and offering proposals for British-supervised reforms of the Chinese government. He had just left Peking for the Yangtse region, when Governor-Generals Liu K'un-i and Chang Chih-tung were instructed by the Throne that, should Beresford present to them his proposal of establishing a Military Bureau in Peking with British advisors, his suggestion must be repulsed. The only thing that could be considered was to follow a previous plan for training 2,000 modernized troops (with British aid) in Hupeh, under Chinese control.[50] In other words, Britain's good will should be cultivated by the granting of favors here and there, but at the same time she must not be given too marked an ascendancy at the capital.

Thus, through the combination of circumstances described above, British business desire for economic expansion, the effort of the British government to counterbalance the gains of other powers in China in order to safeguard her strategic and economic position, and the Chinese officials' aim to achieve some stability by utilizing Britain's rivalry with the other powers, the large number of railway concessions were acquired by British firms in 1898.

A preliminary agreement was as a rule concluded between the interested British syndicate and an agency of the Chinese government. The latter was in most cases the Imperial Railway Administration, but in the case of the Peking Syndicate's mining and railway rights the Shansi and Honan provincial authorities were the respective contracting parties. All demands were accorded diplomatic support by the British Minister at Peking, and the preliminary agreements bore the official approval of the Tsungli Yamen.

Preliminary agreements for two of the concessions—the Canton-Kowloon and the Tientsin-Chinkiang lines—were not consummated until the spring of 1899. But that for the Shanghai-Nanking Railway was concluded in May, 1898, and served as a model for the others. Those for the Soochow-Hangchow-Ningpo and Pukou-Sinyang lines, for example, consisted chiefly of the provision that terms for the loan should be identical with those governing the financing and construction of the Shanghai-Nanking Railway.

The striking features of that agreement were the stringent financial provisions, and the high degree of authority over railway administration vested in the British chief engineer. The issuing price to the Chinese government was set at 90; that is, the latter was to receive £90 out of each £100 loan bond, whatever might be the selling price, with profit or loss from the sale going to the Corporation; [51] the property and revenue of the line were to be placed on mortgage in case of default; and the creditor also enjoyed a variety of other economic advantages, such as the participation in the net profit of the line, among other things. The British chief engineer exercised the power of appointment and dismissal of the entire railway staff below his own rank.[52] These terms, however, were eventually modified to various degrees, as their subsequent history shows.

The fiercest phase of the "battle for concessions" was over, but it only left China and her foreign relations in a state of greater tension than ever before. There were evidences that the Peking government's capitulations were not accepted without question by the various parts of Chinese society, nor did they produce conciliation among the powers. By the middle of 1899, for example, the British and the French were at loggerheads again in the southwest. Both had simultaneously sent railway survey parties to Yunnan, each headed by an official of respectable rank. Neither had acted according to the treaty provisions.

Their presence and the prospective railway, moreover, gave rise to deep resentment on the part of the provincial transportation interests.[53] The two-fold problem of Chinese opposition and power politics was henceforth to become a constant element, with variable intensity, in the fortunes of British railway interests in China.

II

Railways of the Yangtse Delta

BRITISH RAILWAY INTERESTS in the lower Yangtse region consisted of two lines, the Shanghai-Nanking and the Soochow (later changed to Shanghai)-Hangchow-Ningpo railways. Actually they are two branches of a single system serving this agriculturally fertile and commercially well-developed area, but the difference in their relationship with the British creditor was significant. In the case of the Shanghai-Nanking Railway, the terms of the loan were highly objectionable to the Chinese but were accepted with little more than verbal protest. As regards the other line, the provincial interest waged a bitter contention against the British concessionaire, and nearly succeeded in unseating him.

Behind events concerning both railways lay the fact that these lines were considered extremely important in British mercantile circles. But if serious provincial opposition was encountered in one railway, what were the reactions the British received in connection with the other? Which aspects in the Shanghai-Nanking loan contract were the most unwelcome to the Chinese? When provincial opposition arose in regard to the Hangchow railway, on what grounds were the British able to press their claim and obtain a loan contract, despite the fact that the railway was already being built without the aid of foreign capital even as the controversy was going on? Did the Peking government follow a consistent policy throughout these developments?

THE SHANGHAI-NANKING RAILWAY

The Loan of 1903. As soon as the Boer War and the Boxer uprisings were over, the British and Chinese Corporation again took up the matter of railway concessions. Its attention was first concentrated on the Shanghai-Nanking Railway as being the line of primary importance. Byron Brenan, former British consul-general at Shanghai, was chosen to discuss the matter with Sheng Hsüan-huai.[1]

Difficulties arose during the negotiations. They were partly due to the Corporation's wish to exact the best terms it could get, and partly due to the efforts of the Chinese to retrieve some of the rights they had signed away in the preliminary articles. The Chinese, for instance, questioned the Corporation's new demand that it should receive a 5 per cent commission on all materials purchased for the railway, and proposed the appointment of a Chinese government agent to inspect the accounts.[2] These signs of native interest in railways and assertion of rights were not appreciated by the British negotiator. Sheng attributed the delays to Brenan's artful bickering: "Every article had to be fought over. Brenan had long been a consul-general in China and is full of machinations. The British Minister was moreover backing him by repeatedly urging a conclusion." [3]

In negotiating for the final agreement, Sheng had the collaboration of Chang Chih-tung, who was then serving as the acting governor-general of Nanking.[4] These two leading advocates of the railway in China had frequently differed in their ways of approach to a problem and in their tactics of solving it. But in this instance they agreed that the terms for this loan should be more favorable to the Chinese side than the preliminary agreement had provided. There existed a Sino-American agreement regarding the building of the Hankow-Canton Railway containing stipulations that were considered somewhat less disadvantageous to China.

These stipulations included letting the Chinese Railway Administration, instead of the concessionaire, buy the necessary land for the railway, and the appointment of a joint board of control and of a Chinese managing director. This agreement was taken as the model for the new negotiations by Sheng and Chang.[5]

Sheng complained of the exacting terms proposed by the British and Chinese Corporation when the negotiations were opened. They would deprive China of all sovereign rights over the railway, he said.[6] But in the course of discussions certain changes were made. On the whole, the feeling among the Chinese was that the loan conditions were somewhat better than the worst that could have been imposed. Although the total amount of the loan was £3,250,000, and the interest rate raised from 4½ to 5 per cent, the issuance of bonds had to be subject to the needs of the actual work of construction, and the first issue was set at £2,250,000 only. A time limit of thirty-nine months was set for the completion of the line. The time in which China could redeem the whole amount without extra charge was changed from twenty-five years to twelve and a half years. Provision was made against the interference in local affairs on the part of the British chief engineer. All those points were highly recommended to the Throne,[7] and the document was signed on July 9, 1903.[8]

A comparison of the more salient features of the loan's provisions with those of the preliminary agreement shows that the vaunted improvements really did not amount to much. The sum of the loan was in fact increased from £3,000,000 to £3,250,000, which was £1,000,000 in excess of the then current estimates of construction costs. As stated before, the amount actually floated on the market as the first issue was £2,250,000.[9] The issuing price was 90 per cent of the nominal value of each bond,[10] which was the same as that stipulated in the preliminary agreement, and it represented the lowest price on railway loan bonds in China during the period under survey. Security for the loan was the whole property and revenue of the Shanghai-Nanking Railway itself, so that in case of default it was subject to mortgage and control by the creditor. After the railway was in operation the British and Chinese Corporation was to receive 20 per cent of the net profits after deduction of all expenses. Furthermore, in accordance with the demand of the Corporation, a 5 per cent commission was given to it on all purchases of material.[11] This last item represented an additional financial advantage for the concessionaire not stipulated in the preliminary agreement. As to the disposition of the funds raised from the sale of bonds, Article IV provided that the amount needed for the construction of specific sections of the railway should be transferred to the Hongkong and Shanghai Bank at Shanghai, after such sums as might be required for the purchase of materials and payments of contracts in England were deducted and kept there.[12] Here the importance of railway concessions to the industrial earnings of the investing country was plainly indicated.

One of the most serious concerns of the Chinese at this date in their transactions with foreigners arose from their increasing awareness that they were constantly losing Chinese sovereign rights. Therefore the question of the British chief engineer's authority became an important issue. Article VI of the final agreement curtailed this individual's powers considerably as compared with those provided for in the preliminaries (wherein he was vested with the right to appoint the entire staff of the railway's employees), and it was expressly stated in the same article that he should always pay due "consideration" to the Chinese governmental authorities. A Board of Commissioners composed of both British and Chinese was established for the administration of the railway.[13] But as we shall see more fully later, these provisions were not thorough enough to solve the problem of Chinese versus English authority in railway matters.[14]

A Second Issue. As soon as the loan had been floated on the market in the middle of 1904, Chinese desire to redeem the line became manifest. This was expressed from two quarters. The officials such as Sheng Hsüan-huai and Chang Chih-tung approached the question of redemption as a bond-buying proposition. When the bonds were put on sale, the Hongkong and Shanghai Bank asked Sheng how many the Chinese wanted to buy so that these could be put aside. Sheng in turn urged the provincial authorities to encourage investment in the undertaking, claiming that the value of the bonds would surely increase with the completion of the construction. It also appeared that Chinese employees of the railway had been ordered to purchase bonds according to their individual ability.[15] Chang Chih-tung concurred in this policy by saying: "This railroad lies in the richest part of China. We must and should buy in as many bonds as possible in order to preserve our rights." [16]

In the following year redemption proposals of a more radical nature came from a different direction. The new enthusiasm for railway development was stirring the country. This new movement demanded the cancellation of railway contracts already entered into with foreign concessionaires and the formation of Chinese railway companies to undertake the work of construction. In connection with the Shanghai-Nanking Railway, two groups in Kiangsu made their desires articulate. Certain members of the gentry petitioned the Governor of Kiangsu in September, 1905, to allow them to raise the necessary money and construct the railway themselves. Students at the modern "high school" at Kiang-ying also telegraphed the Governor-General of Liangkiang, urging the complete redemption of the Shanghai-Nanking Railway. But whether or not these designs, official or otherwise, could be put into practice was another question.

Faced with the demands of the gentry and students, the railway administrator demurred on grounds of practical difficulty: Sheng held that the construction of the line was already half-way done, and that the British were not likely to give up the concession at this point; nor did he think the Kiangsu people capable of raising the necessary funds for the undertaking. He maintained that the best thing to do was to aim at the gradual recovery of China's control of this line through increasing purchases of bonds.[17] At the same time, the Throne adopted a similar policy of bowing to both the rising nationalist movement and to the power of foreign finance. It declared that the Shanghai-Nanking Railway should be redeemed at an early date; but as to how this was to be done was left to Sheng to arrange.[18] Here the problem stagnated, since Sheng was not sympathetic to any suggestion of direct redemption. In the matter of bond purchase, on the other hand, all he could do was limited to the asking of the provincial authorities to encourage investment. Actually no formal channel was available to insure the implementation of a policy of recovery.

The decree ordering early redemption was occasioned by attacks on the affairs of this railway, attacks which ultimately resulted in the dismissal of Sheng Hsüan-huai as administrator of the Shanghai-Nanking line, and the appointment of a rising young official in the Foreign Ministry, T'ang Shao-i, to that post.[19] Financial mismanagement was the chief point in the Chinese indictment of the Railway Administration. It has been bruited about in the English press that the supply of land, skilled labor, and construction materials had been "cornered" by Sheng's son and other provincial interests, thus increasing the cost of construction.[20] The censors criticized such a state of affairs as wasteful and detrimental to the nation, in that it increased China's financial burden. The airing of the suspicious financial state of the road, and the change of the Railway Administrator were taken by a part of the modern press in China as a sign of the Chinese people's rising interest in national affairs. Special pride was shown in the fact that members of the Kiangsu gentry had actively taken part in the episode by signing a petition against the mismanagement of railway affairs. Outwardly at least, the British mercantile opinion at Shanghai pooh-poohed this interpretation of the situation, and stoutly defended the Corporation's construction record as well as the admittedly excessive estimates of expenditure.[21]

But the new administrator found the conditions in the accounting department in great confusion. T'ang Shao-i reported that the accounts submitted to him by both the chief accountant and by Sheng were unacceptable. The Boards of Commerce and of Finance also admitted that they were not able to ascertain the costs of construction, the revenue of the operating sections, or to estimate the total cost, since Sheng had never made reports to the Boards.[22]

Instead of being able to proceed with any kind of redemption plans, the administration found itself obliged to borrow more money from England. The schemes of speedy redemption mentioned by T'ang's predecessor had proved impractical. But the news of a proposed addition to the existing railway debts brought forth protests from some Chinese officials. Disappointment was expressed that T'ang had not effected immediate improvement in the railway administration, and the additional issuance of loan bonds to the amount of £700,000 was deplored. If the building of this railroad, which had already cost more than other roads per mile, really required more funds, it was then suggested that a part of the profits from the operation of the Peking-Hankow Railway be turned over to fill the needs. In any case, further obligations to foreign creditors, with their attendant disadvantages, such as the 90 per cent issuing price, must be avoided.[23]

It should be pointed out that the additional obligation here contemplated would not constitute a fresh loan, but would be merely a second issue of the 1903 loan bonds. However, according to Article V, paragraph 11, of the loan agreement, the British and Chinese Corporation was to notify the Chinese government before the second issue was made, in order that the Chinese government might have a chance to use its own capital for this railway. In that event the amount so used would be deducted from the total loan of £3,250,000.[24] Early in 1906, then, the agent of the Corporation, J. O. P. Bland, and the British Chief Engineer, Collinson asked T'ang for a second issue of £700,000.[25]

Eager to seize this opportunity to demonstrate China's ability to finance at least part of a railway line, the Peking government and T'ang Shao-i carried on a lengthy discussion. In the end the Board of Commerce concluded that, the additional amount now considered necessary for the completion of the railway being £650,000 (which was the equivalent of 4,700,000 taels), it was beyond the ability of the government treasury to furnish such a large sum. A second issue of loan bonds would thus have to be granted. This new obligation was made to seem less burdensome by the Board's pointing out to the Throne the fact that Chinese subjects could purchase the bonds, and that the price of the bonds to the Chinese government had been advanced from 90 to 95 or 96 per cent. Imperial consent to this second issue was quickly obtained.[26]

Thus, through the lack of available funds, the efforts of the Chinese government to provide capital for the completion of this important railway, and for the reduction of the total loan, were not successful, but as a result of the objections raised against the new issue of bonds, the conditions were changed slightly to the advantage of the Chinese. The price of remittance finally agreed on was 95½ per cent. A British writer on the subject expressed surprise at the difficulties encountered by the British and Chinese Corporation when the question of a second issue was raised. He remarked that 95½ per cent was the best price that China had ever gotten in loan bonds.[27] It was actually more than that. When we recall that, since the £700,000 was only a part of the 1903 loan fund, and that their issue should be governed by the conditions provided in the 1903 agreement, the significance of the change becomes remarkable. It was one of the signs indicating that the Chinese were launching in earnest a railway movement of their own.

The Question of Control. Such a nationalistic tendency found expression in the friction between the Chinese and the British in the matter of personnel and power of control over the Shanghai-Nanking Railway. Here the champions of China's rights over her own government railways confronted the power that held the financial whip. The fact that the "old China hands" were highly satisfied with the loan agreement and regarded it as the first triumph of British finance,[28] meant that it would be considered with apprehension by the Chinese.

The controversy over the personnel of the railway administration revolved around the position of chief engineer, and the composition of the Board of Commissioners. Article VI of the loan agreement provided for the creation of a board of five members, of whom two were to be Chinese and three English; among the latter was the chief engineer, who was to be "nominated" by the British and Chinese Corporation but "approved" by the director-general of the Chinese Railway Administration. His functions were "limited" to the construction and operation of the line, "and the management of affairs connected with the railway." [29] But when the first chief engineer, Collinson, came to get his contract signed, difficulties arose. The British Minister relayed to the Foreign Ministry at Peking a complaint from the British Consul-General in Shanghai, charging Sheng with suddenly demanding that the chairman of the Board of Commissioners be a Chinese. Otherwise, Sheng allegedly threatened, he would not sign the engineer's contract, thereby delaying the beginning of construction.[30]

Sheng's reply to the Foreign Ministry's inquiry indicated the importance which the Chinese attached to the question of personnel. According to Sheng, the British corporation had, first, asked the chief engineer to sign the contract with the Board of Commissioners instead of with the director-general, and, second, had insisted on a Jardine agent's becoming the chairman of the Board. In that case, the chief engineer would not be under the control of the Chinese Railway Administration, and the Board would be entirely dominated by the British. Therefore, he would refuse to sign the contract and the bonds (which were just then awaiting release to the market) unless those two points were settled. He concluded his communication with these words:

> It is the common practice of foreign companies to argue for rights between the lines of an agreement, and one moment's carelessness will bring decades of disadvantages. If the bonds are signed and floated now, the rights will have been irrevocably lost. Please request Minister Satow to ask Jardine's not to raise this unreasonable fuss, so that we may continue our relations in the future.[31]

In fact, the value of a railway agreement was then very often judged by the Chinese in terms of "disadvantages"—and the Shanghai-Nanking loan agreement was, from that point of view, one of the worst. The Board of Finance described it as a railway operating under conditions more disadvantageous to China than the Peking-Hankow line, and the major difficulty lay with the Board of Commissioners. Not only were the Chinese members of the Board outnumbered at meetings, but also those Chinese who could not speak English were helpless.[32] The Board's fairness in the conduct of its affairs, especially where it touched Chinese and British rights, was seriously questioned in a Chinese government report.[33]

Another source of Chinese dissatisfaction was the financial arrangements. By the loan agreement the control of all money matters rested with the English chief accountant. Moreover, the managers of traffic and of materials were foreign, and the purchase of materials was undertaken by the Corporation. Although a Chinese government agent could inspect the accounts of the railway, he was nevertheless without authority over the actual administration of the railway.[34] The Board of Finance proposed adding a Chinese co-manager to most of the departments in order to have "equal authority" with the British in railway administration.[35] Whether or not these co-managers could escape being mere figureheads was a question not considered at that time.

Discussions for the purpose of setting up a working agreement more in favor of China were begun in late 1905 after Tang Shao-i became the director-general of the railway. By 1908, when the whole line had been opened to traffic, a working agreement was concluded.[36]

An investigation of the provisions reveals that despite some modifications, the Chinese government had failed to reduce the real powers exercised by British railway officials. In 1908 the following offices were held by the British: secretary and chief accountant, auditor and assistant auditor, traffic manager, traffic inspector, station inspector, manager of materials, chief engineer and ten assistant engineers, four inspectors of tracks, and other positions making a total of 59 out of 180 officers of middle and higher ranks. The Chinese officers were mostly assistants to English departmental or sectional heads, station masters, or occupants of offices of still lower rank.[37]

As to the composition of the Board of Commissioners—

i.e., the central administrative organ of the railway—the final solution embodied in the working agreement was to have a Chinese official, appointed by the Board of Posts and approved by the British and Chinese Corporation, serve as the head with the title of managing director.[38] This person was to act as the representative of the Board of Posts, and his duty was to supervise generally the working of the railway; he was to sign all checks and orders for imported materials, these to be countersigned by the chief accountant; and he was to receive reports from the heads of the various departments. However, a new post, that of a general manager, was also created in the working agreement. It was specified that the British chief engineer was to hold this post concurrently, and his function was "to be responsible to the Managing Director . . . for the details of the Railway Management, including general control of the various departments and the appointment of subordinate employees of the rank of foremen or under." [39] For appointment of employees above the rank of foremen the general manager was to consult the managing director. When necessary he was to be consulted by the latter about affairs of the railway; departmental reports were submitted to the managing director only through him (excepting the report of the chief accountant, which was sent direct to the managing director). The general manager, moreover, was to make out a budget for the railway every six months or one year, and no item could be added to or omitted from it by the managing director "except after full discussion with the General Manager." Instructions from the managing director to the departments were also to be sent through the general manager as a matter of general practice.[40]

In short, the British chief engineer was still very much the actual administrator of the railway, though acting under a new and different title, and placed under the nominal authority of a Chinese official director. The scope of his functions, so comprehensively stated in Article VI of the 1903 agreement, had thereby received a more concrete definition, but his relation with Chinese authorities remained essentially the same.

THE CONTROVERSY OVER THE SHANGHAI-HANGCHOW-NINGPO RAILWAY LOAN [41]

In the long run, the British and Chinese Corporation reaped an unexpected harvest from the Shanghai-Nanking contract. The more objectionable features of the loan agreement evidently served as a stimulant to the Chinese and helped to quicken the pace of their own efforts at railway development, in order to avoid more foreign obligations. Between 1904 and 1906 Kiangsu and Chekiang became actively engaged in organizing provincial railway companies under the leadership of the gentry-officials.[42] In the course of this activity, friction with foreign concessionaires emerged and came to a head over the question as to which—the British firm or the Chinese companies—had the right to construct the Soochow-Hangchow-Ningpo line.

The Basis of the Conflict. The preliminary agreement of 1898 granted the British and Chinese Corporation the right to finance and construct a railway from Soochow on the Shanghai-Nanking line to Hangchow and Ningpo in Chekiang, on the same terms as the Nanking-Shanghai Railway loan. It was taken by the concessionaire as a compact valid for all time, assuming that the Chinese could fill only a negative role in these matters. But when this negative role changed and assumed a positive aspect, the whole mechanism of the concession system fell into confusion.

From the juridical point of view, the problem was simply this: Peking had given the right of railway construction to the provincial gentry in 1905 and 1906, when it sanctioned the establishment of the Chekiang and Kiangsu railway companies, in spite of the fact that from the begining there was a clear indication of possible conflict with the previous British concession. Yet it was not a case of willful whims on the part of the Chinese government. It was essentially a test to see whether the making of foreign railway loans should be determined solely by the needs of the Chinese, or whether the law of Western business should predominate over the situation, regardless of the right and aspirations of the Chinese to construct their own railways.

The Chekiang gentry's interest in railway development, centering on Hangchow, first manifested itself in 1897, and took definite shape in 1904. The British and Chinese Corporation having shown no active interest in the Soochow-Hangchow-Ningpo Railway by 1903, there was some doubt among the Chinese whether the concession was still to be enforced. Sheng Hsüan-huai, in a letter to the Corporation, declared that if the surveying and construction work on this railway did not commence within six months of his writing, the preliminary agreement would be considered void.[43] This was a unilateral declaration regarding a bilateral contract, and the British and Chinese Corporation chose not to commit itself, and did not reply. But Sheng took this silence to mean tacit acquiescence, with important consequences.

In 1904 Sheng explicitly encouraged the Chekiang gentry to proceed with their railway plans.[44] At that time the line contemplated was only a short railroad in the neighborhood of Hangchow. But with the formal establishment of the Chekiang Railway Company in 1905, the plans expanded. The company was imperially ordered to formulate an overall railway scheme for the province. By 1907 the initial line was incorporated into a provincial rail plan centering at Hangchow.[45] This clashed directly with the British concession.

The situation was further complicated by a sentence in the preliminary agreement of 1898: "in case there should arise local difficulties, it [the agreement] should then be adjusted accordingly."[46] Did this give the Chinese a free hand to change the conditions of the concession as situations demanded? The Chinese railway administrator took the affirmative view and used it as a point of argument, but it carried little weight. When the talk of cancellation was in the air, the British thought it wiser to cling to their claim as a contractual right, and ignored China's finer arguments of right of change. Under these circumstances, what was the policy taken by the Court at Peking?

The Position of the Chinese Government. Having definitely gone along with the provincial railway ambitions, Peking then turned to the question of the British concession. As time went on the government found itself increasingly hard pressed by both sides. How to resolve the conflict between the British financiers and the Chinese gentry without rousing the overwhelming resentment of either became therefore the foremost problem.

In the autumn of 1905 confidence and hope prevailed in China. The recent "redemption" of the Hankow-Canton Railway seemed to encourage the government and people in the thought that it was not too difficult to get rid of undesirable foreign leaseholds on the country's railways after all. "Let Sheng Hsüan-huai negotiate the matter speedily, and [the railway] must be redeemed so that it be developed by our own people," ordered an Imperial Decree dated September 24, 1905.[47]

In cooperation with the provincial authorities, Sheng reiterated the desire to cancel the 1898 agreement. But the British concessionaire offered stiff resistance. After six months of futile talk, Sheng reported to the Throne, justifying the provincial position on two counts: the absence of actual work on the line by the British, and the clause in the preliminary agreement regarding adjustment in accordance with local difficulties. At this point British diplomatic pressure was brought to bear at Peking, and it was intimated that Sheng was not welcome to continue his superintendency of the matter.[48]

The situation was this: Without arguing whether or not their concession had the reason to be continued, the British simply held that it existed and was valid. They began to bypass the railway administration and the provincial interests, and applied their pressure, through the British Minister, directly at Peking.[49] This gradually led to a divergence of viewpoints between Peking and the provinces, and also pointed the way to the compromise that was eventually reached.

By the middle of 1906 the negotiations were transferred to Peking, where for more than a year the Foreign Ministry was besieged by both sides of the contention. The British Minister was persistent in his efforts to secure a speedy conclusion of the loan on the basis of the preliminary agreement. The provincial interests were equally determined in the opposite direction, and had as spokesmen a group of metropolitan officials from Chekiang. But if the evidences of national "awakening" in railway affairs were impressive, the nature of the foreign reaction to it was also unmistakably emphatic. In the English press and in Parliament the sentiment was reiterated that the 1898 concessions must be upheld, while the British mercantile circles in Shanghai protested against the new regulations concerning restriction of foreign mining investment in China.[50] Therefore the controversy over the Hangchow railway assumed the aspect of a test case. The Peking Foreign Ministry tried to base its arguments on a *fait accompli:* that the Kiangsu and Chekiang railway companies had already been formed, that work on the line had already been started, and that the Chinese government could not stop its own people from building their own railways. Sir John Jordan insisted vigorously that the previous agreement still held. The

Foreign Ministry finally was persuaded by Jordan's argument to recognize their legal obligations, and conceded that complete annulment of the preliminary agreement did not seem possible. At this point the Chinese government was ready to agree to a loan; but its terms would have to be more favorable to China than were those of the Shanghai-Nanking Railway. After further negotiation Jordan agreed to this, and to a *modus vivendi* proposed by the Chinese officials, that the loan and the power of control over the railway should be separated.[51]

From its overconfident state of mind at the beginning of the negotiations the Throne now perforce had to be stern with its Chinese subjects, in order that the British could remain quiet. The burden of an edict dated October 20, 1907, was that the Chekiang and Kiangsu gentry-capitalists should desist from their railway venture, and allow a loan for the Soochow-Hangchow-Ningpo Railway to be consummated.[52]

Far from improving the situation, this change of stand by the Peking government touched off a series of protests from the provinces. The official-gentry-capitalists declared that the provincial companies had already accumulated sufficient capital, and therefore needed no loan.[53] In the last quarter of 1907 both the provincial and the Peking authorities were subject to renewed pressure. Under the proposed arrangement with the British, the provinces still had the financial burden of the loan to bear. Also, aside from their patriotism, the gentry saw that their business fortune was at stake, and created such a state of agitation that the Throne became thoroughly alarmed. At the height of the imbroglio an edict was issued ordering the governors and governor-generals to be vigilant; it was possible that these struggles for the railway were only a front for the revolutionary elements to perpetrate their subversive deeds![54]

At the same time, however, the Peking government also saw that it was impossible to conclude the matter without pacifying the provincial contenders. Therefore a third attitude was adopted. The Throne assumed a pleading tone, and asked the gentry to understand that "all mention of our past obligations and of the present way of settling the affair are truly due to the pressure of circumstances."[55] The Foreign Minister invited representatives of the provinces to Peking for a conference. But it also made it clear that the arguments of the western laws of contract had won the case; and that given the unequal relations existing between China and the Great Powers, it was impolitic and impossible to ignore or act contrary to their usages. In any case, Peking was not prepared to do so.[56]

The Outcome. With the Peking government thus orientated, the ground was laid for the final agreement. The continued stormy protests from the provincial representatives, however, was rewarded by a concession in their favor: the loan was to be accredited to the Board of Posts and Communications instead of to Chekiang and Kiangsu, and was to be paid back by that Board.[57] Sheng Hsüan-huai, now acting as mediator between Peking and the provinces, attempted to bring the matter to a close on this basis.

The problem of control of the railway remained to be settled. Modeling it on the system provided by the terms of the Shanghai-Nanking railway loan agreement was out of the question; instead, the newly consummated Tientsin-Pukou railway loan contract was taken as example. The latter agreement, by pledging certain government revenue instead of the railway as security, was regarded as a great advance to the benefit of China. It was believed that by this means the control of the line in question would not be affected by the foreign financier, but would remain in the hands of the Chinese. Therefore, with all sides acquiescing, the Shanghai-Hangchow-Ningpo Railway Loan of £1,500,000 was signed on March 6, 1908, in Peking, by representatives of the Chinese government and of the British and Chinese Corporation.[58]

Compared to the terms for the Shanghai-Nanking Railway loan, the present agreement points to a number of differences in detail. Unlike the Shanghai-Nanking loan, this one was secured not on the earnings of the railway itself, but on the surplus earnings of the Imperial railways of North China, so that in the event of default the Shanghai-Hangchow-Ningpo would not be mortgaged, nor the Chinese power of control lost to the British creditors.[59] In this connection we must recall that at the time of the negotiations, the government at Peking was in no position to institute a claim for the disposition of the provincial railways. This provision, though in line with developments regarding loan terms in the period, must therefore also be considered as much a measure of expediency as of policy. It was also questionable how much real independence was gained by the Chinese. The North China Railways were under financial obligations to, and under the virtual control of, the same Corporation; therefore they had not freed themselves from any possible pressure had the occasion arose for it.

The greatest difference between this and the Shanghai-Nanking loan lay in the terms governing administrative authority. The agreement provided that the Chinese government was to have the rights of construction and control of the railway. The Board of Posts or a managing director appointed by it was to select a British chief engineer who would function under the authority of the Chinese official.[60] Actually, the Peking government for the time was only the nominal administrator of this railroad. Construction and management remained in the hands of the provincial companies until after the Republican Revolution of 1911.

A further concession was obtained by these companies in

the partial re-routing of the line. In order to accommodate a stretch of the line already built by the Kiangsu Company, the northern terminus was formally changed from Soochow to Shanghai. The Cha-k'ou section outside Hangchow, then under construction, was also incorporated into the line to avoid loss by the Chekiang Company.[61] Thus the Shanghai-Hangchow-Ningpo Railway acquired its present course and name.

The net result of over three year's controversy was now clear: The British financiers got their loan; for years the £1,500,000 were kept in banks, producing interest at five per cent for the creditors. But the money was not used for the construction of the railway for which the loan was contracted, because the gentry of the provinces were able to furnish the necessary funds.[62] The provincial railway companies built their railway that linked Kiangsu and Chekiang, an indication of the capability of the gentry-capitalists. The Peking government, however, received much the worst part of the bargain: it was obliged to accept a new foreign loan, and by its vacillating policies lowered even further its own position in the country.

A COMPARISON

Both the Shanghai-Nanking and the Shanghai-Hangchow-Ningpo railways served areas that were considered as part of the Yangtse "sphere" of British influence. Moreover, the former line was generally regarded as the first stretch of a system of rail communications leading toward the opening of the middle and upper Yangtse country to foreign—in this case British—trade.[63] The conclusion of what, for the British, was a successful loan agreement in 1903 symbolized the first fruit of 1898 harvested by the British financiers. The Hangchow railroad was also considered highly important by the British mercantile circle, but the conclusion of its loan in 1908 signified the closing of an era in which British capital alone was able to accomplish the task of railway politics in China. It was the last instance in which demands of British financiers were pressed and brought to a conclusion—even with modifications. To understand the differences between these two railway loans it is necessary that we glance over the circumstances surrounding the loan negotiations in each case.

So far as the British were concerned, the primary element of anxiety at Shanghai was the presence of strong rival foreign interests—especially those of Germany. The fear of foreign competition, first manifested in 1898,[64] was intensified after the turn of the century. Conflict within the international body in control of Whampoo River conservancy work, differences of opinion in the Shanghai Municipal Council, and above all, apprehension of German designs on the Yangtse region, all contributed to a wave of pessimism and alarmist predictions of Britain's "total eclipse in this [Chinese] empire." [65] While negotiations for the Shanghai-Nanking loan were under way, British nerves at Shanghai were rudely jarred by the report of certain German proposals to the Chinese government asking for promises regarding the Yangtse valley in return for the complete evacuation of foreign garrisons in Shanghai left over from the Boxer days.[66] Further fear was aroused by the suspicion that the Continental Powers were conspiring to take over the finances of China, or at least to supplant the British in the Inspectorate General of the Imperial Maritime Customs.[67]

These inquietudes led to a prolonged series of attacks by the British merchants on the London government, which was accused of not rendering to the British in China as much help as that which the Russian, German, French, and Belgian governments were giving their nationals. The delay in building of British-financed railways, particularly of the

Shanghai-Nanking line, was felt to be especially irritating.[68]

The main reason for this divergence of views between the local British merchant and his home government lay in the fact that in England the forces in favor of formal adherence to the principles of laissez-faire were still powerful. Actually, the charges of non-support rang false more often than true. London was ready to, and did, give support to the British financier seeking a concession in China, when the opponent was only the Peking government. But it was not willing to openly oppose other imperialist powers because of the delicate and tense power balance in China. Ordinarily, operating with complete freedom from government restrictions, the British exporter, financier and shipping-house got their proportionate share of increases in the slowly expanding China market. The Shanghai-Nanking Railway loan was concluded at the beginning of a period which saw an increase in the export of British capital abroad,[69] a phenomenon directly coordinated with the period of railway loans in China.

The British and Chinese Corporation was not slow to seize the chance of a fruitful bargain, and as related above, the terms of the Shanghai-Nanking Railway loan became the most advantageous to the creditor. As late as 1920 one Western writer observed that "the amount of Chinese control over this line is very small indeed." [70] Thus the loan agreement of 1903 served two purposes. It formally launched a British-financed enterprise with a number of economic advantages to the creditor; and it strengthened the position of British interests vis-à-vis the other European Powers, and bolstered British aspirations for further commercial penetration of China. Britain's superior position in this area seemed, temporarily at least, to have been secured.

But the Chinese reaction to these events was not expected by foreign investors of the day. The harsh terms of the Shanghai-Nanking contract provided a stimulus for the crystalization of the nascent Chinese interest in railway development. Led by the gentry-capitalists in the provinces, this clashed frontally with British plans. The controversy over the Shanghai-Hangchow-Ningpo Railway loan contained two noteworthy features. First, even though the Peking authorities were willing to concede the loan to the British and Chinese Corporation, the latter was still unable to obtain it without a modification of the terms. Instead of becoming a model for all British railway loans in China, therefore, the Shanghai-Nanking terms became a unique instance. Second, the Chinese who were the most active in the railway movement of Kiangsu and Chekiang were also active in the movement for constitutional government. Names such as T'ang Shou-ch'ien and Chu Fu-hsien were listed among the energetic participants in the agitations for constitutionalism in 1907 and thereabouts.[71]

As stated before, this fact aroused no little apprehension in the mind of the Court, but in the provinces the interests of these elements waxed strong—people who clung firmly to their age-old privileged position as the learned and moneyed gentry were at the same time waging a contest against foreign encroachment in new economic enterprises such as the railway. In proportion to the extent to which the Peking government was willing to compromise with the British concessionaire, the provincial companies opposed its policy. The construction of the line from Shanghai was pushed apace while the controversy continued, and in the last stages of the dispute the companies stated that their total accumulation of capital had reached the sum of $10,000,000.[72] It is not clear whether the technical work was done by foreign or Chinese personnel. Judging from the histories of other rail lines, it would seem that the construction was undertaken by hired foreign engineers. (The sole known exception to this practice was the Peking-Kalgan Railway which, therefore, immediately became a noted landmark in Chinese railway history.) In any event, the Shanghai-Hangchow-Ningpo line was completed without resort to the British loan funds.

Thus in the lower Yangtse region, for some time regarded by the British as the preserve for their interest and influence, the British and Chinese Corporation was faced with different outcomes from its concessions. Although highly satisfied with the terms of the 1903 Shanghai-Nanking loan, it could not make the loan serve as a model for all later enterprises. In fact, the Hangchow railway loan became purely an interest-bearing item in a bank, with the provincial companies financing and managing the railroad until its nationalization in 1914. Even so, the financial and managerial provisions of the Shanghai-Hangchow-Ningpo Railway loan were changed to the better advantage of the Chinese, because without such changes the loan was not acceptable even to the Peking government. Sir John Jordan admitted that he was astonished by the appearance of a new generation of Chinese on the scene when he returned to China in 1906 after an eight-year absence. In the same year W. W. Rockhill, the American Minister to Peking, found the Chinese self-satisfied for reasons he could not fathom, and "impossible to deal with at present." [73] It would be difficult indeed to gauge from one or two instances the scope and depth of the militancy of the Chinese attitude in this period. But the British creditors' different relations with the Shanghai-Nanking and Shanghai-Hangchow-Ningpo railways, resulting from that attitude, were indicative of a new trend of the times.

III

The Southern Trunk: First Stage

By agreements concluded in 1898, a southern trunk line of an estimated 821 miles was to be built with foreign capital.[1] The major part of this line, the railway running from Hankow to Canton, was to be financed and constructed by the American China Development Company,[2] while the concession over the Canton-Kowloon Railway—a distance of about 112 miles—was obtained by the British and Chinese Corporation. A more ideal situation for the British, of course, would have been for them to have established control over the entire trunk line, for then the emporium of the central Yangtse valley would be brought into direct contact with Hongkong, a free port in the British Crown Colony, lying just across the half-mile strait from Kowloon. Failing to get the desired concession from the Chinese government, the British and Chinese Corporation proceeded to negotiate with the Americans with the objective of establishing a joint Anglo-American enterprise over both the Hankow-Canton and Canton-Kowloon lines. The British were apparently confident of the success of their endeavor, for in late 1898 Sir Claude MacDonald, writing to Lord Charles Beresford, included a half interest on the Hanchow-Canton Railway among the British acquisitions of that year.[3] But the Americans maintained a complete hold over that railway, and the British concern failed in its efforts. Then in 1905 an opportunity arose which enabled the pound-sterling to establish a foothold on the Hankow-Canton line: it financed the Chinese government's redemption of this railway from the American concessionaire.

The Question of Redemption. The redemption of the Hankow-Canton Railway was occasioned by the sale of company stock by the American firm to Belgians. This was in direct contradiction to Article 17 of the Supplementary Agreement of 1900 on the Hankow-Canton Railway, which stated that the American concessionaire was not to transfer the rights of the loan to other nations or people of other nationality.[4] But the real cause for the vehemence of the Chinese action lay deeper than mere dissatisfaction with the American's breach of contract. Similar to the case of the Hangchow railway, the existence of provincial interest in the railway strongly influenced the outcome. In addition, the policy of Chang Chih-tung, Governor-General of Hukuang, was a determinant factor. As we shall see, Chang was suspicious of the Belgian connection, and was determined to recover the railway rights for quick construction, even at the price of more loans from other powers.

Not long after the Supplementary Agreement was concluded in 1900, word came to Sheng Hsüan-huai, the Director of the Railway Administration, that the American company had sold 4,000 of its 6,000 shares to Belgian hands and that two of the seven directors of the company were now Belgian.[5] But Sheng was loath to stir up any commotion, and the idea of changing the American concession made little headway with him. Engaged at that time in negotiating the Mackay Treaty and the Shanghai-Nanking Railway loan agreement, he explained that he was reluctant to cause unnecessary trouble, lest it result in disadvantageous terms for the loan agreement.[6] However, Sheng's attitude—throughout the affair he showed a strong inclination to retain the American contract—can certainly be further explained by the following considerations: his coal interest at P'ing-hsiang, which would be highly benefited by the prompt construction of the

Hankow-Canton Railway according to the existing schedule; his smooth relations with the American company; and the fact that he was possibly persuaded by the argument that American company law did not prohibit the sale of such shares to foreigners.[7]

Chang Chih-tung, on the other hand, held different views:

> It is known that Belgium and France are associated and France is in turn the partner of Russia. The Peking-Hankow Railway is already a Franco-Belgian enterprise; now if the Canton-Hankow line falls into their hands again, then territorial rights of China in both the North and the South would be controlled by France, Belgium, etc., and it will be connected with the Manchurian railway of the Russians into one system. . . . What awful menace that will be to China I can not bear to mention.[8]

When the American concessionaire went so far as to allow a Belgian engineer, Cito, to take part in the surveying of the route, matters were brought to a head.[9] Against the background of power politics a plan for cancelling the American concession began to take root in the mind of Chang Chih-tung.

Here enter the interests of the gentry of Hupeh, Hunan, and Kwangtung provinces. But it is not easy to discover the source of the initiative in the movement for cancellation. To what extent was the governor-general urged by the gentry in his determination to replace the American concession? And how much was the gentry's demands for recovery of the railway rights due to their own material aspirations, and how much to the leadership of Chang Chih-tung? Evidence indicates that the two collaborated closely for their mutual benefit. The reality of the gentry's vociferous demands and protests was unquestionable. They were unleashed on the viceregal authorities, and were much quoted in numerous official communications between Chang Chih-tung, Sheng Hsüan-huai, and the governor-general of Liang-kwang. However, Chang claimed in a memorial that the concern of the gentry over the railway concession began only after they had heard of his own suggestion of cancellation.[10]

This reported concern was very likely an effort to convince the Throne of the altruistic nature of the provincial gentry, and of the movement for redemption as a whole, but that the expressions of the gentry-merchants were not always spontaneous or undirected was shown by other incidents. Chang suggested at one time, for instance, that the Hunanese gentry residing in Shanghai should issue a public petition for cancellation, so that the movement might carry more weight in America.[11] At the same time, such incidents indicate the weight of the moneyed gentry in provincial affairs. Some members of this group were really local magnates of finance. The prominent scholar-official Wang Hsien-ch'ien of Hunan, for example, was one of the most active advocates of the cancellation of the Hankow-Canton concession; he cooperated closely with Chang Chih-tung in this undertaking, and in 1905 became the president of the Hunan Railway Company.[12] It was he who eight years previously had led a group that obtained from Governor-General Chang Chih-tung a monopoly for the transportation of minerals between Changsha and Sha-shih on the Yangtse River. That enterprise was placed under official auspices—that is, the protection of officialdom was formally extended, so that "other merchants" would not encroach on this group's privileges.[13]

The project of cancelling the American concession was actively pursued by Chang Chih-tung from the middle of 1904 on. The urgency of the situation was greatly accentuated by the widespread anti-American agitation and boycotts in China caused by the Chinese exclusion laws, and by local friction between the American surveying crews of the Hankow-Canton railway and the Chinese population.[14]

At that date, however, British capital did not constitute

a part of the plan for redemption. In fact, the participation of foreign capital in any form at any stage of the enterprise was regarded by Peking with apprehension as late as August, 1905.[15] Chang Chih-tung first asked the officials and gentry of the three provinces to raise the necessary funds for purchasing the outstanding stocks of the railway. The latter devised various plans in order to obtain the money through the government: the gentry of Hunan suggested levying additional grain and salt taxes; those of Kwangtung proposed issuing bonds and soliciting capital from abroad; and the Hupeh gentry suggested the sale of public grain stored in local granaries.[16] For a time it appeared as though the official-gentry cooperation was destined to be fruitful. Upon the request of the Hunan gentry leaders, Lung K'an-lin and Wang Hsien-ch'ien, Chang Chih-tung asked the financial commissioner to transfer the revenue derived from grain sales in both Hunan and Hupeh to Shanghai to be used for the purchase of the Hankow-Canton Railway bonds.[17]

At the same time, however, another factor was complicating the scene—the ripening of an "American replacement" plan which had the support of Sheng Hsüan-huai. This plan called for regranting this railway concession to a new American syndicate represented in China by one A. W. Bash who, indeed, was the same person who had signed the original agreement in behalf of the American Development Company in 1898.[18] This situation produced a clash of opinions between Sheng Hsüan-huai and Chang Chih-tung, the latter being determined to recover the concession from any and all American control. The fact that Bash had formerly represented the Development Company deepened Chang's suspicion that some people were trying to pull the wool over his eyes in their attempt to prevent the termination of the concession.

Toward the end of 1904, therefore, Chang queried the authorities of Kwangtung and Hunan regarding the financial prospects in their provinces. He made it clear in the communications that he wanted to ascertain the situation in order to counteract Bash's maneuvers. The answers sufficiently strengthened his hand. The governor-general of Liangkwang and the governor of Kwangtung replied that the gentry in that province were planning to institute the sale of savings bonds, and it was estimated that $1,000,000 per month could be realized in terms of bond value. The answer from Hunan was still more reassuring. The gentry leaders telegraphed Chang, telling him that the railway expenditures would be underwritten by the proceeds from grain reserves, and further, that the gentry-merchants could make up any deficiency that might occur.[19]

With the provinces thus behind him, Chang Chih-tung reiterated with Sheng Hsüan-huai his stand against "American replacement," and turned the argument of popular opinion on Sheng. During January, 1905, the two exchanged polite but acid remarks over the railway problem. It cannot be ascertained whether Sheng had definitely committed himself to Bash, but he did say that he wanted to have no part in sending communications to Minister Liang at Washington regarding cancellation of the original concession. Since he was the director-general of the Railway Administration, it was not difficult for Chang to chide him for this uncooperative attitude, pointing out that the Railway Administration, which had signed the agreement of concession, should be the proper agency to deal with the situation now, and that Sheng could not back out of the difficulty due to personal prejudices.[20]

At the same time, it was probably highly trying for Sheng to be at the head of the Railway Administration and yet find himself unable to exert any influence in the controversy—the traditional forces of provincial gentry-official interests were too deep-seated and powerful. Furthermore, although Sheng was the head of a specialized agency, yet the existing system gave him no recognized right legally to contest the views of the veteran governor-general through whose provinces the greater part of the Hankow-Canton Railway passed. With these intrinsic political factors added to the rising national consciousness of the Chinese people, the general excited state of mind against the United States in 1905 mentioned above, and the fact that Sheng himself was then already in bad grace with the government owing to the Shanghai-Nanking Railway scandals, it was not surprising that his conflict with Chang Chih-tung should have ended in victory for the latter.[21] The Throne also, in its effort to rally some popular support through "reform" measures, was favorable to the idea of complete redemption. Therefore an Imperial decree named Chang the negotiator for the redemption of the concession with the assistance of Minister Liang Ch'eng at Washington, while Sheng was "forbidden to concern himself with it," [22] thus vesting the sole responsibility for the final outcome in Chang's hands.

Meanwhile, negotiations had been going on in the United States, which involved many a high personage in international finance. The parleys resulted in a two-fold arrangement. First, it was agreed that instead of "cancellation" there should be "redemption"; second, the Chinese would purchase with cash the loan bonds, the company shares, and the whole existing property of the railway at a price to be named by the Development Company.[23] The sum finally fixed upon for the redemption was $6,750,000.[24]

But the funds were not forthcoming from the provinces. By the late spring of 1905 Chang Chih-tung saw that Hupeh and Hunan could not meet their obligations. A plan was suggested of raising some funds by additional minting of copper coins in Hunan, with the gentry declaring that so long as the railroad could be recovered, they would not consider the cost.[25] But the plan apparently came to naught. Chang had wired the high provincial authorities at Canton to inquire whether Kwangtung was making any headway in meeting its allotments,[26] and Governor-General Ch'ing was said to have replied:

The gentry of Kwangtung are scattered and unorganized. Those who advocate [the redemption] do not have the money, and those who have the money do not concern themselves with [it]. We definitely cannot rely on the efforts of the gentry, yet government resources are extremely limited and can not be responsible for such a great item . . .[27]

It appears that at this juncture Chang and Ch'ing came to an understanding that the project would have to be financed by a foreign loan. A suggestion by Liang Ch'eng, that J. P. Morgan be allowed to purchase the concession for China on mortgage, was nevertheless turned down by Chang because he did not want to place this railway in the hands of "the most powerful individual in America." [28]

The British Loan. The draft agreement for the Hankow-Canton redemption at $6,750,000 was signed in Washington on June 7, 1905, pending approval by the American China Development Company shareholders, which was not given until August 29.[29] During that interval Chang had broached the subject of a loan with his friend Fraser, the British Consul-General at Hankow, who was able to negotiate for some funds with the Government of Hongkong. However, owing to certain demands that Fraser raised with regard to British interests in Kwangtung province, Chang could not proceed with speed.[30] By the middle of August, nevertheless, the elements of an understanding with the British official had been reached, and Chang Chih-tung urged the Peking authorities to stand firm against renewed attempts by the Belgian and American financiers—through the King of Belgium and J. P. Morgan—to scotch the plan of redemption.[31]

But when at last the shareholders' approval did arrive, a new difficulty had to be surmounted by the Chinese. On

August 31, Chang Chih-tung learned from Liang Ch'eng that the first payment, set at $2,090,806, must be made on or before September 6, otherwise the Development Company would refuse to sign the final agreement for the redemption. This evoked some acid remarks from Chang on the cunning of American tactics which sought to take advantage of the Chinese government's well-known impecuniousness; but the condition had to be met immediately and successfully, or all efforts would come to nothing.[32]

The urgency of the situation was apparent. Yet Fraser just then was away on a vacation and Chang Chih-tung was wary of seeming to be in too helpless a condition, lest it encourage the British to make more demands in exchange for the loan. Fortunately, the Government Currency Exchange of Hupeh (an agency of the provincial government within Chang's jurisdiction) was sufficiently trusted by foreign financial circles, and on Chang's order it borrowed, on its own credit, 3,000,000 taels from the Hongkong and Shanghai Banking Corporation to fulfill on time the first redemption payment in New York.[33]

Remittance of that first payment insured the final conclusion of the redemption agreement. Now that the line was actually taken back by China, the British decided that they ought not to let the opportunity pass without establishing some hold over it. Therefore the Hongkong Government Loan for Redemption of the Canton-Hankow Railway Contract for the sum of £1,100,000 was consummated within the same week. On September 2, Chang asked the permission of the Throne to sign the agreement with the Development Company.[34] Two days later he cabled Liang Ch'eng that funds were on their way to him; on September 4 and 5, the formalities of imperial approval and notices to the British Legation were rushed through at Peking, and the loan agreement with the Hongkong government was signed on September 9. Three days earlier, on September 6, the agreement of redemption had been signed in the United States.[35] In the final discussions for the loan agreement Fraser agreed to drop the demands regarding Kwangtung. Chang described the situation by saying that the British Consul-General was eager to help China achieve her undertaking, seeing that the question of redemption concerned the general political situation.[36] It is clear, however, that Fraser had accomplished just as much for British interests and rights as the Governor-General had apparently done for the Chinese.

The terms of the loan contract were more lenient than those of previous loans. The £1,100,000 were to be amortized in ten years with an annual interest of 4½ per cent.[37] The amount was to be paid to the Chinese in full, that is, without the customary discount; of that sum £400,000 should be remitted to the Hongkong and Shanghai Bank in payment of the money that it lent to the Hupeh Currency Exchange, and £700,000 were to be remitted to Liang Ch'eng to finish payment for the redemption.[38] The loan was secured not on the railway or its property, but on the opium revenue of the three provinces of Hupeh, Hunan, and Kwangtung, and the annual payments were further insured by hypothecating the equivalent amount of internal revenue bonds for that purpose.[39]

The most significant feature of this loan, however, was not contained in the text of the agreement. It was embodied in a letter from Chang Chih-tung to Consul-General Fraser, bearing the date of the signature of the loan agreement. In it preference was given to British nationals in the future railway developments in Hupeh and Hunan:

As regards funds for the future construction of the Canton-Hankow Railway, in case it is necessary to borrow abroad in addition to the amount China may herself provide, the first application shall be made to England, and if the British tender is, as regards interest and issue price, equal to the tenders of the other countries, British financiers shall have the first option of undertaking the business; if in the above and other respects the tenders of other countries are fairer and more favorable than England's, China will be free to choose the fairest and most favorable and make other arrangements for borrowing.[40]

One half of the engineers would be from the nation that lent the money, and the other half would be Japanese; in the purchase of railway materials abroad British firms were to be preferred in a way similar to the loan. Furthermore, if within the jurisdiction of Hupeh and Hunan provinces other railway enterprises called for foreign loans, they were to be determined by the same method.[41]

This provision was naturally not welcomed by the Chinese. Chang Chih-tung consented to it because he wanted to obtain the much-needed loan from Hongkong, the substance of the assurance to the British was in fact first informally given by Chang three weeks previously, when the redemption price was agreed upon.[42] But Ch'ing of Canton objected strenuously to it on grounds of national interest when Chang asked for his assent, and although Fraser's original condition regarding "other railway enterprises" in the future included those of Kwangtung, ultimately in the provision the latter had to be omitted.[43] Opposition to both the conditions of the loan and preference for future British loans also sprang up from among roused Hupeh students in Tokyo, and Chang had to make lengthy explanations to the Throne in defense of his own policy and conduct in answer to severe criticisms directed at his "secret understanding" with the British.[44]

Once the railway was reinstated in Chinese hands, the problem then arose: with what capital was it to be constructed? General patriotic feeling in China was running high at the time of the redemption; great rejoicing was exhibited in Hunan province in late July over a premature press announcement of the cancellation of the American concession, while a dismal picture for foreign business in the Hankow area for the year 1905 was painted by Fraser, who attributed the phenomenon to "Chinese objection to foreign trade" and to the Chinese "rights recovery" movement.[45] In such an environment a further large-scale foreign loan was, temporarily at least, out of the question.

Chang Chih-tung, however, had grave doubts regarding the ability of the provinces to raise enough funds for the construction of the trunk line. It was estimated that the cost for Hunan, including its share both in the redemption loan and in construction, would be over 20,000,000 taels, and provincial opinion together with Chang were disposed toward speedy construction of the railway with a foreign loan. It was particularly Chang's aim to put the line on a normally operating basis, hoping thus to attract large investments from the gentry-merchants and thereby paying back the loan. But under strong objections from the Foreign Ministry this plan had to be given up. Fraser was informed that the Hankow-Canton Railway would be built with Chinese capital raised in the provinces, and there for a brief interval the matter rested.[46]

THE CANTON-KOWLOON RAILWAY LOAN OF 1907

In contrast to the inconclusive hold the British obtained over the Hankow-Canton line, the final Sino-British loan agreement for the Canton-Kowloon Railway was consummated in 1907. Here we are concerned with the 90-mile section of the railroad between Canton and Shumchun, the town on the border of the British-leased territory of Kowloon. This was the length of the line covered by the loan agreement. The rest of the line, 22 miles between Shumchun and Kowloon, was constructed by the government of Hongkong.[47]

The basis for the conclusion of this loan agreement was the preliminary agreement of 1898. But the British and

Chinese Corporation was dissatisfied with its terms, while the loan itself was contracted not without vigorous opposition from the Chinese officials. The Corporation was disappointed that the terms were not modeled upon the Shanghai-Nanking loan provisions, as stated in the preliminary agreement.[48] Early negotiations regarding the Kowloon railway bogged down, it was reported in December, 1904, over the questions of control and division of profits.[49] But another cause was also present, although little known at the time. It was the fact that some of the Chinese officials objected not only to the British corporation's obtaining too lucrative and influential a share in the railway, but that on grounds of national defense they were opposed to seeing this railway built at all.

In 1899, the year after the concession was granted to the British and Chinese Corporation, it was suggested to the Throne that the Canton-Kowloon Railway should not be built, as it would reduce to impotence stragetic points which were important for the defense of Kwangtung province. That suggestion was vetoed by the Director-General of the Chinese Railway Administration, Sheng Hsüan-huai, who thought such a move would involve China and England in a diplomatic dispute which ought to be avoided. Furthermore, he held the existence or nonexistence of a railway would make no essential difference in the situation for China, since the Kowloon leased territory had now been extended to Shumchun, and British power was practically pressing on the walls of Canton, anyway.[50] This railway was therefore accepted by the Chinese as an unavoidable evil; and, considering the repeated invasions that Canton had suffered at the hands of Britain during the nineteenth century, an evil it remained in the minds of many officials. So far as our present knowledge goes, active gentry-merchant interest in this short line was nil.

Parleys having borne no fruit for the British and Chinese

Corporation in 1904, the matter was taken up by the British Legation in the summer of the next year, when Chang Chih-tung was looking for foreign financial aid in order to redeem the Hankow-Canton trunk line. The consummation of the Canton-Kowloon loan agreement was urged by Consul-General Fraser as a condition for the Hongkong government loan.[51] But that such pressure originated with the British Legation at Peking rather than with Fraser himself is plainly indicated by two considerations. First, at about the time that Fraser made his suggestion to Chang Chih-tung, a member of the British Legation staff took up the same subject with Sheng Hsüan-huai;[52] second, Fraser would have been stepping out of his line of duty in meddling with a matter not lying within his proper jurisdiction had there not been instructions from above.

Fraser's demand was met by a rejoinder from the Canton authorities that the Redemption Loan and the Canton-Kowloon Railway were entirely unconnected affairs.[53] They also asked Sheng Hsüan-huai to impress upon the British Minister that Kwangtung province would raise its own funds for the construction of this railway, and that foreign capital was not welcome.[54] In reality, however, there was very little resistance to British proposals for concluding the Canton-Kowloon Railway loan. The main contention, that China would build the railroad with her own funds, was reiterated by the Chinese Foreign Ministry to Sir Ernest Satow in July, 1905. But it was withdrawn during the same month by the Kwangtung authorities themselves when they realized the futility of such action in the face of Britain's determined interest in this region and of the preliminary agreement.[55]

What was left for posterity to see was a series of telegraphic exchanges between the Foreign Ministry, Chang Chih-tung, and the governor-general and governor of Kwangtung, each assuring the others that he was standing firm against British movements and exhorting the others to consider national welfare above everything, while they were all dealing with a situation not within their power to control. Fearing to bear the onus down the ages of being the man whose Hankow-Canton redemption scheme had made the Canton-Kowloon loan inevitable, Chang Chih-tung vigorously deplored the construction of this latter railway as one that would undermine the value of the maritime defenses of Kwangtung. He further suggested that, should its construction be unavoidable, three remedial measures must be provided for China's self-defense: to build the Chinese section of the line on a different gauge from the British, to open a new treaty town on its route (so that other powers than England would also have interests in this region to serve as a balance to British dominance), and to fortify the territory along the railway.[56] How many of those suggestions were practicable—especially that relating to the gauge—was questionable, perhaps even to Chang Chih-tung himself. They certainly were given little attention by the other Chinese officials, who were now turning their attention to the matter of control, and who maintained that the Canton-Kowloon Railway, if built, must at least be built under Chinese auspices[57]—that is to say, the ultimate authority over the railway affairs during construction, and later in operation, must rest with China and not with the British concessionaire as in the case of the Shanghai-Nanking Railway agreement.

In the meantime, Chang Chih-tung had protested against the inclusion of the Kowloon railway as a condition for the Hankow-Canton redemption loan, and, as indicated above, that issue was later dropped by Fraser. However, the delay in obtaining a final agreement for the Kowloon line soon roused the ire of the British mercantile community in Hongkong.[58] When a deadlock was produced in 1906 by the triangular disagreement among the Canton authorities, the British and Chinese Corporation, and the director-general of the Chinese Railway Administration, the matter was moved up to Peking for settlement.[59]

The final agreement for the Canton-Kowloon Railway loan was signed in Peking on March 7, 1907, with T'ang Shao-i representing the Chinese Foreign Ministry, and J. O. P. Bland the British and Chinese Corporation.[60] So far as financial control was concerned, the British maintained a tight grip: the loan was for a sum of £1,500,000 at 5 per cent interest, priced at 94, to run for thirty years. It was secured on the property of the railway and the rights of first mortgage over it was guaranteed. All earnings of the railway were also to be deposited in the Hongkong and Shanghai Banking Corporation.[61] These did not constitute any appreciable improvement over the Shanghai-Nanking railway provisions for the Chinese.

But the Chinese officials got some consolation out of the provisions regarding the administration of the line. Unlike the Shanghai-Nanking Railway, the governor-general was named as the person holding the final authority over matters concerning this railway, with the foreign engineer-in-chief placed under him as to duties and authority.[62] There was no such equivocal Anglo-Chinese administrative body as the "Board of Commissioners" to cloud the issue of control. Construction began immediately in 1907, and the entire line from Canton to the British terminus of Kowloon was opened to traffic in 1911.[63]

In summary, two salient features are noticeable in the early history of the southern trunk line. First was the strength and nature of the provincial railway movement. It was without doubt a force to reckon with, and contributed decisively to the outcome of the redemption plan. However, here in contrast to the case of the Hangchow railway, the gentry's role derived not from their sound financial abilities, but rather from their close link with the high provincial authorities. This gentry-official collaboration was succinctly illustrated by Chang Chih-tung's rejection of Peking's appointment of the director of the Hunan Railway Company in 1905, saying that the local leaders who had actively taken part in the redemption plans should be maintained in the important positions of the railway establishment.[64] This situation was conformable to the power pattern of traditional Chinese society, and it enabled the redemption project to be carried through. But it was decidedly backward in finance. Perhaps the close connection with the officials acted as a deterrant to voluntary investment of private capital in the venture, with the result that the redemption could only be made valid on the strength of a British loan.

Furthermore, the comprehensive character of British action was obvious. The fact that the issue of the Redemption Loan was linked with that of the Canton-Kowloon Railway in the discussions in 1905 implied that both railways were of more than local interest to the British. The assurance regarding future needs of foreign capital for the Hankow-Canton line was made not to specific financial groups, but to a British consul-general on the basis of nationality alone. To be sure, Sir Ernest Satow had inveighed against "political railways" in China amid the uncertainties of the Russo-Japanese War.[65] But where no keen foreign competition was encountered, Britain did not hesitate to gain and maintain control over the financing and construction of Chinese railways, albeit such control was held by British financiers rather than government agencies. The negotiations and agreements of 1905 and 1907, therefore, marked a further extension of British influence and interest in central and southern China.

IV

The Southern Trunk: Second Stage

In its final consummation, the financing of the Hankow-Canton Railway was linked up, through a foreign loan, with that of the Hankow-Szechuan Railway. The latter originally was an official project initiated by Acting Governor Hsi-liang of Szechuan in 1903, in the hope of forestalling foreign ambitions in the Upper Yangtse region.[1] In other words, the opening of south and southwestern China was placed together as one general undertaking, and this was brought about primarily by the working of different foreign interests in these areas. Despite a Chinese attempt at financing the Hankow-Canton line with provincial funds, the history of this railroad eventually became that of the Hukuang Railways Loan of 1911. Here we witness the crystalization of a new policy toward China launched by the powers, that of the international consortium, in order that the "open door" might be maintained.[2] It was a positive step taken by the major powers with interests in central and south China to prevent the preponderance of any one power in Chinese affairs.

It is here necessary to inquire into the circumstances that brought the Hukuang Railways Loan into being. Specifically, what was the nature of provincial efforts, and of foreign—especially British—interests regarding these trunk lines after 1905? How did the provincial gentry react to the Peking government's policies, and to the loan? In what way was the consortium brought into being? These questions touched on the essential elements that constituted the Hukuang railways problem between 1905 and 1911.

ATTEMPT AT CHINESE FINANCING OF THE RAILWAYS

The general policy prevailing at Peking in 1905 was that the Hankow-Canton Railway should be constructed with funds raised in the provinces, and that foreign participation was to be excluded.[3] Chang Chih-tung, since July of that year the director-general of the railway,[4] was doubtful of its feasibility from the beginning. Nevertheless, for more than two years the officials and gentry of Hupeh, Hunan, and Kwangtung became engaged in an attempt at placing their railway plans on a functioning basis.

An administrative structure was set up in November, 1905, when Chang Chih-tung presided over the inaugural ceremonies for the Hankow-Canton and Hankow-Szechuan Railways Company in Wuchang.[5] The practical problem of establishing a working order was faced by the various people concerned with the railways. The difficulties they encountered (and engendered), which eventually led to the conclusion of the Hukuang loan, can be analysed from the following phases.

First, there existed a state of confusion in regard to the organization and control of these railways. Chang Chih-tung's theory was that railways were "major affairs of state" and that the government should be entitled to a reasonable share in the enterprise. He was not slow to point out that without the government's efforts the redemption would not have been possible.[6] To insure the successful construction of the lines he thought a system should be set up which made them "merchant enterprise under official supervision" on the basis of equal interest. This called for official-merchant co-operation, but it was easier said than achieved. Especially important was the fact that the Szechuan-Hankow-Canton railways were the first major trunk-lines handled by the Chinese themselves, for which they had no precedents to serve as a guide. Operating within the limits of traditional

Chinese society, every step taken in this modern venture was a test, which had repercussions later in the loan and nationalization questions.

The adjustment of official and merchant-gentry interests roused much controversy. Starting from his own premise, Chang criticized the regulations drawn up by the Kwangtung authorities as being too lenient to the merchants. He held, for instance, that the director of the railway company, though elected by the trustees, ought to be approved by the governor-general, the governor, and the official director-general of the railways; all the actions of the director must likewise be approved. Matters that touched on the general interest of the province, or inter-provincial business relations, should also be first approved by the director-general. Chang made it clear that he considered "unfair" the turning over of all financial and engineering matters to the hands of the company director.[7] Yet one of the major difficulties later encountered by the authorities was the objections of the Kwangtung merchant-gentry to the allocation of the railway administrative authority, as well as that of merchant and official shares in the financing of the project.[8]

Another aspect of the problem was the lack of the concept of centralized control. When Chang Chih-tung mentioned "government" or "official" (*kuan*) rights, he had in mind only the provincial authorities—a reflection of the age-long practice of the territorial nature of provincial jurisdiction. Nor was there any effective attempt at organizing a central body of the provincial interests which should plan and speak for all concerned. In official exchanges the unit under consideration was always "the Hupeh section of the Szechuan-Hankow Railway" or "the Hunan section of the Hankow-Canton line." During Chang's redemption efforts he treated the whole Hankow-Canton Railway as one unit, but that attitude immediately drew charges of "monopolizing railway rights" from his critics. In self-defense Chang found it necessary to reveal what utter lack there was of any kind of central control over the 700-mile railway.[9] It was suggested now that the responsibility for the construction of the different sections of the lines be allotted to the provinces concerned, much as would have been the case with separate nations. Kwangtung was to aid Hunan, and Szechuan to aid Hupeh, in building parts of their respective sections, which were to be "redeemed" by the debtor provinces after twenty-five years. Szechuan also was to have jurisdiction over the section it built in Hupeh until the redemption had taken place.[10] It is true that an inter-provincial agreement was drawn up early in 1905 by the representatives of the three provinces, in which the general principles and regulations governing the Hankow-Canton line were stated.[11] But no sooner had it been concluded than that the Kwangtung capitalists balked at one of the provisions prohibiting the construction of branch railroads before the completion of the main line.[12] The purpose of this prohibition was to channel the funds toward investment in the trunk line; Chang remained unmoved on this point notwithstanding the intercession of the Kwangtung officials in behalf of the local merchants.[13] Yet the conflict of local versus over-all interests was made apparent by this clash of opinion.

Directly affecting the progress of the project was the kind of relation existing between the authorities and merchant-gentry of these provinces, which differed according to the financial strength of the merchant-gentry in each province. It ranged from open conflict in Kwangtung to an almost negligible showing of gentry interest in Hupeh. In the former province there were enough moneyed people to respond to the idea of railway construction, but their chief interest was twofold—to build short branch lines first, so as to realize profits on their investment in the quickest possible fashion, and to ward off excessive official participation or control. Canton, with its historic background as the south

China trading mart where merchant capitalists congregated, was the center of these activities. When Governor-General Ch'ing began levying taxes for the railway, the merchants termed the share allotted them as "extortion" while protesting against the government's authority over the railway. As this independent attitude continued, relations worsened, until a gentry leader was imprisoned and an impasse produced early in 1906.[14] The controversy was subsequently solved by the provincial authorities' renouncing of their control over financial and personnel matters of the railway, their function then being limited to that of protection and regulation.[15] Though the officials never relinquished their close connection with the project—such as supervising with a police force the election of the director and deputy director of the gentry-organized railway company—the Kwangtung part of the railway was considered as a "merchant enterprise." [16] In spite of somewhat stormy intra-gentry relations, railway shares were issued. Investments were reported to be heavy, with the pledges amounting to $40,000,000 in 1907. But the sum actually paid up by 1908 was only $8,000,000.[17]

Hunan presented a different scene. Here the moneyed gentry, having cooperated with the provincial authorities to good advantage in the past, continued to rely on official support. But among various groups the jockeying for positions occurred. The directors of the General Hunan Merchants' Guild presented a petition to Chang Chih-tung and the Board of Commerce in the spring of 1906, asking permission to form a private Hunan Provincial Railway Company and undertake the construction of the Hankow-Canton line. They set the goal of $20,000,000 for the company, of which a $2,000,000 foundation was to be raised first among the sponsors. But it is significant that even this group of late-comers, initiators of a "merchant managed" enterprise, did not feel secure on their own merit as merchants. The names they proposed as the director and assistant directors of the projected railway company were not drawn from their own ranks, but from among the gentry-officials who had figured prominently in the redemption negotiations, including Yuan Shu-hsün, newly appointed Prefect of Shun-t'ien-fu, and Yü Shao-k'ang, former Judicial Commissioner of Kiangsi.[18] Their petition however was turned down by Chang Chih-tung on these grounds: that the business assets of the petitioners were found to be insufficient for this undertaking; that the regulations these merchants had tentatively formulated were too disadvantageous to the government, and therefore unacceptable; and that issues concerning this railway, since the beginning of the negotiations for the redemption, had always been determined by the authorities in consultation with the "higher gentry," and could not be yielded to a few late-comers at the latter's pleasure. The approved personnel of the railway administration was listed by Chang Chih-tung. It included Yuan Shu-hsün and Yü Shao-k'ang, in important positions. In addition, several persons active in the redemption effort were also placed in high offices, as well as Wang Hsien-ch'ien, who, although "lacking in understanding of commercial matters," was nevertheless an influence in provincial circles. Wang was made Honorary Director. But the group represented in the Merchants' Guild was not entirely neglected. The leading petitioners received appointments as councillors of the railway company, whose task it was to help raise funds, while their powers were strictly limited.[19] "Government supervision of merchant enterprise" was set up in Hunan accordingly.[20]

Yet this apparently close gentry-official collaboration in Hunan did not effectively promote capital recruitment. The explanation lies in the fact that the gentry now considered themselves entitled to official help; the duty of raising funds was passed up to the provincial authorities—which meant letting the latter devise some way of getting the money from the general populace. In 1908 the new Hukuang Governor-

General requested and received the Throne's permission to levy an additional salt gabelle to the amount of four coppers per catty—this devise having been suggested by the gentry. The Hunan railway administration was then only aiming at collecting $6,000,000 from private investments.[21]

In Hupeh Province the project was undertaken entirely by the authorities, no major merchant-gentry interests having been encountered. The management of the enterprise was placed in the hands of the Judicial Commissioner. The Hupeh Provincial Currency Exchange, the government agency which loaned the necessary redemption funds to Chang Chih-tung in 1905, was practically the sole investor with $4,000,000 put into the project, the shares in private hands amounting only to $600,000.[22] And in Szechuan the provincial gentry and the authorities, after considerable dispute, reached a working agreement to raise funds through taxes both direct and indirect. The gentry and the officials agreed upon a 3 per cent levy on grain; at the same time it was also suggested that additional copper coins should be minted at Chungking, the profits of which were to be set aside as capital for the railway company.[23] Except for Kwangtung, therefore, the official bureaucracy was a crucial factor in the promotion of the railway projects. But in all the provinces with all their variegated methods the sums actually obtained were inadequate, and before long it was obvious that the undertaking would be delayed.

Anxious to see construction of the railways begun, Chang Chih-tung in 1906 sent a number of Japanese engineers to survey the Hupeh sections of both the Hankow-Canton and Hankow-Szechuan railways.[24] Coupled with this step was Chang's unchanged view that a foreign loan for both lines was necessary. Only three weeks after the redemption of the Hankow-Canton Railway in 1905 he had expressed this view to the Judicial Commissioner of Kiangsi, who conveyed it to President Ch'ü Hung-chi of the Foreign Ministry in a lengthy and carefully drawn telegram. Chang's contention was that, so long as the managerial rights and property of the railway were not conceded to the foreign creditor, there could be no harm in borrowing from abroad for the construction of the railway.[25] Soon afterward Chang was openly urging Peking to consider a British loan for the Hankow-Szechuan Railway, but he had to desist for the time being because of the objections of the Foreign Ministry. Negotiations with British financiers, which he had undertaken, also had to be abandoned.[26]

The British, in the meantime, did not lose touch with Chang, nor were they forgetful of their priority over the Hankow-Canton Railway in the way of foreign assistance. When word came, for instance, that the Kwangtung company was about to engage American engineers to survey the route, the British consul-general in Hankow protested to Chang who in turn remonstrated with the Kwangtung authorities, holding that such a departure from the 1905 agreement with the British ought to be corrected immediately.[27]

From 1903 on, the British were equally interested in the Hankow-Szechuan line along with the French and Americans. In 1905 when the Chinese Central Railways Company was jointly formed by the British and French groups, the British government began to press actively for the concession of this line. They asked the American capitalists whether they were interested to participate in the project,[28] but the inquiry drew no response from the Americans. An agreement had been reached, however, after 1904, by the Chinese government with the British and the American Ministers in Peking, in which the latter were assured that British and American capital would be preferred should it become necessary to enlist foreign aid in financing this railway.[29] The apparent inability of the provinces themselves to proceed speedily with the construction of the two lines offered an opening for the advent of foreign financial interests which enjoyed the diplomatic backing of their own governments.

THE HUKUANG PRELIMINARY AGREEMENT

In 1907 Chang Chih-tung was exerting his efforts to obtain outside funds for the development of the railways in Hupeh. Two attempts were made by him toward that end while Chinese representatives were negotiating for the Peking-Hankow Railway redemption loan, and for the Tientsin-Pukou Railway loan, but in both cases he was unsuccessful.[30] When J. O. P. Bland, representing the Hongkong and Shanghai Banking Corporation, approached him for railway loans in the provinces, Chang had to refer him to the Peking government, while telling the Board of Posts and Communications that a loan of 10,000,000 taels would result in the immediate construction of the lines in Hupeh.[31] Furthermore, with the keen foreign interest in those lines hovering in the background, Chang Chih-tung proceeded on his own authority to negotiate for a £2,000,000 loan with the British Consul-General Fraser, and was apparently making some progress in that direction.[32] However, the situation remained uncertain when the Peking government began to shift its policy: Chang was appointed a Grand Councillor, and had to leave his viceregal post for his new office in Peking.[33]

That change of place was important to the future course of events in the Hukuang loan. It moved Chang from a local jurisdiction to a point from which he was later able to exercise a general supervision over the provinces, and treat the problem of the two railways as an entity. As a part of its "reform" measures the dynasty was then engaged in the centralization of authority. Chang Chih-tung's case offers a good illustration of how this policy could work, for not only was an influential governor-general removed from the provinces to the Court of Peking, but his influence and prestige were also utilized for the promotion of the centralizing of railway affairs. By Imperial Edicts Chang was appointed Director-General of the Hankow-Canton Railway in July, 1908, and of the Hankow-Szechuan Railway, Hupeh section, in January, 1909. Supreme power over these railroads was vested in him, while all officials in the three provinces were ordered to obey and aid him in his effort.[34] The inability of the provinces to undertake the projects was by now apparent to all. Since Chang had made no secret of his ideas regarding foreign loans, his dual appointment must be taken as an indication of the government's definite approbation of a loan policy. It was not surprising, then, that the Foreign Ministry granted him permission to borrow from abroad soon after Chang's Hankow-Canton appointment.[35]

In his conduct of the Hukuang negotiations, Chang Chih-tung has been charged by Western writers with duplicity in his admission of the German interest into this field.[36] An investigation of the details from all sides reveals that the situation was far more complex, and that, above all, the British were not totally in the dark regarding German interest in those railways. Nor was the ultimate outcome, the international loan, the result of a preconceived plan of any particular person. It was rather the product of changing circumstances, and an expedient devised by the parties concerned as new situations arose. Chang Chih-tung himself for a considerable period was opposed to the entrance of more foreign powers than necessary into this field. Before he left Wuchang in the summer of 1907 he received suggestions from several quarters with regard to a railway loan, and among them was the Deutsch-Asiatische Bank. Chang however refused to discuss the matter with its representative, and advised Peking to reject the German request, because "there is a previous agreement with the British Consul-General and it is not advisable to change the matter now." [37]

Up to the last part of 1908 Chang continued to believe in the feasibility of a purely British loan, which was to be a simple financial transaction, with few or no strings attached as to railway rights. He was also opposed to the inclusion of the French financial interest in this loan, as had been suggested by the British.[38] His reasoning was possibly this: the British rested their claim for a loan on the agreement of 1905, while the other powers did not possess a basis for claims; if those powers were allowed to participate in the enterprise, it would encourage a new battle for concessions. That must be avoided. Therefore he turned down the loan offers of all foreign interest except that of the British, and he was anxious that an arrangement could be speedily agreed upon.

Having obtained the Foreign Ministry's consent, the next step for Chang was to urge both the British and the provincial authorities to commence loan negotiations. However, a major future difficulty was already foreshown here —the railway interests of the provincial gentry-merchants. For the time being, Chang sought to reduce the objections from this direction by reiterating that the proposed loans were necessary for the railway construction. Some months later he declared that the loan terms would not infringe on China's railway rights.[39] Meanwhile Consul-General Fraser was asked to send a representative of the British financial group to Peking, and to recommend a competent British chief engineer as soon as possible.[40] Chang assured Fraser that he intended to contract the loan only from British sources. For the two railways in both Hupeh and Hunan, he would borrow £3,500,000 and that

> . . . either the British and Chinese Corporation or the Hongkong and Shanghai Banking Corporation will be acceptable. But in this loan China will deal only with British banks and will not recog-

nize banks of other nationalities, nor will China recognize the action of any other power that interferes with this matter. In that case you [i.e. Fraser] will be expected to refute the contentions of that power.[41]

Chang envisioned for the Hukuang loan a duplication of the Tientsin-Pukou Railway loan terms, which were regarded as more favorable to Chinese management and control than previous railway loans. After Bland, representing the British and Chinese Corporation, had arrived at Peking for the negotiations, Chang repeated his request to the provinces, and nominated two persons as the desirable delegates, since they had had experiences in the negotiations for the Tientsin-Pukou loan agreement. He even optimistically predicted that the negotiations would take but a few days, as nothing more would be required than the application of the Tientsin-Pukou provisions to the new loan.[42]

The idea of securing the prompt conclusion of the Hukuang loan on better terms was not only an idea of Chang's. Sheng Hsüan-huai, then a vice-president of the Board of Posts and Communications, also advocated the speedy settlement of the matter. Sheng was not, in fact, satisfied with the Tientsin-Pukou terms, declaring that in the matter of construction materials they had failed to give priority to Chinese iron and steel. He proposed the inclusion of more stringent provisions regarding the purchase of materials and the fiscal management, so that they would not again fall into the hands of the concessionaire.[43]

The negotiations between the provincial delegates and Bland were begun in early December, 1908,[44] and they took longer than the "few days" promised by Chang. Intransigent as to the loan terms to be exacted from the Chinese government, Bland's attitude and tactics finally induced Chang Chih-tung to change his stand regarding a purely British loan, and to adopt the policy of a multilateral transaction. By his own account, it was at this stage that the German interest was used as a lever to pry the British from their insistence on hard terms.[45] Possibly the precedent of the Anglo-German relations in the Tientsin-Pukou loan influenced the choice of this expedient. But the records show that the Anglo-Chinese negotiations were launched into rough waters from the beginning. Contrary to Chang's expectations, Bland refused to accept the Tientsin-Pukou terms. In foreign circles it was reported that the funds of the Tientsin-Pukou loan had been misappropriated due to the lack of foreign control, and that was the reason for the stand taken by Bland.[46] But Chang Chih-tung reiterated the fact that Bland's demands were of such a nature as to make Chang's consent to them impossible:

> First he [Bland] wanted to place the construction on a contract basis, aiming at monopolizing the construction rights; then he wanted the chief engineer to sign for all expenditures, aiming at interfering with China's authority in appointment and purchase. His demands were so improper that they were really beyond the realm of reason.[47]

Considered in the perspective of railway developments in the previous five years, Bland's demands actually amounted to an attempt to turn back the clock. So the negotiations extended into months, with neither the British nor the Chinese yielding to the other.

When the discussions with Bland had developed into a deadlock, Chang then thought of putting to positive use the German interest in this loan. He now proceeded to sound out German terms, a thing that was within his right to do, since the agreement of 1905 definitely assured the comparison of foreign offers before China should make her decision. In his letter to Fraser dated February 14, 1909, Chang Chih-tung informed the British Consul-General that he was sounding out the banks of other powers for prices. Since Bland, in addition to his insistence on harder terms, had also violated the 1905 agreement by refusing to disclose the British price for the loan, Chang would now go ahead to negotiate with the other banks. It appeared that Bland had been told that the use of other foreign capital was possible, and he had dismissed it as a futile Chinese threat. According to Chang, the British agent left a meeting on February 13 ("yesterday" in Chang's telegram) in a fit of temper, and parted with the remark that

> without the chief engineer's signing [for all expenditures] he would refuse to undertake the loan. If there is another power that wanted to undertake it, then China could go ahead and settle with that power. And furthermore, not only would he refuse to undertake the Hankow-Canton Railway loan, but he would also be unable to undertake the financing of the other [Hankow-Szechuan] railway.[48]

It is notable here that Chang Chih-tung was careful to separate Bland from British interest in general, and that he laid the blame for the impasse only at the door of Bland. He stated, moreover, that he would be willing to continue the negotiation with other British agents. Chang was actually loath to place these railways entirely in the hands of the Germans. Therefore while he made the Germans feel that they would be preferred for the loan,[49] and obtained from them an issuing price better even than that for the Tientsin-Pukou loan, he was at that time mainly looking toward an Anglo-German joint enterprise, in order to preserve, as he thought, the equilibrium in the Yangtse valley.[50] In other words, Chang was trying to engineer a division of interest among the powers, so as to prevent the predominance of any one power in this region.

The Deutsch-Asiatische Bank, represented by H. Cordes, was quick to seize this opportunity of participating in these major railways. From then on events moved fast. On February 20 Chang sent a three-point proposal to Liang Tun-yen for transmission to Bland: if the latter accepted the conditions in this ultimatum, then negotiations could continue, otherwise not. Chang's conditions were these: (1) The function of the chief engineer was to be limited to the sphere of engineering matters; he would not be allowed to sign for the purchase of materials and railway expenditures. (2) Loan conditions were to be similar to the Tientsin-Pukou agreement, with no extra demands allowed. The use of Chinese material was to be emphasized. (3) The agreement was to be settled within two days. On the third day the British offer as to price, interest rate, and so forth, was to be publicly compared with those of other powers.[51]

Those conditions clearly showed the insecure position of the British claim over the Hukuang Railways once these lines were opened for foreign competitive bidding. But the gravity of this message as well as the position of British capital in China were both misjudged by the British agent. The ultimatum met with no active response. In his later account of this episode, Bland intimated that his principals, the British and Chinese Corporation, were not drastically opposed to German participation, although the British Minister at Peking had protested to the Chinese government in February, 1909.[52] This leads us to conclude that Bland had continued to insist on more British controls in the loan terms even when he was aware of German entrance into the field. Thus, his bungling of the affair for the British was partly due to his overconfidence in the competitive power of British capital in China, and partly due to a divergence of view between the Corporation and himself as to financial method.

In a letter to Liang Tun-yen, Chang Chih-tung recorded the events of the last days before the conclusion of the agreement with the Deutsch-Asiatische Bank on March 8, 1909, which information was to be forwarded to Sir John Jordan.[53] In response to Chang's urgent request, Bland had promised either to present his terms for the loan on March 5, or to make known their intentions on the same day should the British wish to withdraw from the enterprise. On March 6, at eleven o'clock in the morning, Bland "determinedly" stated that, if the loan were to be modeled on the Tientsin-Pukou agreement, the British and Chinese Corporation would not be able to undertake it. Four hours later on the same day Chang and Cordes came to an agreement regarding the German loan. But then Bland telephoned the Chinese negotiators after seven o'clock that evening, asking for one more day to consider the matter. The Chinese complied with his request. They waited until the night of the 7th, when Chang decided to close the matter with the German agent. It was the step that replaced British dominance over the central Yangtse region with international finance.

Upon protests from the British government, Chang again expressed willingness to negotiate with other British agents for a modified settlement. Earlier he had reached an understanding with Cordes that, in case of too vigorous British protests, the Hankow-Canton line could be conceded to them, while the German interest would be shifted to the Hankow-Szechuan Railway.[54] The Hongkong and Shanghai Bank accordingly sent E. G. Hillier to undertake the negotiations, who proposed the inclusion of the Banque de l'Indo-Chine.[55]

The two-fold results of these negotiations were well known. They led, first, to the Berlin Compromise of May 14, 1909, wherein the German, British, and French financial and railway groups agreed to share the Hukuang Railways loan.[56] By this instrument the British, with the French, were allotted their hold on the Hankow-Canton-Szechuan railways, while the German position in the Yangtse valley was formally established. Secondly, China's assent to it was given on June 6, when the Hukuang preliminary agreement was signed in Peking. The signers were the Hupeh officials Kao Lin-jui and Tseng Kwang-yung, representing Chang Chih-tung; E. G. Hillier for the Hongkong and Shanghai Banking Corporation; Maurice Casenave for the Banque de l'Indo-Chine; and H. Cordes for the Deutsch-Asiatische Bank.[57] The terms were highly recommended by Chang, who pointed to their three-fold improvement over previous loan conditions: (1) The power of control remained with the Chinese government, the chief engineers were to be selected by the Chinese director-general, and the final authority of appointment and purchase also rested with him. (2) The financial provisions were better than those of the Tientsin-Pukou loan. The loan was to be for £5,500,000 at 5 per cent, with issuing price set at 95, and the loan term at only 25 years. Following the practice in recent years, the payment was secured on certain internal revenues, such as the salt and grain tax and the likin of the three provinces, instead of on the property of the railways. (3) Moreover, the multi-power character of the loan seemed to insure the Yangtse valley against monopoly by any one nation.[58]

The allocation of engineering rights to the three powers was as follows: the British group received the Hankow-Canton line, and the Germans were given the Hankow-Szechuan line up to Ichang. West of Ichang it was to be an Anglo-French section, but that part was just then in a state of uncertainty, as the people representing Szechuan railway interests had expressed their desire to build that section of the railway themselves.[59] The division of tangible construction rights, therefore, belonged to the British and the Germans, the former gaining an upper hand again over the southward trunk line, whereas the latter became entrenched on the railway running along the north bank of the Yangtse River.

That their gain, economic and political, was fully appreciated by the Germans was evident. To the accompaniment of the Kaiser's "Bravo!" and "Good!," Bülow described German participation in this loan as a welcome event, since it broke down England's railway monopoly in the Yangtse valley, and opened new opportunities for German capital and industries in the heretofore British "sphere of interest." [60] The German Minister in Peking expressed the same view, pointing out the significance of China's demonstration of independence from Anglo-French financial power. "Furthermore," he said jubilantly of the Deutsch-Asiatische Bank, "through this loan it has become the leading bank [in the Far East], and has run down the long-established high position of the Hongkong Bank." [61]

In contrast to the jubilation in Berlin, Paris was disturbed and London put on an injured air. But the real currents flowing between London and Hongkong were somewhat difficult to gauge. In Paris, Clemenceau's fear upon hearing of the possibility of German entry into the Hukuang loan was made known to a London *Times* correspondent in this sentence: "There is a cleft in the *entente*." [62] That was on February 1, two weeks before Chang Chih-tung's letter informed Fraser of his negotiations with other foreign banks, and nearly three weeks before Chang addressed the ultimatum to Bland.

However, there was an interesting point in Clemenceau's conversation which has so far roused little attention. The French Minister-President held that he was "much astonished at a proposal which . . . His Majesty's Government had made, that the Germans should be allowed a share in a railway loan in China." [63] He said he got this bit of information from "a Mr. Addis," whom he did not know, and whom the London Foreign Office did not seem to know. Now the same document showed that the activities of Addis were known to the member of the British Embassy in Paris who wrote this memorandum. Addis was, in fact, an agent of the British and Chinese Corporation, and a signer of the four-power agreement regarding Chinese railway loans in November, 1910.[64] He was therefore a person belonging to Britain's high financial circles, and the news he imparted in those crucial days of the Hukuang negotiations should be considered as containing some element of truth. It is not clear to whom the British government actually made the alleged proposals. But the situation prevailing in the last weeks of the Bland negotiations indicated that the Hongkong Bank and the London government were fully cognizant of rival foreign interests in the Hukuang Railways. Furthermore, they appeared to have been ready, at that date, to accept the idea of joint enterprise and forego an exclusively British enterprise, in order to accommodate their position to the requirements of world relations, as well as to avoid a complete loss of the concession.

In England a certain degree of public interest was aroused by the turn of events, but the Foreign Office maintained a cautious attitude. From March 1909 to April 1910 numerous questions were asked in the House of Commons with regard to the Hukuang negotiations, but no emphatic concern was expressed by the Foreign Office officials. Among other things, the fact that the 1905 agreement with Chang Chih-tung permitted the Chinese to choose from among foreign loan offers imposed silence on London. On March 15 and 18, 1909, Sir Edward Grey twice refused to make any statement regarding the matter, because, he said, negotiations had not yet reached a decisive state.[65] This referred to the three-power talks rather than the Anglo-Chinese negotiations. In the next month we learn that protests had been lodged with the Peking government. But the British government objected to the Sino-German agreement only on grounds of violation of "the spirit" of the 1905 agreement.[66]

During the ensuing months the British Foreign Office definitely and unreservedly accepted the situation in central China. McKinnon Wood, the Undersecretary for Foreign Affairs, made these points clear in Parliament. First, he indicated that inasmuch as the 1905 agreement "did not exclude competition from foreign firms as to the terms to be offered to the Chinese Government," the latter could not be said as to have broken its engagement with Britain.[67] Second, he drew attention to the changes that had occurred in international politics in China: "It is quite true that the old principle of spheres of influence has been given up. The new system is that of division among the various nations interested."[68] The desire of the British government to preserve the Far Eastern status quo became more and more frankly proclaimed. Speaking of the Hukuang negotiations in September, 1909, Grey said, "The subsequent negotiations resulted in a compromise, the object of which was to secure more control and avoid competition."[69] The argument used by the Germans as the basis of their participation in the loan—that the 1898 Anglo-German agreement delimiting their "spheres" in China concerned only the *building* of railways and not railway loans—was accepted as valid by McKinnon Wood and the British financial group alike.[70]

But such a policy was gall to an "old China hand" like Bland. Having failed to secure the entire Hukuang loan for British capital, and having been asked by Chang Chih-tung to go back to England and never again to meddle with this affair,[71] Bland placed the blame for the outcome on the Hongkong Bank. He could not grasp the reason why the Bank could be so unpatriotic as to collaborate with the German group, and condemned its "cosmopolitan" tendencies. The Germans and the Chinese behaved in "bad faith," he charged, and the London government was said to have handed over the weighty matter of foreign policy to a cosmopolitan financial group.[72] This is further proof of Bland's lack of support from the financial policy makers for exclusive and stringent British control in these railways, and it stemmed from his inability to understand the relative position of British capital vis-à-vis that of other powers. The fact remains, however, that world politics as seen from London had assumed a different pattern from the late nineteenth century. In order to maintain her economic and political interests in the Far East, both the financiers and the government of Britain realized that it was important to try out a policy of cooperative enterprise with other Western nations.

A claim introduced by the United States relating to American participation in the Hukuang loan delayed Imperial ratification of the preliminary agreement. The American claim was made primarily on the ground that the Chinese government had assured Minister Conger in 1903 of preference for British and American capital for building the Hankow-Szechuan line; and furthermore, that the pledging of likin as security for the loan affected America's treaty rights regarding likin collection in the provinces.[73] These representations, however, were ignored at first by Chang Chih-tung, who did not wish to jeopardize the success of the negotiations. Not until the day on which the preliminary agreement was signed did he dispatch a letter to the Foreign Ministry, refuting the American claim.[74] His main contention was that although in 1903 (and later again in 1904) the United States was assured of the preference for British and American capital for the Szechuan railway, China was still left with the right to choose from firms of various nationalities.

The validity of this argument was borne out by the document.[75] H. P. Fletcher, the American Chargé in Peking, also thought Conger's interpretation of those assurances stronger than the text had warranted. But the Peking Foreign Ministry made no attempt to question the American claim, and the United States government proceeded to agitate the matter in London, Paris, and Berlin.[76]

Early in June a financial group was formed by the leading bankers of New York, to serve as the instrument of the State Department, with Willard Straight acting as the group's representative abroad. His duties involved negotiating with the banks of the three European Powers in London, and the conclusion of the matter with the powers and China in Peking.[77] The American group insisted on having one-fourth of the entire loan for both railways and would not take less. Chang Chih-tung's determined opposition to such an arrangement was overridden by the pressure President Taft exerted directly on the Manchu Prince Regent. The result was that the total amount of the loan was increased to £6,000,000, with the banks of the other powers recognizing equal American participation in finance and purchase of materials.[78]

Prior to this the British also had raised serious objections to American participation in the loan. The former, having just secured a hold over these railways through the policy of cooperation with Germany, were not willing to see a new competitor added to the venture without a struggle. It was significant that from the beginning general British press opinion was reported as being more favorable to the idea of American participation than the Hongkong Bank, the latter having declared that American entrance into the field was "neither required nor desired." [79] The London Foreign Office dismissed the American claims as invalid, and referred to the enterprise as a "business" matter.[80] On the other hand, the United States rested its argument for participation entirely on national and political grounds.[81] Through forceful diplomatic backing at Peking the American group finally achieved its aim. But when Chang Chih-tung died in October, 1909, the final Hukuang agreement was still unmemorialized, and its conclusion was further delayed by factors both Chinese and foreign.

THE FOUR-POWER HUKUANG AGREEMENT AND THE NATIONALIZATION POLICY

The consummation of the Hukuang loan agreement again consisted of a two-fold process: first achieving an agreement among the four powers as to their respective shares in the construction of the railways, then securing the consent of the Chinese government. In both stages progress was slowed down, at first by the conflict of interests of the various financial groups, and secondly by the divergence of view between Peking and the provinces. Complete agreement among the four powers could not be reached until May 23, 1910, after seven months of tortuous negotiation; and the final agreement was eventually signed by the groups and the Board of Posts and Communications one year later, on May 20, 1911.[82]

In brief, the crux of the four-power controversy was this: the three other powers were discontented with the predominant British share in the engineering rights. The British government's plan was to take into consideration only the Hankow-Szechuan Railway for four-power division of construction rights, but leave the Hankow-Canton Railway exclusively for the British and Chinese Corporation. According to this plan, the estimated 2,400 kilometers of the Szechuan line would be divided as follows: Germany 600, American group 800, the Chinese Central Railway (British and French) 1,000.[83] But first the Germans, then the French, and then the Americans in turn objected to such an arrangement.[84] None supported the separation of the two railways, as it would sharply limit the mileage allotment for each group, and the discussion was carried on between the protesting countries and London for some six months. Sir Edward Grey, however, persisted in his policy of separation. Utilizing the 1905 Hankow-Canton Redemption loan as the political basis of Britain's present claim, Grey said, "I observed with surprise that the Hankow-Canton line should be mentioned apparently on an equal footing with the Hankow-Szechuan line as if the two lines formed part of one undertaking." [85]

In the inter-group agreement of May 23, 1910, the British nevertheless succeeded in getting their lion's share. Equal division of the Hankow-Szechuan line was adopted, making the allocation of mileage for engineering rights as follows: The British received 900 kilometers on the Hankow-Canton Railway and 600 on the Szechuan extension, making a total of 1,500 kilometers. The Germans were allotted 800 kilometers on the Hupeh section of the Hankow-Szechuan line, with about 200 kilometers assigned to an American engineer. The Americans would receive a further 400 kilometers on the Szechuan extension; and France was to have 600 kilometers on the same line. The nationality of the purchasing agent was to follow that of the chief engineer for each section, but finance and materials were both to be equally divided among the four groups.[86]

Now that an agreement had been reached among the financiers of the powers, they turned to present their united front to Peking by urging the completion of the Hukuang loan negotiations. Meanwhile, domestic discontent against the Peking government had daily increased, accentuated by the latter's foreign railway loan negotiations.[87] As the year progressed the international financial and political cordon around China was made more secure by the conclusion of the Quadruple Agreement of November 10, 1910, and of the currency reform loan of April 1911. These two instruments further solidified the Hukuang consortium, provided a working agreement among the foreign financiers, and widened their scope of control to include all foreign loans for railway, currency reform, and Manchurian industrial developments.[88] But these activities of the powers were strikingly out of context with the trend of events in China, where the Hukuang loan negotiations were further weakening the position of the Ch'ing dynasty in the country.

Conflict between Peking and the provinces had intensified. In 1908 an Imperial Edict had ordered an investigation of the progress made in all railways, pointing out especially the unsatisfactory conditions that prevailed in gentry-merchant undertakings.[89] The strained relations then existing between the Peking government and the provincial gentry were clearly shown by Chang Chih-tung's assurances to the provinces that their interests and rights would not be encroached upon by his appointment as director-general of the railways.[90] On the one hand Chang gave a written assurance to the foreign bankers, that they would not deal with the local capitalists, that the later would not be allowed "to interfere" as in the case of the Shanghai-Hangchow Railway. On the other hand he realized that the provincial gentry would fight against the surrender of their interests, therefore he continued to advocate government-merchant joint enterprise.[91] He sought by this approach to allay the gentry's objections while still maintaining an effective measure of government control over the railways, including the contracting of foreign loans.

But provincial opposition to the loan was already sharpening. Chang Chih-tung himself had first estimated that the Hunan provincial authorities could obtain over 2,400,000 taels annually from likin revenue and salt and grain taxes to pay off the services on a £2,000,000 loan.[92] Now Hunan declared itself entirely capable of building its own section of the Hankow-Canton Railway. The newly constituted Provincial Assembly resolved that Hunan should hasten the construction by adopting specific procedures, such as cancellation of the preliminary Hukuang agreement, making the railway a wholly merchant-managed enterprise, improving the organization of the railway by employing railway school graduates, and increasing the training of railway personnel. A program for fund raising was also formulated.[93] Earlier reports from Szechuan had also indicated the possibility of constructing the line step by step with provincial resources, and it had been used by the British, French, and German banking groups as an argument for delaying American participation.[94] Provincial pressure on the Peking government became so strong that in early 1910 it granted the Hupeh gentry the right to form a railway company and issue stocks. This elicited a series of inquiries and protests from the powers, which, though not yet quite able to agree among themselves, were nonetheless vigilant to keep the Hukuang railways under their control. Their governments showed anxiety over Peking's sanction for the founding of the Hupeh Railway Company which, as it was pointed out, was contrary to the preliminary agreement of June 6, 1909.[95]

With the conclusion of their bankers' agreement of May, 1910, the four powers were able to bend their combined efforts toward Peking. No less than seven identical representations were sent to the Chinese Foreign Ministry by the Ministers of the powers between July 13, 1910 and May 8, 1911. These communications repeatedly urged for the prompt conclusion of the Hukuang loan, and as insistently expressed the four governments' concern over the formation of the provincial railway companies.[96] Their notes however failed to elicit any answer from the Peking government, which was faced with a situation similar to that of the Shanghai-Hangchow-Ningpo Railway controversy, only this time the prospects were much more menacing. In seeking to find a safe way out between the closed ranks of four Great Powers and the burning hostility of three provinces, the Peking authorities tried to avoid ratifying the 1909 preliminary agreement. In that effort they fell back on a provison which they maintained was written into the preliminary agreement, which provided for the alteration of the loan contract in case the Board of Finance objected to it.[97] The weakness of this contention was that this provision existed only in the Chinese text, whereas Article XXV of the same agreement stipulated that in case of dispute the English version should rule. Therefore the validity of the Chinese claim to change the loan conditions was refuted by the powers without difficulty.[98]

The real cause of the hesitation of the Chinese government—the fierce objection of the provinces toward the loan—was completely disregarded by the foreign bankers, and taken lightly by their governments. The financial groups declared that the Board of Posts and Communications "exaggerated the danger of local trouble in order to obtain easier terms, and that China should be able to carry out original terms without risking serious disturbances, and that she should be pressed to do so by the four Governments." [99] Meanwhile in Peking, as the Foreign Ministry was plied with diplomatic notes from the four powers, the Board of Posts found it necessary to temporize with the provinces. Not only was the Hupeh Railway Company established with the Board's sanction, but two months later it also gave encouragement to the railway company of Hunan province. Early in 1911 the Governor of Hunan informed Peking that his province would accept no foreign loans.[100]

Nevertheless, the combined pressure of the powers on Peking authorities proved effective. The Board of Posts, with Imperial approval, revoked its sanction of the Hupeh Railway Company, on the grounds that it was able thus to secure certain modifications in the terms of the loan. These included the omission of a branch line in Hupeh in exchange for the addition of a section from Ichang to K'ueichou on the Szechuan border; the provision for the Chinese right to deposit half of the loan during the construction of the railways, with the Chiao-tung and Ta-ch'ing banks; the specific mention of the use of Chinese material; and the exclusion of Szechuan and Kwangtung extensions from the loan agreement.[101] The final agreement for the Hukuang Railways loan of £6,000,000 was concluded on May 20, 1911, in Peking. Sheng Hsüan-huai, as President of the Board, signed for the Board of Posts and Communications, E. G. Hillier for the British interest, R. St. Pierre and Casenave for the Banque de l'Indo-Chine, Cordes for the German bank, and Willard Straight for the American group.[102]

Save for the few changes mentioned above, the loan contract adhered fairly closely to the terms contained in the 1909 agreement. In case of further need for foreign capital, the contracting banks were to be preferred by the Chinese government for another loan not exceeding £4,000,000.[103] The agreement reaffirmed the authority of the Chinese government over these railways, and when construction was completed it could employ foreign engineers without reference to the banks.[104] As an indication of the government's earnestness, Sheng Hsüan-huai wrote various Chinese officials within a month of the signature of the agreement, asking for information on a competent German chief engineer and for the past accounts of the Hankow-Canton Railway.[105]

But the provinces showed they were no less earnest in their opposition to the loan. This sentiment was intensified by the policy of nationalization of China's major railways, which was promulgated on May 10, 1911.[106] According to the nationalization plan, all major trunk lines were to be taken over by the Peking government, while branch lines were to remain in private hands. Following the promulgation of the policy, the extra taxes levied in Hunan and Szechuan in the name of railway enterprise were ordered abolished.[107] A means to purchase provincial railway stocks was also devised by Sheng. The Kwangtung railway stock, for instance, was to be purchased by the government at 60 per cent of their face value, the other 40 per cent to be paid in non-interest bearing government bonds.[108]

This close association of the Peking government's centralizing program with the conclusion of the four-power loan cleared the air for those who had long become dissatisfied with the Dynasty as well as with the growth of foreign economic power in China, and the resultant explosions lent their force to the revolution of 1911.

In spite of their poor record in railway construction and lack of concrete results,[109] the provinces were uncompromising in their opposition to the government plans. Aside from the question of the loan, the railway promoters were struck by the cessation of a lucrative source of income owing to the abolition of the extra levies, while at the same time the gentry-merchants refused to place their investments into the hands of a government in which they had little faith. The Hunan gentry held protest meetings which impressed the provincial governor as formidable, and Kwangtung stockholders refused to accept the government bonds, causing panic in the market by demanding cash payment on the certificates.[110] In Szechuan the agitations reached the greatest heights. There the anti-nationalizers were branded by the authorities as subversive elements, riots followed, petitioners were killed, the chairmen and other officers of the newly convened Provincial Assembly were arrested, and the Manchu dignitary Tuan-fang was sent to suppress the uprising with an army.[111] But exactly five months after the promulgation of the nationalization policy, the revolution of October 10, 1911, broke out in Wuchang, and Sheng was soon reprimanded and dismissed from office.[112] It was obvious that China's regeneration required more thorough measures than the building of railways with foreign loans.

What distinguished the Hukuang railways loan from others was the way in which a variety of economic and political forces operated in relation to it, making it "the crux of the contentions between the provinces and the Central Government, between the Government and the Powers interested, and among the Powers themselves." [113] Its final significance lay in the compromise among the powers, in which Britain retreated somewhat from her previous predominant position, with the interests of the other powers more or less evenly distributed. It lay also in the extent to which both the foreign powers and the Peking authorities misjudged the real state of popular opinion in China, which hastened the downfall of the Manchu Dynasty. Lastly, the historian is faced with the problem of evaluating the validity of the government's efforts at centralization. Assuming that a more centralized and effective government was a practical need in China, the Peking government's failure in 1911 certainly was a reminder that the outcome of any policy must not be judged by its content alone, but also by the method with which it was brought about, and the circumstances in which it operated.

V

Projects and Conflicts in North China

In the area between the Yangtse and the Great Wall, railway politics presented a situation different from the one we have observed in the preceeding chapters. First, in the northern provinces of Shantung, Chihli, Honan, and Shansi, there was a lack of active gentry interest in the building of railways. The weak showing of the moneyed gentry on the scene may be explained by the relatively low development of commercial centers in these provinces as compared to the more commercialized areas of southern China. This led to a situation in which the railway plans rested completely in the hands of the government, as the officials wound their way around the stakes put forth by foreign financiers. Only briefly did a Three Provinces Association figure in the Tientsin-Pukou negotiations, but this organization was more notable for its ready acquiescence to the official view than for any demonstration in behalf of a well-defined group interest. Consequently in the development of railway negotiations and loans, very little gentry-capitalist activities were involved.

Second, the rivalry among the powers was much more sharply drawn in north China, principally because of the strong positions obtained by Germany, Russia, and France through their respective concessions. Rather than being the predominant financial power here, as she was in the Yangtse valley and southward, Britain was from the first only one of the nations competing for economic advantages. Therefore the railway policy adopted by the British soon became either tacit retreat, or collaboration with another power, whichever that would best suit the circumstances.

The initiative regarding the railway projects lay largely with the foreign interests. But a common factor did present itself in this area with that of the other parts of China, that is, the attempt of the Chinese government to improve the conditions of loans contracted with foreign concessionaires—this being the only thing it was capable of doing, wedged in as it was between the general opinion of the country and the pressing demands of the powers.

PROJECTS ON THE NORTH CHINA PLAIN

The present section will deal with a number of British railway plans that failed to materialize with the exception of one short line. These include the Hopeh extensions of the Imperial Railways of North China, the Tsechou-Pukou project, and the ninety-mile Taok'ou-Chinghua line which was built by the Peking Syndicate as a mining railway.

During the Boxer war the British-financed Imperial Railways of North China were administered by British and Russian authorities, the former having jurisdiction over the section within the Great Wall (Peking-Shanhaikuan), and the Russians taking charge of the part between Shanhaikuan and Newchuang.[1] In 1902, following the Peace Protocol of 1901, both sections were returned to Chinese civil authorities. The restoration agreements with the British were signed on April 29, 1902, by the British Minister Sir Ernest Satow, and Yuan Shih-kai and Hu Yü-fen, administrators-general of the Northern Railways.[2] But the terms of the agreements soon drew objections from Russia, and in the end the British government was obliged to acquiesce in the modification of some of the provisions. Those dealt with the questions of foreign military personnel in relation to railway affairs, and the construction of branch lines.

The 1901 Protocol had provided for the stationing of military posts on this railway by the powers; in Articles II and III of the present restoration agreement a British co-director was appointed, whose responsibility was to arrange for the requirements of foreign military traffic with the Chinese administrator. Japanese and German military authorities were given the right each to appoint a deputy co-director, and commanding officers of the contingents of the various powers might appoint station-masters at important points after arranging with the British co-director.[3]

These provisions clearly put certain aspects of the administration of the railway into the hands of a British military officer. Lessar, the Russian Minister at Peking, promptly addressed a protest to the Foreign Ministry. If that provision could not be amended, added Lessar, then Russia would demand equal right with Germany and Japan in appointing a deputy co-director on this section of the railway.[4] The Chinese government undertook a negotiation with the London authorities about possible modifications. Eventually the Chinese Foreign Ministry was able to pacify Russia with the assurance that the British military co-director was not to be admitted into the railway administration.[5]

An additional agreement for the regulation of management of the Peking-Shanhaikuan Railway was also signed on the same day with the restoration agreement. At the end of the regulations, as if by an afterthought, was appended the fifth article which called forth a significant series of foreign protests, for it touched on a subject that lay within the realm of national policy. First, it confirmed "the intent" of Article III of the 1898 Northern Railways loan agreement, which stipulated that, should foreign funds be needed for the construction of branch lines, China would first apply to the British and Chinese Corporation.[6] Furthermore, the Chinese officials agreed here that the construction of certain branch lines within eighty miles of the present railway—including a line northward to the Great Wall and a Tientsin-

Paoting line—should not, in view of the interests of the Imperial Northern Railways, be allowed to fall into other hands.[7] It is recalled that this railway was built with a British loan, that the "interests" of the line were those of the British and Chinese Corporation as the investor with rights based on the 1898 agreement. The Chinese government by the present provision, therefore, was bound never to admit foreign—especially Russian—interests to participate in certain specified railroad projects within the area served by this main line. It is clear then why other powers regarded this article as representing an advance of the British position in north China and raised vigorous objections. These powers were Russia, France, and Belgium, which already possessed railway interests in this part of China.

Russian objections were directed against the contemplated branch line from Peking northward to the Great Wall. Minister Lessar requested the Chinese Foreign Ministry to have the provisions regarding that line altered.[8] It was said that in the previous year the Chinese authorities had committed themselves to Russia regarding the construction of such a railway. Lessar probably meant the alleged "secret treaty" of February, 1901, in which a general mention was made of future railways in Manchuria and Mongolia. It should be noted, however, that in 1899, a few weeks after the conclusion of the Anglo-Russian agreement in relation to their railway spheres in China, an exchange of notes took place between the Tsungli Yamen and the Russian Minister in Peking, in which it was agreed that future railways "from Peking to the north or to the northeast toward the Russian border" would be built with Chinese capital and under Chinese supervision; in case they were constructed by any foreign syndicate, it should be Russian, and in no case would another nation be allowed to construct the railway.[9] Legalistically speaking, such a commitment ran counter to the Sino-British loan agreement of 1898, and the Anglo-Russian railway agreement of 1899, which used the Great Wall as the dividing line of the respective spheres. Li Hung-chang in 1901 also denied the diplomatic binding force of the new agreement with Russia.[10] Nevertheless, the Russian pressure in 1902 bore fruit. Prince Ch'ing soon assured Lessar that the line to the north would be constructed by the Chinese government, "without application of foreign capital for this purpose," and that the revenue of such lines would never serve as security for foreign loans.[11]

The railroad in question soon was built by Chinese engineers under the leadership of Chan T'ien-yu (Jeme Tien Yow) as a government enterprise, and was known as the Peking-Kalgan Railway, which opened for traffic in 1909. Capital for the construction of this line was derived from the profits of the North China Railway, though this slight manifestation of independence was enough to cause uneasiness among the British.[12] It is a well known story how the successful construction of this line was hailed by the entire nation. Built over difficult terrain with efficiency and speed and without foreign help, the Peking-Kalgan seemed to give the needed reassurance to the Chinese in their railway enthusiasm. It also indicated that the Anglo-Russian rivalry in north China was for once utilized by the Peking authorities for a constructive purpose.

The mention of a Tientsin-Paoting branch line in Article V of the additional agreement of 1902 touched off protests from Belgium and France. These Powers had established interests in the Peking-Hankow Railway, on which Paoting was a large station. On the grounds of protecting the earning capacity of this trunk line, Belgium and France sent strong protests to the Chinese government. Further, the Belgian chief engineer was reported to have asked the director-general of the Chinese Railway Administration for an assurance that the building of the branch line would be entrusted to the Peking-Hankow Railway Company.[13] Under such diplomatic pressure, the Peking government finally sought and secured Britain's assent to drop the matter of this branch line.

Such immediate alterations in a formal instrument signed by representatives of the British and Chinese governments, testified not only to the strength of Russian and Franco-Belgian influence in Peking, but also to the readiness of Britain to compromise with rival powers in China. On a larger scale, another British project also foundered on the rock of the Peking-Hankow interest, which in these years still maintained a monopolistic role for itself in north-central China and would not tolerate any suggestion of a new railway touching on the trunk line.

Ever since the Shansi mining and rail transport concessions had been granted to it in 1898, the Peking Syndicate paid heavy attention to the development of a railway that would unite the mining area and the Yangtse valley into one British sphere. Its projected line was to run from the mining center at Tsechow in Shansi to Pukou opposite Nanking, traversing the territory of four provinces, and with a total length of at least 450 miles. The Syndicate based its right of railway construction on Article XVII of the 1898 agreement,[14] which permitted the building of a "branch" railroad to transport mineral products.

But the basis of the Syndicate's claim was questionable. Article XVII mentioned no specific river terminus for the mining railway.[15] Sheng Hsüan-huai reported, however, that Sir Ernest Satow, following the precedence of Sir Claude MacDonald, interpreted the term *ho-k'ou* in the Chinese text to denote the river port of Hsiang-yang in Hupeh province. (In the English version of the agreement the official rendering of this term was "water navigation.") Later Satow asked that the terminus be changed from Hsiang-yang to Pukou for better navigation, but it was suggested in Peking that this should be rejected, because a line linking Tsechow with Pukou would constitute a great foreign-controlled trunk line across the central plains of China.[16] Of course, the same objections could have been raised with regard to Hsiang-yang. But the lack of it impressed the British with China's tacit consent to the principle of a major railway, and in 1902 the subject was brought up for discussion in earnest, the Peking Syndicate having now commenced its mining operations.

Since the proposed line would cut across the Peking-Hankow Railway, Sheng Hsüan-huai consulted M. Jadat, the Belgian chief engineer. Jadat rejected the plan outright. He contended that such a railway would greatly injure the Peking-Hankow by siphoning off the latter's business from two provinces.[17] This strengthened Sheng's hand henceforth in opposing the British project, the argument being that the income of the Peking-Hankow must be protected, since on it depended the repayment of the Belgian loan. Chang Chih-tung, farther away from the Franco-Belgian interest than Sheng and more favorably inclined toward the British in this period, tended to compromise. But not even the intervention of the British Minister at Peking could counteract the Franco-Belgian opposition and bring Sheng to accept the propositions.[18]

In 1903 the Syndicate proposed to utilize the Peking-Hankow Railway down to Yen-ch'eng, and thence build the Syndicate's railway to Pukou. But the French and Belgian governments disallowed this plan also.[19] At the same time, the Yen-ch'eng-Pukou line was in conflict with a plan of the British and Chinese Corporation, which provided for a railway to be built from Sinyang (100 miles below Yen-ch'eng on the Peking-Hankow Railway) to Pukou.[20] This complication aided Sheng, who in June of 1903 advised the Foreign Ministry to reject definitely the Peking Syndicate's request.[21] For the time being the interest of the Peking-Hankow prevailed. The Pukou-Sinyang Railway has never been built, although a loan agreement for its construction was concluded in 1914 between the government of the Chinese Republic and the British and French interests known as the Chinese Central Railways Company, Ltd.[22]

Of the Peking Syndicate's grandiose plans for an independent Honan-Hupeh-Kiangsu rail system, only 90 miles in Honan province were realized, but after the opening of traffic its legal ownership was transferred from the British concessionaire to the Chinese government. This transfer was prompted by practical considerations on the part of the former, and was gladly undertaken by the Chinese government at a time when desire to recover railway rights was running high.

This line, linking Chinghua in the mining area with Taokou on the Wei River, cut across the Peking-Hankow Railway at Hsin-hsiang. Its construction was begun in 1902 over the Honan Governor's objections,[23] only on condition that it should engage in no other traffic except the shipping of the Syndicate's minerals. This was to protect the business of the Peking-Hankow Railway.[24] Such restrictions, however, were already implicit in Article XVII of the 1898 Honan Mining Agreement.

Halfway through the construction the Chinese government received proposals from the British Minister, asking to place the Taokou-Chinghua railway on a loan basis.[25] That meant letting the Peking Syndicate construct it under the nominal ownership of China, with funds that were considered a "loan" to the Chinese government, which the latter would pay back on an amortization scheme. Sheng Hsüan-huai was rather wary of this plan; he pointed out the difficulties of ascertaining the amount of money already spent, and also the line's meager business. He feared that China might incur too heavy a financial burden and even losses if she undertook the railroad.[26]

It is reasonable to conclude that the apprehensions expressed by Sheng were precisely the reasons which prompted the British to ask for a change of the railway's status. Deprived of normal freight and passenger traffic, the road would depend on the exportation of minerals and importation of mining machinery for its income, which would be extremely slight. Furthermore, its eastern terminus on the bank of Wei River connected it with the Grand Canal—the waterway with the illustrious name, but of uncertain value for transportation at that date.[27] The Peking Syndicate therefore found it hardly practical to keep this railroad its own venture. If it was placed on a loan basis, the Chinese government securities would guarantee the Syndicate against losses, while the usual loan terms would maintain British influence in that region for a few decades, besides providing the Syndicate with highly profitable financial advantages. The British concessionaire, therefore, had much to gain and only a nominal ownership to lose in such a transaction. As for the transportation of minerals, under existing circumstances the use of the Peking-Hankow Railway was unavoidable if any sizable market was to be reached in central China or down the Yangtse. Under Chinese government ownership the Taokou-Chinghua Railway would rest on an equal footing with the larger trunk line, and it would probably be easier to arrange terms with regard to rates.

The Chinese authorities took the opportunity of the negotiations in 1903–1905 to regain some of the comprehensive rights signed away in 1898. They insisted that a mining agreement be concluded with the railway agreement. Between 1904 and 1905 Sheng Hsüan-huai eventually was able to conclude four articles of agreement with the British agent, making the Shansi iron mining and smelting a joint Anglo-Chinese enterprise, and restricting the export of iron from Shansi to "Chinese government products." [28] After further argument over the degree of Chinese control of the Syndicate-appointed general manager, a loan agreement and a railway working agreement were signed on July 3, 1905, some six months after the line had been opened to traffic.[29]

As is to be expected, this transaction was termed "redemption" of the railroad by Sheng, although in effect the "loan" was an installment paying plan by which the Peking government compensated the Peking Syndicate with interest.[30] Until the loan was repaid the Syndicate retained virtual control over the entire railway, with the property and earnings of the line hypothecated as security for the payment of the loan.[31] In addition, an exchange of notes between Sheng and Jamieson, agent for the Syndicate, established the latter's right to provide the Railway Administration with a loan in case of future construction of the Chinghua-Tsechow section. That right was invalidated three years later, however, when the Shansi mines were redeemed by the provincial government.[32]

BILATERAL ENTERPRISES

The following pages will deal with the Tientsin-Pukou Railway loan of 1908, and the Anglo-French loan of the same year. They are instances in which British capital found it necessary to combine forces with that of another power, and fundamentally the same forces operated as in the case of the Hukuang Railways loan.[33] Here on the north China plain, however, the British found it only necessary to join with one other power in each of the railways concerned, the Tientsin-Pukou and the Peking-Hankow, where Germany and France were the predominating influence respectively.

In Chapter I we have seen how, as a compromise in their conflicting national interests, the British and German concerns secured a joint concession over the Tientsin-Chinkiang Railway which passed through the provinces of Chihli, Shantung, and Kiangsu.[34] In 1902 the negotiations for the final loan agreement were begun, but it was not until 1908 that it could be concluded. The negotiations were significant in two aspects: the way in which the idea of "redemption" of the concession was treated by the Chinese officials in charge, and the somewhat improved loan terms that were accorded to China.

On the western half of the north China plain, the Peking-Hankow Railway was constructed by a Belgian company. The great bridge over the Yellow River was completed in the autumn of 1905, and the entire line was opened to traffic on November 13 of that year.[35] Soon British capital won for itself a place in the Anglo-French loan, which was contracted by the Chinese government in 1908 so that it might redeem this line from the Belgian interests. Technically speaking, however, the loan was a purely financial transaction and not a railway loan.

Minor difficulties at first hindered the progress of the Tientsin-Pukou negotiations. For instance, the draft submitted by the representative of the German bank put the amount of the loan at £8,000,000 instead of the £7,400,000 stated in the preliminary agreement; the German Minister also asked for the right to build two branch lines westward to Honan, a request that the Chinese government was reluctant to grant.[36] Meanwhile, the German-built Tsingtao-Tsinan Railway was completed in 1904, and Shantung province was astir with new activities. The advance of foreign economic penetration was marked by the official opening of new trading towns along the railway to facilitate larger commercial transactions.[37] But the negotiations for the loan proceeded slowly, and not until 1905 was the draft of the final agreement placed before the Chinese authorities.[38]

Before the agreement could be concluded, however, the situation was complicated by a Chinese proposal to cancel the concession, and to build the railway with Chinese funds. But there was lacking a vigorous gentry-capitalist movement for this railway and the policy of Yuan Shih-kai—then Governor-General of Chihli and in charge of the negotiations—combined with the weakness of provincial interest in the end served to eliminate any real obstacles to the loan.

In March, 1907, Chang Chih-tung formally opened the question of cancellation; he objected to the existing Anglo-German arrangement because, he contended, the Tientsin-Chinkiang line was a railway that affected the "fundamental safety" of the country. He proposed that the gentry of Chihli and Shantung should be rallied behind the cause of redemption, the government should invite the participation of local capital in the project, and the construction of the northern section, which was closest to the capital, was to begin immediately.[39] To show its favorable response to this idea the Throne appointed Chang to manage the Tientsin-Chinkiang Railway affairs jointly with Yuan Shih-kai.[40] They were to supervise the matter on the policy level, while Liang Tun-yen of the Foreign Ministry carried on direct negotiations with the British and German banks.

Chang Chih-tung's appointment contained no little contradiction in itself, since Yuan had already been in charge of the negotiations for several years, and his views did not coincide with those of Chang. The suggestion of cancellation was rejected by him outright, and after a short exchange of views Chang abandoned his original proposals completely. Yuan's objections were based on two grounds. First, he held that as a matter of policy the Anglo-German concession should be retained, because it could serve as a remedy for the Shantung treaties previously entered into with Germany,[41] wherein exclusive railway rights were given away. The abrogation of the Anglo-German concession would automatically restore Germany's monopoly of railway rights in this province, which he considered a greater evil. Second, where were the provincial funds necessary for the construction of this railway? Unless the Peking government could amass 40 to 50 million taels, Yuan declared, it should not lightly speak of cancellation.[42]

In those weeks Chang Chih-tung showed much inconsistency in his views. Paramount in his mind was an intense distrust of the Germans. He told Lu Ch'uan-lin how, as soon as the news of possible cancellation had gone out, the British had repeatedly come to ask for more information; but the Germans acted as though they had heard nothing at all. This, he said, indicated the existence of some "cunning scheme" with regard to Shantung railway rights.[43] It is clear that for a short time he still held that the best solution to the problem would be cancellation, although he soon began to doubt its feasibility.[44]

When he found that Chang was persistent in his advocacy of cancellation, Yuan brought in the argument of diplomatic considerations. China was too weak to defy two Great Powers at once, and break off her legal engagements with them. The fate of Korea was cited as a warning.[45] Chang was not slow to be persuaded by this line of reasoning, and promptly showed a change of his own position by denying that he himself had ever wished to cancel the Anglo-German agreement.[46] From that time on the two high officials worked in cooperation for the preservation of the equilibrium of Anglo-German interests, but the concession was to be retained on the basis of improved loan terms.

The actual relationship between Chang Chih-tung and the gentry of these provinces constitutes an interesting problem for the historian. Had there been a genuine redemption movement among the gentry, and if so, were they responsible for Chang's early proposals for cancellation? Or was such a movement mainly inspired by Chang, with the gentry cooperating with his policy? Chang had spoken of rallying the gentry behind the cause, but that in itself did not eliminate the possibility of the gentry's having taken the initiative. Judging from Chang's readiness to agree with

Yuan Shih-k'ai, and from his other expressions of opinion, we may infer that he urged for the cancellation as a formal gesture under some pressure from the gentry. Certainly it is clear from his utterances elsewhere that Chang in this period was placing a great deal of hope in foreign loans as a means of financing railway enterprises. In his letter to the Three Provinces Association (of Chihli, Shantung, and Kiangsu), rejecting the idea of cancellation, Chang Chih-tung pointed out as an example that not "one foot" of the Hankow-Canton line had been built since its redemption two years ago.[47] He asked the gentry to desist from their demands. This was indeed a novel situation in which an official persuaded the people not to agitate for the recovery of railway rights. But besides the Hankow-Canton problem, the prolonged and futile negotiations for the cancellation of the Soochow-Hangchow-Ningpo concession were undoubtedly also factors that induced Chang to take that stand.

The policy adopted by Chang and Yuan, in the course of their deliberations, was to seek partial redemption of the power of control formerly granted to the foreigners. Chang was pleased by the information that both Sir John Jordan, British Minister in Peking, and J. O. P. Bland, representing the British concessionaire, were friendly to the plan of introducing changes in the detail of the loan provisions.[48] H. Cordes of the Deutsch-Asiatische Bank showed a similar attitude. During an interview between him and Chang Chih-tung fifteen articles were tentatively drawn up, in which the concessionaires undertook to modify the terms regarding the amount of the loan, the issuing price, the security for the loan, the period of amortization, and other items to the better advantage of China. However, this conciliatory attitude on the part of the financiers was coupled at the same time with a firm refusal to deal with the gentry-merchants of the provinces.[49]

By this time the provincial representatives had accepted

the idea of a loan, but they proposed modifications in the conditions, such as a drastic reduction in the amount of the loan, and the employment of a Chinese chief engineer. Later in the year they reverted their stand back to cancellation. But the Chinese officials, under the pressure of the British and German ministers who were urging for a speedy conclusion of the loan, silenced the provincial demands with the verdict that they were impractical.[50] Actually there had been no doubt among foreign circles in China that the concessionaires would maintain their hold over this railway.[51] The final agreement signed on January 13, 1908, was based on the general plan discussed by Yuan and the bankers, and drafted by Chang and Cordes in 1907.

Tactically, the Chinese officials aimed at separating the loan from the power of control over the railway. This was aided by the Foreign Ministry's willingness to pledge certain likin revenues of Chihli, Shantung, and Kiangsu as security, so that no mortgage was to be given on the railway.[52] In the final agreement this was achieved through two sets of regulations which caused this contract to be regarded by contemporary observers as one that marked a new stage in China's railway politics. In the first place, the Chinese government's right of control was recognized. The mixed Boards of Commissioners, provided in the preliminary agreement for the supervision of construction and management of the railway, were replaced by the Government Railway Administration. The selection and appointment of the British and German chief engineers for the southern and northern sections of the railway, respectively, were to be done solely by the Chinese government, and the chief engineers were to carry out the orders of the Chinese managing director of the line. The British and German banks had no authority to oversee the terms of the chief engineers' contracts.[53] These provisions most forcibly impressed foreign observers. The

American Chargé d'Affaires in Peking, reporting on the Tientsin-Pukou loan agreement, said,

> . . . the placing of the entire ownership and control of the road in the hands of the Chinese Government marks an important departure from the lines followed by the preceding railway agreements. This provision was made necessary by the outcry against foreign control of railways and, in view of the awakened national spirit, will likely be copied into all future railway agreements.[54]

Second, the financial terms were improved over those stipulated in 1898. The total amount was reduced from £7,400,000 to £5,000,000, and the time shortened from 50 to 30 years. The issuing price also was increased from 90 to 93 per cent, and a share of 20 per cent of the net profit of the line to the syndicates was commuted by an outright £200,000 commission from the first issue of bonds.[55] Instead of a first mortgage on the railway itself as security for the loan, the latter was secured by the likin and internal revenues of Chihli, Shantung, and Kiangsu to the amount of 4,700,000 taels per year. These revenues were to be turned over for administration by the Imperial Maritime Customs in case of default of payment.[56] The concessionaires were therefore prevented from assuming direct control of the railway. However, they retained other economic advantages, such as preference for British and German building materials, and the 5 per cent commission on all purchases abroad.

This comparative leniency in loan terms was to become the new standard for loan negotiations, as was indicated in the histories of the Hangchow and Hukuang railway loans. This turn of events could be partly accounted for by the prevalent Chinese nationalist sentiment, and the desire of the concessionaires to meet the situation with the least injury to themselves. But other factors which, from the concessionaires' point of view, impinged more heavily on their interests were also at play to bring about the changes.

These factors were based on the Anglo-German rivalry. It is undoubtedly true that the Anglo-German cooperation over the Tientsin-Pukou Railway concession could be regarded as the classic example of the cosmopolitan trend of British finance, within the limits of international balance.[57] But it was also obvious that as soon as the movement for cancellation was bruited about, the British and the Germans each sought to maintain their respective hold on the concession through strategic expressions of good will to the Chinese government. Sir John Jordan made it known that alterations in practical details could easily be arranged, so long as the concession was maintained.[58] Cordes was "anxious to please," and at the same time assured Chang that the Deutsch-Asiatische Bank gave up the 20 per cent share of profits in order to promote good relations with China.[59] Both banking groups were loath to lose the concession as an economic venture. Both the British and German governments were unwilling to see it cancelled, for in that event Britain would have had to watch the growth of a consolidated German railway system in Shantung, and Germany would have lost her chance to extend her influence down to the Yangtse region. It was possible, too, that Chang Chih-tung's early espousal of cancellation was a technique of pressure against the concessionaires. When the ministers of the two powers indicated their willingness to change some of the terms, the Chinese officials then decided the best solution would be to let the British and Germans construct the railway first, and to redeem the road in the future.[60]

Following this line of reasoning, Chang Chih-tung and others promptly suggested a plan of recovery, soon after the loan agreement was signed. They thought this railway could be made into a government-merchant joint enterprise at the end of ten years, when payment of the principal of the loan was to begin.[61] Under that system the interest of the provincial gentry-merchants in the railway was to be divided by provinces, the share of each province being proportionate to the length of the railway that ran through its territory.[62]

But once rebuffed by the authorities in their initial attempt to enter the field of railway enterprise, provincial interests made slight showing of themselves. Provincial subscriptions to the loan bonds of 1908, although encouraged by the government, amounted only to a pledged £250,000 after a year. In July, 1909 it was reported that these pledges had not been paid, and that the Chinese government had had to borrow the money from a German bank in Tsinan at 7 per cent in order to purchase the bonds.[63] Before any plan of redemption could be executed, therefore, additional loans had to be contracted in order to complete the railway, since no substantial financial contribution was forthcoming from the provincial gentry. A second loan of £4,800,000 was agreed upon with the Chinese Central Railway and the Deutsch-Asiatische Bank in 1910, on terms similar to the 1908 loan.[64]

In the case of the Peking-Hankow Railway, the Chinese government was able to bring about the purchase of the line from its Belgian concessionaire. This was accomplished by consummating a joint Anglo-French loan which, however, was not explicitly a railway undertaking. It took the form of a purely financial loan from the British and French banks to the Board of Posts and Communications. Yet the points remain that the interest of the British in this trunk line dated back to 1898, and that the present transaction represented a deal by which British capital was admitted into underwriting the operation of another major railway in China.

While the British had been perturbed since 1898 when the Peking-Hankow concession was awarded to the Belgian syndicate, the Société d'Étude des Chemins de Fer en Chine, the Chinese also attached great importance to this railway, it being the first rail enterprise of such scale to be carried through in the country.[65] A soon as traffic was opened in 1905, Sheng Hsüan-huai and T'ang Shao-i immediately urged that the Peking government plan for an early redemption of the line, in order to regain all the rights of control then in the hands of the concessionaire.[66]

Already before this date Sheng had advocated the speedy redemption of the 112,500,000 franc loan, since the original loan agreement had provided that the entire sum could be redeemed any time after September 1, 1907.[67] The subject was broached with the Belgian agent in 1906 and met with no opposition. At the same time, the Peking-Hankow Railway flourished, with the gross income for 1906 $2,000,000 in excess of that for the previous year. The net profit of $1,600,000 was put aside for the service of the loan.[68] No one, however, had considered it possible to repay the entire loan from railway profits, and early in 1906 Sheng had suggested contracting a foreign loan to eliminate the Peking-Hankow Railway debt.[69]

As a matter of fact, a part of the redemption fund was furnished by the Peking government itself. This was done by having the Board of Posts and Communications borrow 5,000,000 taels from the Board of Finance, and by using the 1906 profits of the Peking-Hankow line.[70] But these covered only a minor part of the required amount. The difference, then, was covered by a loan between the Board of Posts and Communications on the one hand, and on the other hand the Hongkong and Shanghai Banking Corporation and the Banque de l'Indo-Chine, concluded in October, 1908.

Little material is available on the details of the negotiations for this loan. It is clear, however, that from the first the Chinese had determined to free the railway itself of all future foreign control, and that the loan was to be contracted as a simple financial transaction, without impinging on rights or privileges over the railway. A part of the memorial of the Board of Posts, recommending the Anglo-French loan agreement for Imperial sanction, is worth noting:

> Regarding the present loan, Your Majesty's Board has steadfastly followed the principle that neither the creditor nor the contracting bank should have the least right to interfere with [the railway] affairs. Nor would it be specified for what purpose the money is to be used. After more than a twelve month's planning, and having negotiated with several banks, we have found that only the terms proposed by the said two banks are suitable . . . The present contract only provides for the methods of payment and amortization: it does not touch upon the management of affairs or the specific use of the loan funds. Therefore, the previous loss of power of control due to foreign loans is hereby completely avoided.[71]

The Throne's rescript gave approval to the entire proposition. It also avoided mention of the railway, referring to the loan only as "a foreign loan," and authorized the officials of the Board of Posts to sign the agreement.[72]

Since there was no preliminary understanding binding the contracting parties to its conditions, the terms of this contract must be considered as the best that could be arrived at for both sides under existing circumstances. These include the following financial provisions: [73] the loan was for £5,000,000, to be raised by the two contracting banks on equal shares, and to run for thirty years. The price to the Chinese government was set at 94—a better rate than usual, but still lower than that for the 1907 issue of the Shanghai-Nanking Railway loan. The interest was 5 per cent for the first fifteen years, and 4½ per cent thereafter. The commission to the banks was £2 for every £1,000, or 0.2 per cent, the lowest rate yet obtained. On the other hand, payment of the interest and principal of the loan was unconditionally guaranteed by the Peking government, and was secured on specified internal revenues and new taxes in the provinces of Kiangsu, Chekiang, Hupeh, and Chihli, up to 4,250,000 taels each year. However, the American Minister in Peking,

Rockhill, thought the real value of the hypothecated revenues was of small account, since the Chinese government's general guarantee "is unquestionably all-sufficient." [74]

But the freedom of disposal of the loan funds, much advertised in the Board of Posts memorial, was more apparent than real. It is undeniable that the wording of the first article of the agreement was notably vague. Eighty per cent of the loan money, it said, was to be used by the Chinese government in Europe "for the redemption of certain railway loans," and the remaining twenty per cent would be employed by the Board of Posts "in productive work of public utility within the department and functions of that Board." [75] But since the Peking-Hankow Railway was then the only Chinese railroad in a condition to be redeemed, the purpose of the loan was considered sufficiently defined for the banks to undertake it.[76]

The Peking-Hankow Railway was officially transferred from the Belgian syndicate to the Chinese government authorities on January 1, 1909, after the redemption funds had been paid on December 28, 1908.[77] Great relief was expressed by the Board of Posts at this successful conclusion of events, for jurisdictionally an important trunk line was placed under the control of the Chinese government for the first time.

From opposing camps therefore the British and French interests had now joined forces in order to eliminate friction, with a major loan to Peking undertaken on equal shares. Already in 1905 the new stage of *Weltpolitik* in China was pointed out when the French interests were admitted into the British syndicate, the Chinese Central Railways, Ltd., with the approval of the London and Paris governments.[78] France was laden with railway concessions in the Peking-Hankow area: besides her connection with the Peking-Hankow line, she also had shares in the Chengting-Taiyuan and Kaifeng-Chengchow railway loans.[79] Britain's participation in the present loan therefore represented the opening of a new market for British capital, as well as another step in the readjustment of foreign preponderance in China.

However, the share of British capital in the Peking-Hankow line increased in later years. In 1908, simultaneously with the conclusion of the Anglo-French loan, the Board of Posts and Communications had issued a $10,000,000 Government loan for partial payment of the redemption of this railway.[80] In 1910 half of that sum, or £450,000, was purchased by Dunn, Fisher and Company of London, and the bonds were floated jointly by this company and the London City and Midland Bank, Ltd. The Chinese government undertook to guarantee the repayment of capital and interest of the loan in sterling.[81] Two years later, the City Safe Deposit and Agency Company of London made a loan of £150,000 to the Chinese Republican Government, which was further secured on bonds of the 1908 Anglo-French loan.[82] It thus turned out that British financial firms became the largest investors in the loan bonds for the redemption of the Peking-Hankow Railway.

In sum, both bilateral enterprises resulted primarily from the rivalry of foreign interests in north China. While these interests achieved some degree of balance through the policy of compromise, there was also an observable reduction in the extent of financial advantages that were usually obtained by concession powers from loans. The Chinese officials were wont to point with pride to the concessionaire's lessened direct control over the railways. But since the loans were secured on other Chinese internal revenues, the advantages to the Chinese fiscal system must still be considered as negative.

VI

Plans for the Northeastern Provinces

BEYOND the Great Wall world attention was focused on Manchuria during the Russo-Japanese War of 1904–1905. After the close of hostilities the Peking government attempted to carry out the reconstruction of the region by a two-fold process: on the one hand there was to be a new system of railway transportation linking together the more important cities, while the administrative offices were to be revamped for the introduction of a strong Manchurian policy.[1] On the other hand, the rivalry and conflicts among the powers over Manchuria were to be utilized in such a way as to produce a power equilibrium. This would, it was hoped, end the domination of either Russia or Japan, and establish circumstances under which Chinese projects could be realized.

On China's side, therefore, railway plans for Manchuria were parts of an over-all regional scheme and as such they were directly affected by the vissicitudes of government policy. They suffered also from a lack of active local interest and support from among the relatively sparse population, for it seemed that gentry-merchants of substantial means, such as were found in Kiangsu, Chekiang, and Kwangtung, were not much in evidence in Manchuria. Even when local gentry became initiators of railway projects, the Chinese authorities were appealed to for aid. A case in point was the delegation of gentry and merchants who arrived at Peking in 1906 to confer with the authorities regarding the Kirin-Changchun railway. The government undertook to provide 800,000 taels.[2]

But by their very nature the government plans brought their own contradictions, and served to defeat their own ends on the plane of power politics. The following pages will discuss the Hsinmintun-Fakumen plan of 1907, the Chinchow-Aigun project of 1909, as well as the "Knox plan" of 1909–1910, the last being an American project that had received the acquiescence of the Peking authorities. None of these plans could be fulfilled.

THE HSINMINTUN-FAKUMEN RAILWAY PROJECT

After the Russo-Japanese War friction still remained between China and Russia, but there was a sense of imminent menace from the direction of Japan. Rockhill was correct when he discounted any likelihood of China's becoming a mere follower of Japan in the event of the latter's victory in 1905: "China is in as great a fear of Japanese preponderance as it ever was of Russian or German." [3] When the new Manchurian administration under the governor-generalship of Hsü Shih-ch'ang was installed in 1907, plans for the development of the provinces were pushed ahead amid clashes with the Japanese—in Mukden, along the Korean border, over mining rights.[4] The situation was critical, and one Western observer of Chinese affairs held that China one day would have to "fight for Manchuria or lose it." [5]

As a part of the reconstruction movement in Manchuria, the Hsinmintun-Fakumen Railway inevitably assumed a leading place in the government's plans. In 1906 Ch'eng Te-ch'üan, Military Governor of Heilungkiang, submitted to Peking a carefully drawn proposal for the construction of a Hsinmintun-Tsitsihar Railway, the justification being the strengthening of national defence in that region as well as promoting commerce. His plan received serious attention at Peking, and he himself had been commended by the Throne for his diligence in resisting foreign encroachment. In 1907 he was appointed Acting Governor of Heilungkiang in the new Manchurian administration.[6] However, at that time the aim appeared to be the building of this railway with material produced by the Hanyang Iron Works in Hupeh, and financing it by capital raised from Chinese sources.

When the railway plan was to be put into operation, however, the Hsü administration realized that it was necessary to invite the participation of foreign capital. It veered toward the Anglo-American interests in order the more effectively to counterbalance the Russo-Japanese predominance. After failing to get help from the American railway magnate Harriman,[7] Hsü Shih-ch'ang and T'ang Shao-i, the latter now the Governor of Fengtien, concluded a contract with the British firms Pauling and Company and the British and Chinese Corporation, on November 8, 1907, for the construction and financing respectively of the Hsinmintun-Fakumen railway, the first fifty-five miles on the 400-mile line between Hsinmintun and Tsitsihar.[8]

Hsü and T'ang suggested that the whole line be treated as a branch of the Imperial Railways of North China, because in that way it could technically avoid being a Manchurian project. Thus other foreign powers—implying the Russian and Japanese governments—would then have no excuse to object to its construction. Furthermore, this first section lay to the west of the Liao River, "and it does not touch upon Japanese interests in any way." In case Japan should create obstacles regarding this matter, the Foreign Ministry was urged to reject her claim upon those grounds.[9] The estimates of the cost of the line followed that of the North China Railways, £6,500 per mile, and it was decided not to make public, for the time being, the project for the two longer sections beyond Fakumen.[10]

When the Manchurian administrators mentioned "obstacles," they had in mind the ominous inquiry that had already been directed at Peking from Tokyo in August 1907. The Japanese Chargé had asked the Foreign Ministry for information on these points: first, the reported plan to extend the North China Railways northward from Fakumen; second, the reported raising of a foreign loan by Manchuria. He declared that Japan would not agree to the building of railways that would parallel or be detrimental to the interest of the South Manchurian Railway.[11] It was then more than a year after Japan's domination over the southern part of the Manchurian provinces had been officially established by the organization of the closely related Kwantung Government General and the South Manchurian Railway Co.[12] China was in fact attempting to solidify her *de jure* rights, with the hoped-for support of Britain and the United States, in those parts where Japanese dominance had not yet established itself. Therefore the official Chinese rejoinder to the Japanese protests was that the question of a foreign loan was China's own business; as for the railways, they would be in any case a part of China's own communications system and would not impinge on the South Manchurian Railway, nor would they be injurious to it.[13]

The above was basically the position maintained by the Chinese government in the dispute that subsequently developed. Yet the recognition given to Japan's alleged right to protest against Chinese railway plans, implicit in the official reply, led to ultimate failure. The Japanese government repeated its protests in October and December, 1907, and the ensuing discussions became deeply involved in the question of interpretation of the minutes of the 1905 Sino-Japanese treaty conference at Peking, and in the definition of the terms "neighborhood" and "parallel." [14] Although Hsü Shih-ch'ang and T'ang Shao-i were pressing for Imperial ratification of the Pauling contract, urging it as a matter that concerned the recovery of Chinese sovereign rights in the northeast, and that it must not be stopped by Japan's objections,[15] and although the Peking Foreign Ministry for a time maintained a determined front against the Japanese Legation, it soon became obvious that the outcome was by no means certain.

The diplomatic spotlight was now on London. In an effort to persuade Whitehall to give its support to the project, the Chinese Minister in London was instructed to explain the situation to the British Foreign Office, pointing out especially that in 1905 Japan had undertaken not to hinder China's plans for the development of her own territory.[16]

Some British observers continued to cling to the original provisions of the 1898 loan agreement for the North China Railways, in which Britain's interest in Manchuria was admitted.[17] But the new alignment of power in the Far East in 1907 was such that it soon became clear London would withhold its support of the British contractors in the Hsinmintun-Fakumen Railway. In fact, by June, 1908, Japan was sufficiently assured of Britain's passivity to send a very uncivil note to the Chinese Foreign Ministry, reiterating the theme that the Fakumen line would divert traffic from the South Manchurian Railway, and that pursuing the plan was "unprincipled conduct" on the part of China "which the Imperial Japanese Government could not tolerate." However, if the route were changed so that it would connect directly with the South Manchurian Railway, and become one of the latter's branch railroads, the Japanese government would then give consent to such a project.[18] A few months later proposals were again made for either the construction of a Japanese line across the Fakumen railway, terminating at Liao-yuan half-way up to Taonan, or changing the route of the Chinese project. Both were rejected by Hsü Shih-ch'ang and the Foreign Ministry who regarded them as means of killing the Chinese plan and of extending the Japanese sphere of interest.[19]

All quibbling as to the mileage between parallel points on

the Fakumen and South Manchurian Railway lines was actually irrelevant to the main issue. Hsü Shih-ch'ang, upon leaving his post at Mukden, contended that failure for the project stemmed from the inefficacy of the Chinese government itself. He believed that the Japanese would not have insisted on calling the Hsinmintun-Fakumen Railway a parallel line to the South Manchurian, had the Peking authorities been more determined and the officials more serious about their tasks.[20] So far as the Chinese were concerned, the matter involved was no less than the basic question of China's right to pursue development plans within her own territory.

Another aspect of the matter was the inability of the British Foreign Office to aid such plans for fear of risking the Far Eastern equilibrium which was based on the Anglo-Japanese Alliance. This view was not taken by the British public who were thinking in terms of the value of individual economic concessions; nor was it expected by the Chinese.[21] The London Foreign Office, however, acquiesced in Japan's contention that the projected railway was a parallel line to the South Manchurian Railway. By describing the problem as one between Japan and China,[22] London declared her intention of not interfering with the "sphere" of Japanese predominance. Her ally was gratified by this stand. Prince Ito acknowledged to the British Minister at Tokyo that "the British Government had acted with justice and admirable fairness" in the matter of the Hsinmintun-Fakumen Railway.[23] It was reported that Morrison, Peking correspondent of the London *Times,* had been sent to London by the British contractors to "fix" the Foreign Office,[24] but his weight was easily overbalanced by the considerations for empire politics.

The Peking government, unused to the idea of opposing Japan's encroachments alone, decided to yield. In September, 1909, it signed an agreement with Japan concerning the railways and mines of Manchuria. The first article of the document provided that, should China decide to construct a Hsinmintun-Fakumen railway in the future, she should arrange beforehand with Japan.[25]

THE CHINCHOW-AIGUN PROJECT

The Pauling contract was dropped, and the Manchurian reconstruction plans under the administration of Hsü Shih-ch'ang likewise had failed. Would another railway project, starting from some point west of Hsinmintun and reaching farther north, have the chance to succeed despite Russia and Japan? [26] What if it were carried out with the joint support of both the British interests and an anti-Japanese America? Hsü was soon replaced as governor-general by Hsi-liang, a vigorous Manchu with an anti-opium record in Yunnan. He became the advocate of a Chinchow-Tsitsihar-Aigun railway, and within a few months had secured the support of the British and American interests both for its financing and construction.[27] The British contractor was still Pauling and Co., and the American group consisted of New York financiers represented by Willard Straight.

Prior to the Russo-Japanese War a certain unity of purpose had existed among Britain, the United States, and Japan in their opposition to Russian expansion in eastern Asia.[28] But this situation changed after 1905. Contrary to Theodore Roosevelt's hopes of seeing Russia and Japan contained by each other's position in Manchuria and Korea,[29] Japan became the predominant power in this region. It was not long after Portsmouth that the United States Minister at Tokyo began complaining of the disadvantageous position in which the Japanese had put American business and diplomatic interests in Manchuria: towns opened by the Japanese military authorities to Japanese merchants were closed to other nationals; the opening of

American consulates in Mukden and Dalny was obstructed. The British also felt the restrictions on foreign trade and shipping, and in 1906 the American and British governments simultaneously protested to the Japanese government against such acts of discrimination.[30]

The role of active antagonist of Japan however was assumed by the United States, partly because underdeveloped Manchuria offered her a chance of vast economic expansion, while the European powers were already deeply involved in the other parts of China; and partly because, unlike Britain, she was not obliged to consider maintaining a condition of equilibrium with Japan. In 1906 Willard Straight, then twenty-six years old, was appointed American Consul-General at Mukden. Now Straight had connections with the Roosevelt family, was familiar with E. H. Harriman's grandiose plans for railway expansion, and had become a confirmed Japanophobe since his brief stay in Korea in 1906. During his two years at Mukden he eagerly pushed forward American interests, his actions included the consolidation of American consulships in Manchuria and the setting up of a propaganda agency specifically aimed at countering Japanese efforts in the same field. In short, he became "a thorn in the side of Dai Nippon." [31]

Straight also kept in contact with Harriman, ready to launch a development project in Manchuria that would tie up with American financial and railway interests.[32] Since the Japanese Foreign Ministry had in 1906 turned down the Harriman-Katsura agreement for the formation of an American-Japanese South Manchurian Railway Syndicate, in which China's rights in Manchuria were completely ignored by both parties, the next thing that suggested itself to Harriman was to purchase the Chinese Eastern Railway from the Russians. He would also obtain a concession from China to build a railway from Chinchow to connect with the Trans-Siberian Railway. That would serve as a solid foothold for the United States in this region against the Japanese interest.[33]

At this juncture American and Chinese diplomacy temporarily merged. While Britain was getting more entangled in European affairs, the Anglo-Japanese Alliance was regarded with increasing apprehension by China.[34] The Hsinmintun-Fakumen affair in 1907 revealed further that Britain was inclined to be passive in regard to the northeast. All this increased the potential value of American support of China, and in the spring of 1908 T'ang Shao-i, Governor of Fengtien, memorialized in favor of an American loan of 20 million taels. This information was passed on to the State Department by Minister Rockhill.[35] In July Straight, whose recent fracas with a Japanese postman had threatened to create an international incident, was recalled to Washington. It is significant that instead of being a reprimand, this recall really placed Straight in a role that was most effective for the carrying out of American policy. It appeared that Harriman had persuaded Washington to try out some of his projects. On his return there Straight was consulted by the State Department regarding railway and industrial developments in Manchuria,[36] and in the next year he became the chief American representative on the Hukuang loan negotiations.

While T'ang Shao-i failed in his loan proposal and in his mission to the United States, Harriman's interest in Manchurian railways continued. By 1909, when the United States was contending for a part in the Hukuang loans, a larger American interest in China was thought to be indispensable for dealing with the British and European groups on an equal footing.[37] Despite the Root-Takarhira convention of November, 1908, the sense of competition with Japan was keenly felt—such, for instance, as existed in the field of the textile trade in all China.[38] Even the scholarly Rockhill, who had not always agreed with Straight in the latter's cavalier tactics in Manchuria, showed a degree of sensitiveness when dealing with the Japanese that was highly illuminating.[39]

Under these circumstances the Manchurian railway projects of 1909 assumed an increasingly complicated aspect. Upon learning of China's plan to start a railway from Chinchow, Japan proceeded to exert her pressure. First, Pauling and Co. in London was approached by a counsellor of the Japanese Embassy, who asked for the right of Japan to participate in the construction of the Chinchow-Tsitsihar railway, promising in that event to withdraw Japan's opposition to the whole project. Pauling, however, refused to negotiate, declaring it was a matter to be decided by the Chinese government.[40] Through articles that appeared in the London *Times* on August 19, 1909, George Pauling made it publicly known that his firm intended to hold on to the contract.[41] The Japanese meanwhile also intimated to the Peking Foreign Ministry that their government was determined to obstruct the construction of the Chinchow-Taonan line which, according to Minister Ijuin, was also a route parallel to the South Manchurian Railway. The Foreign Ministry's reaction to such remonstrances was to advise moderation on the part of the Chinese.[42]

The provincial authorities in Manchuria, however, were less willing to adopt a policy of "watch and wait." The pressure of Japanese power was more directly felt and caused greater apprehension in Manchuria than in Peking, and Hsi-liang summed up an interview with Prince Ito in these words: "Implicitly he regards China on the same level as Korea, and his words and expression unconsciously suggest aggressive ambitions." [43] Hsi-liang and Governor Ch'eng of Fengtien pushed forward the Chinchow-Aigun project during the summer of 1909. The route was surveyed, while Governor Chou of Heilungkiang already was reminding the Foreign Ministry that this railway must be built beyond

Tsitsihar, Russian objections notwithstanding, in order that the coal industry might be benefited.[44]

It appeared that, before heavy Japanese pressure had been applied at Peking, a confidential Imperial order had been issued to the Manchurian authorities, asking them to arrange for the opening of trading towns and contracting of foreign loans in Manchuria.[45] Accordingly the railway project was carried forward. Straight by now had returned to China as representative of the American financial group, and proceeded to negotiate with Lord ffrench, agent of Pauling and Co. The outcome was the preliminary agreement of October 2, 1909, on the financing and construction of the Chinchow-Aigun Railway, concluded between the British firm, the American group, and the Chinese authorities. Straight's parting remark to the Chinese dignitaries was, according to Hsi-liang, "Don't worry about Japanese and Russian objections." [46] The agreement was referred by edict to the Board of Posts, the Board of Finance, and the Foreign Ministry for study and report.[47]

Compared with other foreign loans for Chinese government railways, the Chinchow-Aigun preliminary agreement embodied a unique feature, in that the political aim of the project was explicitly indicated. Articles VI and VII stated that during construction the railway company, legally a Chinese government undertaking, was to be organized by British, Chinese, and American interests and composed of the nationals of these three countries; the Chinese were to have the majority interest in the control, and "under no circumstances shall persons of other nationality than those herein mentioned have any voice in the management or control of the company without the full permission of the Imperial Chinese Government." [48] While this provision attested to the desperate attempt of Hsi-liang to attract foreign support, it also represented a significant triumph for the American and British participants in that their voice in the management and control of the railway company was formally assured.

This agreement was hastily drawn, the amount and price of the loan and other details being left for later settlement. The road was to be built on a contract basis, and the Mukden officials did not argue closely about the economic advantages to be accorded the financiers and contractor. The chief engineer was to be an Englishman appointed by Pauling and Co. but formally approved by the Chinese Railway Administration.[49] The line was to be constructed in two sections, Chinchow-Tsitsihar and Tsitsihar-Aigun, and was to be financed by two separate issues of loan bonds.[50] Security for the loan was to be the railway itself, and 10 per cent of the net profit was to go to the company. Straight and Lord ffrench also signed an Anglo-American supplementary document on October 6, 1909, in which an agreement was reached by the two groups respecting their mutual financial interests.[51]

Here a divergence of view between the provincial and Peking authorities showed itself. Doubtful of the efficacy of British policy in this area, and probably also skeptical as to the possibility of real Anglo-American cooperation while the controversy over the latter's participation in the Hukuang loan was raging, the Peking officials were inclined to be cautious. At the same time, evidences of Russian and Japanese vigilance were not wanting. For instance, soon after the conclusion of the October 2 agreement Korostovetz, Russian Minister at Peking, addressed an inquiry concerning the proposed Anglo-American loan. Though the Foreign Ministry replied that "this is China's domestic business, and foreigners need not concern themselves with it," [52] the import of the inquiry was not lightly regarded in Peking.

Thus, after fifty days of deliberation over the Chinchow-Aigun preliminary agreement, the three government ministries in November memorialized the Throne against it.[53] Their main contentions were that the problem of Manchuria called for a comprehensive regional development plan, not merely a railway, and that the present agreement gave away too many economic advantages to the British and Americans. This line of reasoning was subsequently countered by Hsi-liang who held, "Nominally it is a commercial railway, but actually it embodies political and diplomatic strategies . . . With us the primary aim is the saving of the nation, and not merely the profitable development of resources." He pleaded again for the speedy ratification of the agreement before international complications appeared; his memorial, however, was again referred to the ministries for further consideration.[54] For the time being the October 2 agreement remained on the shelf, and before long it became a part of the larger issues of the neutralization of railways in Manchuria.

THE KNOX PLAN AND THE POWERS

While the Chinchow-Aigun project hung fire, the United States Department of State was launching another enterprise, the "Knox plan" for the neutralization of Manchurian railways. The proposal was first made to London by the American government. According to the plan, China was to purchase the Manchurian railways of Russia and Japan with a loan furnished by "interested powers," and regain legal ownership of the lines. For the duration of the loan the railroads were to be placed under the supervision of the nationals of the participating powers, the administration of the railroads would thus be international. Close cooperation of Britain and the United States was to serve as the foundation of the whole plan.[55]

It would be erroneous to regard the Knox plan and the Chinchow-Aigun project as two separate matters. Throughout the negotiations it became increasingly clear that the Chinchow-Aigun project was but the first step toward a more general American plan of changing the political balance in Manchuria. Indeed, Knox had observed that the special interests of Britain and the United States rested only on the existing contracts concerning the Chinchow-Aigun Railway.[56] And in case the original Knox plan could not win the cooperation of Russia and Japan, the alternative proposed by Knox was to have Britain and the United States give diplomatic support to the Chinchow-Aigun project, inviting at the same time the interested powers "friendly to the complete commercial neutralization of Manchuria to participate in the financing and construction of that line," and in such additional lines as future commercial developments might require. China meanwhile was to be loaned funds to purchase existing lines that might be offered for inclusion in this system.[57] The emphasis on commercial development here testified to the ultimate long-range nature of the American interest; it was the end for which the Chinchow-Aigun and the neutralization plan were the means.

Harriman had proposed including Russia as one of the original partners of the undertaking against Japan. Such maneuvering in power politics, however, was disregarded by Knox.[58] He sought instead to have Britain and the United States take the initiative, thus placing both Russia and Japan on the defensive. Rather than breaking the Far Eastern front of these two powers, as it was hoped at first, it soon became apparent that Knox's policy actually served to solidify it.

In reply to Knox's proposal, Sir Edward Grey expressed agreement with the principle of the plan, but doubted whether time was yet ripe for the negotiations; he also showed special concern over Japan's interests and position in Manchuria.[59] But Knox waved aside these reservations. In early November Rockhill, now Ambassador to St. Petersburg, had already been instructed to inform the Russian Foreign Minister of the general outline of the neutralization plan.[60] After receiving Grey's reply Knox decided it was time to start the plan going, and on December 14 instructions were sent to the American representatives at Paris, Berlin, Tokyo, Peking and St. Petersburg, formally to present the neutralization plan to the various governments.[61]

In the Russian capital the group led by Izvolsky, the Foreign Minister, was opposed to the plan for reasons of the wider economic, political and military interests of Russia. Tokyo reacted in a similar fashion. After an exchange of views Izvolsky was able to announce in January, 1910, that "Komura found it possible to express the conviction that Japan would on no account permit the South Manchurian Railway to pass into foreign hands." [62] On January 23, 1910, Russia and Japan in official communications simultaneously rejected the Knox plan; Japan, however, also expressed willingness to participate in the Chinchow-Aigun project.[63]

In Peking the neutralization plan and the Chinchow-Aigun project were presented as two aspects of the same problem. Chargé Fletcher presented the former to the Foreign Ministry on December 21, 1909; the advantage of the plan was shown to be the elimination of political questions incidental to railway development. Later when the Peking government was urged to act on the agreement of October 2, the Chinchow-Aigun project was described as "the foundation stone in China's recovery of railway rights." [64] At the same time, both the American and British governments were urging the Chinese authorities to accept Japanese participation in the Chinchow-Aigun project.[65]

London, however, appeared to be regarding the Knox plan and the Chinchow project as two separate matters. While she had succeeded in getting the United States to push for Japanese participation, Britain remained basically noncommittal with regard to the larger plan, save to express the desire to be informed of Russia and Japan's responses to the Knox proposal.[66] The attitude of the British Ambassador in Tokyo was described by his German colleague as being "reserved, cool, and skeptical." [67] As to Germany, she had no intention of becoming embroiled with the Entente Powers in the Far East, and based her agreement to the Knox plan on Japanese and Russian approval. France never took the proposal seriously, and also conditioned her acceptance on similar action by Japan and Russia.[68]

That the Peking government aimed to use the railway projects as a means of recovering its sovereignty in the northeast was well understood by the powers,[69] and the open split among the latter put Peking in a situation wherein it was obliged to make a decision. While the prospects for the first Knox plan darkened, the British and American Ministers in Peking were instructed by their governments to urge the ratification of the Chinchow-Aigun agreement. They also strongly advocated the participation of Japan and other interested powers in this railway. In other words, the alternate plan contained in Knox's November 6 memorandum was to be put into operation. However, the American Chargé was instructed to emphasize especially the importance of the Chinchow-Aigun project to China's hopes for the whole Manchurian territory, and to declare that the success of the neutralization project "which means so much to China," depended in a large measure upon an early public ratification of the Chinchow project as signed in 1909.[70] The United States, determined to pursue its plans in this part of China, attached special importance to the Chinchow line in an effort to insure itself of the possession of a material asset in Manchuria. This would serve as the base for operations should the neutralization plan materialize. If not, it still would constitute an enterprise capable of competing with the Japanese and Russian-controlled lines.

From January 12 to 20, 1910, the three leading ministries of the Chinese government—the Foreign Ministry, the Board of Finance and the Board of Posts—consulted each other as to the advisability of ratifying the Chinchow-Aigun agreement. The Foreign Ministry expressed its approval of an early ratification, persuaded no doubt by the evidence of American support. From the viewpoint of diplomacy, the Ministry believed both the Knox plan and the Chinchow project would be helpful to China.[71] The Board of Posts concurred in this view. However, it drew attention to two additional points. The first was dissatisfaction with the loan provisions. The Board held that the joint Anglo-American-Chinese undertaking, instead of being a Chinese enterprise financed by foreign loans, was actually detrimental to Chinese rights, since the loan conditions concerning such matters as personnel and purchase of material were below the standard terms of railway loans in recent years. The possibilities of some changes in the route to avoid entanglement with the South Manchurian Railway and certain other projects for Manchurian development were also mentioned. The Board proposed, therefore, that the general agreement be signed, but that the detailed provisions should be modified. It was also in favor of promptly memorializing the Throne for ratification.[72] The Board of Finance agreed with the other two ministries. On January 20 the three ministries jointly memorialized for the sanction of the Throne, and received Imperial approval of the Chinchow-Aigun agreement. In this memorial, the political and economic importance of this railway to Manchuria was outlined. The final terms of the contract, however, were to be concluded along the lines of recent railway loan terms. This was to be done by the Manchurian authorities after discussing the matter with the American banking group. In addition, the three ministries advocated the establishment of a Frontier Colonization Bank with Chinese resources, as supplement to the railway project in the regional development plan.[73] In notifying the American Legation of the ratification, Prince Ch'ing made clear the Chinese condition with regard to changes in the terms of the contract.[74]

From then on the Manchurian projects became mainly a tug-of-war between the American interest and the Entente Powers, in which Britain's decision assumed vital importance.

As soon as the ratification of the October 2 agreement became known, protests poured into the Peking Foreign Ministry from the governments of Japan and Russia, supported by France. In brief, Japan objected to the Chinchow-Aigun project on the old ground of a parallel railway, and Russia was opposed to its touching her frontier at Aigun, but both claimed the right to be consulted.[75] The protests were begun on January 31, when the Japanese Minister Ijuin sent a note to the Foreign Ministry, saying that China should obtain the consent of Japan before making any decision regarding the Chinchow-Aigun Railway—otherwise unpredictable dangers would arise in the relationship between the two countries.[76] Following upon this Russia, on February 2, made similar representations at Peking and at Washington. Minister Korostovetz's note to the Foreign Ministry contained similar objections and warning to China as the Japanese note, while in Washington the United States was asked not to conclude the Chinchow-Aigun loan before the Russian government had had a chance to express its views.[77]

Shortly after this, an interview between Chargé Fletcher and Max Muller of the British Legation at Peking revealed that both their governments had instructed them to ask the Chinese Foreign Ministry to consult Russia about the Chinchow Aigun project. There was however an interesting footnote to the British attitude: speaking of the British representation to be made to Liang Tun-yen, Fletcher requested Muller to make it in such a way as to leave no doubt that Great Britain was heartily in favor of the railway scheme.

That, reported Fletcher, Muller promised to do.[78] This indicated that on the American side there had begun to develop the feeling that Britain's stand in this matter needed to be reinforced.

It was soon after this conversation, however, when Britain made it clear that she would abide by the final decisions of Russia and Japan in the Manchurian question. The British representation to the Chinese government went farther in behalf of Russia and Japan than Washington wanted it to go. It advised the Peking government that, without consulting these two powers, it was to make no definite settlement of the Chinchow-Aigun project. That was a view expressed also by the French Minister at Peking. In fact, Muller was reported to have warned the Chinese government, on February 9, to be cautious lest it be dragged into trouble by the Americans. Nor could England participate in the undertaking until Russia and Japan had been consulted. The effect of Britain's over-all political ties on her general policy was again plainly revealed, and Knox was reported to have become highly dissatisfied with the attitude of London.[79]

While the formation of a closer Russo-Japanese Entente was becoming daily more obvious, and was closely watched by German diplomats, Washington persisted in support of the original project.[80] Toward late February Russia countered with a proposal of a Mongolian railway to replace the Aigun project, but the proposal was not presented to the Chinese until one week after it was laid before the State Department. The plan called for the building of a Kalgan-Urga-Kiakta line, to be connected with the Trans-Siberian by a branch line, and the Urga-Kiakta section was to be financed by Russia.[81] While in her note to the Chinese government Russia objected to the Aigun line on the grounds that it would injure the commercial value of the Chinese Eastern Railway, in the memorandum to the State Department she charged that the Aigun line would be injurious to Russia's strategic interests as well. Russia thus made plain her desire to keep the Manchurian status quo. Her proposal in effect would shift the railway from Manchuria to Mongolia and place it partially under her control. To the Peking government the Russian note added this curious reasoning: "since the Chinchow-Aigun Railway contract was concluded with foreign capitalists, containing no political implications, then it would not be impossible to shift its route and construct it elsewhere." The reply from the State Department was equally plain in its desire to break the status quo. The United States rejected the 1899 Anglo-Russian agreement regarding railway rights as contrary to the principle of the "open door," and asked Russia to lift her objections so that work could be commenced on the first stretch of the Chinchow-Aigun line. Since Russia by proposing the Mongolian line showed a desire for cooperation in Chinese railway matters, Knox hoped that she would find the Aigun project not contrary to broad Russian policy.[82]

Japan, meanwhile, in an effort to make the Chinchow-Aigun line a part of the Japanese system, also proposed a plan similar to the Russian one. Ijuin made a two-point suggestion to the Peking Foreign Ministry, declaring that Japan would consent to the Chinchow-Aigun project on these conditions: first, Japan was to participate in financing the project and providing a part of the materials and engineers, and second, the Chinese and Japanese governments were to agree to the building of a branch railway connecting the Aigun line with the South Manchurian Railway.[83]

The combined opposition of the four Entente Powers to any Manchurian project which did not have the approval of the Russian and Japanese governments produced fear and hesitation in Peking. In March, 1910, the Foreign Ministry argued with Hsi-liang whether it was advisable to negotiate at that time the details of the Chinchow-Aigun loan contract, or whether Russia and Japan should be satisfied before continuing with the original project. The Foreign Ministry held that the negotiations should wait for a prior settlement with these two powers which had "seen through" China's objective of strengthening her position in Manchuria through this railway. Hsi-liang opposed this view, declaring that the opposition of Russia and Japan was not unexpected, but that China must not be intimidated. Hsi-liang's plan was to send his delegates to Tientsin and negotiate the detailed provisions of the contract with Straight, but he promised not to settle anything definitely without the approval of the Foreign Ministry.[84] This controversy lasted into the summer, when Straight went to St. Petersburg in an effort to win over Russia to the Chinchow-Aigun project. The State Department was also seeking to bring about Russia's approval of the plan.[85] A renewed inquiry from Hsi-liang, however, elicited only the unenthusiastic response from the Foreign Ministry that he might proceed with the conclusion of the loan and building contracts after an agreement had been reached with the Russian and Japanese governments.[86]

While the Peking government drew back, and the United States was trying to win the acquiescence of St. Petersburg to the railway projects, Russia and Japan were taking positive steps further to fortify their positions in northeastern China. The uneasiness caused by the Knox démarche in the previous winter had stimulated a desire in both the Russian and Japanese governments to have their respective positions clarified and placed under stronger guarantee. This desire was intensified when, despite the similar replies that were sent to Knox in January, 1910, by both governments, the separate proposals that each had made regarding a change of railway routes in the ensuing months indicated that, given the opportunity, neither power would hesitate to enlarge its own interests by incorporating the American proposal into its own system.

This mutual apprehension resulted in the Russo-Japanese agreement of July 4, 1910, consisting of one public and one secret convention. The significance of the former lay in the fact that it made public the arrangement for delimitating their spheres in Manchuria that was contained in the secret convention of 1907. Now it was specifically stated that they would cooperate with a view to the improvement of their railways in Manchuria; it also was a warning to other powers against their attempting to disturb the status quo in that region.[87] It signalled the other great powers that the Russians and the Japanese intended to stay in that part of China.

The secret convention went further. Each power was given a free hand in the sphere that had been marked out in 1907 for its domination—Russia over northern Manchuria and Japan over southern—and each was not to hinder the development of the other's "special interests" in the latter's sphere. Mutual and cooperative defense for these interests was agreed upon in case they became threatened.[88] This convention served the purpose of a mutual guarantee between the two powers themselves. Their suspicion of each other's intentions had in fact never ceased, even at the time of the conclusion of the agreement.[89] The secret provisions therefore were made in order that neither one would be deflected from its established policy, join the American camp, and participate in ventures that would be dangerous to the interests of the other.

Within the Chinese government the potential threat to China that was embodied in the new Russo-Japanese accord was fully realized by some officials. The most articulate about the situation were Sheng Hsüan-huai in Peking and Hsi-liang in Mukden. Toward the beginning of July, word came of a possible settlement with Russia through the efforts of Straight and ffrench. At the same time the disturbing news of the entente between Russia and Japan came to China's attention. Hsi-liang feared that if Russia's designs were thwarted in the northeast, she might take action in China's northwest. The remedy, as he saw it, would be the immediate construction of both the Chinchow-Aigun and the Urga-Kiakta railways by the Chinese government, leaving Russia no chance to demand railway rights in Mongolia.[90] Sheng Hsüan-huai was at that time advocating the policy of contracting foreign loans for the resuscitation of the Ch'ing government. In his view an American loan, with perhaps the cooperation of Germany, was the instrument with which the government of China could save its rights in the northeast. By that time Britain had been written off as a possible source of aid for China in Manchuria.[91]

In August, 1910, it was reported that five Russians had been sent by their government to northern Heilungkiang, under the pretext of inspecting the commerce of that area, to survey the route of the Tsitsihar-Aigun railway, while Washington urged that Peking come to a decision on the Chinchow-Aigun question.[92] But it was not clear whether or not America and Britain had yet arrived at any specific arrangements with Russia. In the winter of 1910–1911 the United States renewed its effort to draw Russia into cooperation. Straight pointed out to Korostovetz that Japan was the real menace to the peace of the East, while Knox intimated to ffrench that some changes in the route of the Chinchow-Aigun line might be acceptable if Russian objections to the present project could thus be overcome.[93] But the efforts of Straight and ffrench, by placing the railway matter on a predominantly commercial plane, was out of gear with Russian interests. While the Peking authorities tried another expedient in getting outside aid—the currency reform and Manchurian development loans—the Chinchow-Aigun railway project lapsed into oblivion.

Conclusion

FROM THE BATTLE for concessions in 1898 to the signing of the Hukuang loan agreement in 1911, the railway movement in China underwent significant changes and development. At the same time, though British interests in this field on the whole continued to advance, the advances were accompanied by certain modifications as regards method and strategy in relation to other powers. We may sum up the events of these years as of three-fold significance: the efforts of Chinese gentry-capitalists and officials to promote railway construction amid domestic and diplomatic changes; the way in which special foreign interests operated their claims of "spheres" in a decadent empire; and the methods by which Britain sought to reconcile her interests with those of other powers in China, so that conflict might not be precipitated in the Far East in a world of high diplomatic tension.

On the Chinese side the scene was in the main one of a split between the gentry and provincial interests and the dynastic government. For a number of reasons the former were generally advocates of Chinese enterprise in railways, while the latter, from 1898 on, showed an increasingly clear tendency to accept, and to seek, foreign participation and aid. However, there did not always exist a clearly defined system of relationships between the gentry interests and government officials. While in some cases the gentry-capitalists were instrumental in the realization of railway policies, such as the Hankow-Canton redemption plan, yet in others the officials apparently were able easily to over-ride the opinion of the gentry when the latter's demands were contrary to government policy. For example, the Tientsin-Pukou loan was contracted with the British and German financiers, although there were evidences of gentry opposition to it, and in 1906 it was reported in the press that cancellation of the concession, according to the wishes of the merchants and gentry of the provinces, was imminent.[1]

The relative economic strength of the gentry capitalists in different provinces was a contributing factor to the differing manifestations. Their ability to carry out railway plans ranged from the actual financing and construction of the Shanghai-Hangchow-Ningpo railway to the virtual absence of gentry interests in the Manchurian plans. In some instances the gentry-merchants depended primarily on the cooperation of the provincial authorities for the raising of capital through extra taxes, notably in Szechuan, Hunan and Hupeh. Here the official-gentry relationship in the traditional power structure was utilized to serve the purpose of modernization; but aside from benefiting the railway promoters concerned, the results were negative.

It was plain that the old financial methods, and traditional concepts of provincial interests, were inadequate to meet the demands of the new enterprise in railways. In another respect, the policy of the Ch'ing government was also to prove unfit for the furtherance of national welfare through modernization. Could China's problems be solved by railways built upon a pile of debts and mortgages? Were the various powers likely to be used by Peking in its effort to save itself by playing one group against another? The Chinese officials' attitude regarding Britain showed that such action was attempted. From 1898 on, the idea of a power equilibrium, in terms of concessions in China, had occupied the minds of some officials. After the Russo-Japanese war it became particularly evident, and in Chang Chih-tung one sees an advocate of the pro-British line in foreign relations. After the British loan for the redemption of the Hankow-

Canton Railway, and the consummation of the Tientsin-Pukou contract, British influence came to be regarded with some favor by others of the government. Hence the extension of British investment into Manchuria was welcomed by the provincial administration and Peking—the latter though with some hesitancy. The failure of the Fakumen and Aigun projects did not lessen the significance of these plans.

In this connection another aspect of the Ch'ing government policy became evident. Foreign loans were to be contracted not only for the construction of individual railways, but also were to serve as the bases of regional development, and furthermore, of the resuscitation of the dynasty. Sheng Hsüan-huai, commenting on the deadlock over the Chinchow-Aigun project in 1910, exposed this view fully. He held that France helped Russia, and Britain supported Japan in this controversy, basing his belief on the fact that France and England were the creditors of the other two powers. It was regrettable, Sheng concluded, that China, while contracting an American loan, should not be able to seize the opportunity and utilize American support for diplomatic and political ends.[2] According to this reasoning, foreign loans should have been a means with which the Ch'ing dynasty could hope to strengthen its rule in the country.

The general situation in China indeed gave cause of worry to the dynastic government. Between 1906 and 1908 seven armed revolts had taken place in the provinces of Kwangtung, Hunan, Anhui, and Kiangsi, six of which were directly or indirectly connected with the revolutionary party T'ung-meng Hui.[3] While national discontent and unrest reached the boiling point, the dynasty leaned increasingly more to a policy of seeking foreign aid. Foreign loans for railways came to be regarded as inevitable. But this put the government in a contradictory position with both the gentry-capitalists and the foreign concessionaires. As to the former, it increased the conflict within the country, and precipitated the political revolution of 1911. As regards the latter, while Peking was obliged to argue for better loan terms, and sometimes even give support to provincial redemption movements against the foreign concessionaires, it nevertheless was not able to withstand the pressure exerted by the powers. At the same time, the conclusion of loans brought about the participation of the government in all major railway projects. This proved to be also a convenient instrument for the foreign interests which preferred to hold some central organ to account to dealing with various—and often hostile—provincial interests. Thus, on more than one occasion the foreign banking groups were assured by Chinese officials that the gentry would not be allowed to deal in the loan under discussion.

In the end what the Chinese officials could point to were the "improved" loan terms, of which the Tientsin-Pukou Railway loan was especially held up as an example. Its main difference from previous loans was the separation of the railway revenue and property from obligations of loan payments, thus precluding the possibility of the railway's becoming mortgaged to the foreign creditor in case of default. The Tientsin-Pukou terms were taken as a model by the Chinese negotiators for the Hangchow and Hukuang railway loans. But according to their provisions, the loans were secured on other parts of China's government revenue, primarily the income from the internal transit tax and the opium taxes. These were important items of the government's revenue, and their hypothecation affected the nation's financial independence no less than the potential mortgage on the railway lines. In so far as foreign debts were contracted, they must be paid in some way. But to hail such loan terms as being great economic changes in China's favor, as most officials did at that time, was certainly unrealistic. The lack of any program for a basic improvement in the nation's economy was indicative of the short-shift nature of the Ch'ing policies. We have seen that as late as 1910, while debating on the Chinchow-Aigun issue, the Board of Posts still thought that the important concern for the moment was the changes of certain specific terms in the contract, as though "improvements" in such matters as the issuing price or interest rate could bring forth qualitative changes in China's position vis-à-vis the Great Powers.

On the international side, the period under survey presented two different financial methods with which the British promoted and maintained their railway concessions in China. These represented the adjustments that British capital made to changing conditions of foreign investment. The first method was that of simple British concessions, under the terms of which British financiers were the sole contractors for the financing and construction of Chinese government railways. Loans for the Shanghai-Nanking, Canton-Kowloon, Shanghai-Hangchow-Ningpo, and the Taok'ou-Ch'inghua railways were concluded on this basis. For the British mercantile circle these were the more satisfactory sort of transactions, since the contracts placed entire railway lines under the exclusive control of British capital.

However, after the Russo-Japanese War the alignment of power blocs had been precipitated to such an extent that certain readjustments were deemed necessary. This was manifested by Whitehall and the major British financiers' adoption of a trend that was already emerging in 1898: the policy of cooperation with other powers that had economic interests in China. In 1898 the attempt of the British group to effect a joint Anglo-American enterprise on the Hankow-Canton line was not successful, but thirteen years later the four-power Hukuang Railways Loan came into being. Prior to that, in 1908 the Tientsin-Pukou Railway loan established the actual precedence for joint enterprise, and the Anglo-French loan of the same year furnished funds for the redemption of the Peking-Hankow line from the Belgian concern.

If such "cosmopolitan" trends were denounced by old-time British expansionists like Bland, the other aspect of British policy in the period under survey—withdrawal from controversial projects—met with even less support from this group. The changes made in the Sino-British Restoration agreement in 1902, regarding the building of branch lines of the Imperial Railways of North China, was indicative of future British policy. The Manchurian projects from 1907 on revealed this policy still more forcibly, and the position of the London government was then more clearly defined, since the pattern of diplomatic alliances and ententes had already assumed final shape, and all foreign dealings had to take into account the matter of Anglo-German competition for empire.[4] The Far Eastern entente of Britain, Japan, and Russia was a highly delicate affair on which London depended for the maintenance of a state of equilibrium in China; and Sir Edward Grey's repeated statement, that the Liberal Government would not deviate from the foreign policy laid down by its Conservative predecessor,[5] should surprise no one, since the foreign relations of a country generally follow the broad trends of its basic needs, and seldom change drastically with the changes in party government.

The withdrawal of Britain's naval strength from the Pacific, in fact, was fully appreciated by Japan. For instance, during the First World War one of the leading newspapers in the latter country expressed deep resentment over the cooperation of British forces with the Japanese in operations at Kiaochow and the South Pacific, declaring that Japan "neither needed nor wanted any cooperation at all." [6] But for Britain's part, in order to keep the Far Eastern power bloc intact, certain concessions had to be made to the claims of Japan and Russia over China's economic development plans. In Parliament a lengthy debate was roused by the Chinchow-Aigun Railway issue, during which Grey summed up the British position in these words:

All that I am defending is our attitude of neutrality . . . while we have every wish to see British and American finance to cooperate in railway construction in China, yet in regard to this particular railway we can not but think it reasonable that China should consult both with Japan and Russia, if she intends to have this railway made by foreigners. In face of the Anglo-Russian agreement of 1897 [*sic*], the only reasonable course for us to adopt would be to maintain a neutral attitude until the Russian and Japanese objections to the railway have been removed.[7]

The failure of Anglo-American collaboration in the Manchurian projects was due not so much to intent as to circumstances surrounding the action of each. Harking back to the days when England and the United States had a community of interest in opposition to the Russian power in northeastern Asia, the United States in 1909–1910 overlooked the fact that the pattern of world politics had changed in recent years. While Russia and Japan now saw in the United States a rival for Manchuria, they were both allies of England. London could hardly risk the stability of her alliances for the sake of cooperating with America in China. It is important to remember that returns for this risk were slight. The United States was as yet neither ready nor willing to give support to England in the latter's diplomacy in Europe, Africa, or other parts of Asia.[8]

In the last analysis, the railway movement in China at the turn of the century was a combination of two elements: in the long run it was part of a national effort for modernization of the country; immediately it was also partly a protest against increasing foreign economic domination. But given the existing conditions—the dispersed agrarian economy and the dearth of ready capital, the contradictions between the government policies and gentry interests, the Western financial groups eagerly seeking a channel of investment in the China market—it is difficult to visualize general and rapid achievements in China within this short period. But had the gentry-capitalists been given more room by the Peking government to develop their plans, the economic outcome might have been different. The building of the Shanghai-Hangchow-Ningpo and the Peking-Kalgan Railways proved that it was possible for the Chinese themselves to undertake railway projects on their own. With every additional accomplishment the people themselves would have gained new experience and confidence in further undertakings.

As the records stand, within our period of survey the British financial agents were able to contract, either singly or jointly with other powers, loans for Chinese railways covering some 3,704 miles of railroads. Compared with the figures for a later date, that mileage amounted to 38 per cent of the national total in 1935 when 9,773 miles of railways were in existence in China, including Japanese-occupied Manchuria.[9] But the conflicting purposes of the gentry-merchants, the Ch'ing government, and the foreign investors could not be long maintained in a precarious balance, and the Republican Revolution of 1911 sounded the warning note that the old order was changing.

Notes

Abbreviations Used in the Notes

BDOW	G. P. Gooch and H. Temperley, *British Documents on the Origins of the War*
BPP	*British Parliamentary Papers*
CCWCSL	*Ch'ing-chi wai-chiao shih-liao*
ch.	Chüan (subdivision in a Chinese volume)
FRUS	*Foreign Relations of the United States*
GP	J. Lepsius, A. M. Bartholdy, and F. Thimme, *Die Grosse Politik der Europaische Kabinette 1871–1914*
TCLCSL	*Ta-Ch'ing li-ch'ao shih-lu*
THHL	*Tung-hua hsü-lu*

Introduction

1. Herbert Feis, *Europe, the World's Banker 1870–1914* (New Haven, 1931), pp. 5–15, 23, 28, 32, 84. C. K. Hobson, *The Export of Capital* (New York, 1914), pp. 7–15, 54–55, 59, 159.

2. See for example Lord Charles Beresford, *The Break-up of China* (London, 1899), p. 15. *The Threatened Decline of Great Britain in China,* pub. by the China Gazette (Shanghai, 1903), pp. 4, 21–22, 43–44. C. A. Middleton-Smith, *The British in China and Far Eastern Trade* (London, 1920), pp. 41 ff., 81 ff.

3. Sir Robert Hart, *These From the Land of Sinim* (London, 1901), pp. 61–62. C. F. Remer, *The Foreign Trade of China* (Shanghai, 1925), pp. 123–125, 161, and *Foreign Investment in China,* (New York, 1933), p. 407.

4. R. C. K. Ensor, *England 1870–1914* (Oxford, 1944), pp. 275–276. Yen Chung-p'ing *Chung-kuo mien-yeh chih fa-chan* [The Development of the Chinese Cotton Industry] (Chungking, 1943), chapter 5.

5. William L. Langer, *The Diplomacy of Imperialism* (New York, 1935), II, 416; see also Nathan Pelcovits, *Old China Hands and the Foreign Office* (New York, 1948).

6. Beresford, pp. 12–13, 15, 32. *British Parliamentary Papers, China No. 1 (1899)*, p. 190, no. 278. W. W. Willoughby, *Foreign Rights and Interests in China* (Baltimore, 1920), p. 282.

7. For these concessions see next chapter. The Tsungli Yamen was the abbreviated version of the name for the Board for the Management of Foreign Affairs (Tsung-li ko-kuo shih-wu ya-men), established in 1861. It was reorganized in 1901 as the Ministry of Foreign Affairs (Wai-wu Pu). Brunnert and Hagelstrom, *Present Day Political Organization of China* (Shanghai, 1912), pp. 104–107.

8. *China No. 1 (1899)*, pp. 346–347, Enclosure 3 in no. 459.

9. *Ibid.*, p. 4, no. 5.

10. Pelcovits, p. 230.

11. J. V. A. MacMurray, *Treaties and Agreements with and Concerning China*, I, 534–536, especially Articles I–III, V–VI.

12. Cheng Lin, *The Chinese Railways Past and Present* (Shanghai, 1937), pp. 38–52.

13. Tseng K'un-hua, *Chung-kuo t'ieh-lu shih* [History of Chinese Railways], (Peking, 1924), pp. 94–95, give a tabulated comparison.

14. *China No. 1 (1899)*, pp. 141–142, no. 214.

15. Quoted in Pelcovits, p. 264.

16. T. W. Overlach, *Foreign Financial Control in China* (New York, 1919), pp. 66, 68. J. O. P. Bland, *Recent Events and Present Policies in China* (Philadelphia, 1912), pp. 260–261. Feis, pp. 83–89, 96–99.

17. *China No. 1 (1899)*, p. 141, no. 214.

18. Pelcovits, p. 266.

19. W. W. Rockhill, Rockhill Papers, Mss., Harvard University, A. R. Burkill to Lord Lansdowne, March 21, 1904. A. L. P. Dennis, *Adventures in American Diplomacy, 1896–1906* (New York, 1923), chapter 14, *passim*.

20. Rockhill Papers, memorandum from A. R. Burkill to Rockhill, March 30, 1904. Italics added.

21. *Ibid.*, Sir Ernest Satow to Rockhill, July 7, 1904.

22. *Parliamentary Debates*, 5th series, vol. XVII, p. 1390, G. Stewart speaking on Chinese railway question, June 15, 1910.

23. Chao Feng-t'ien, *Wan-Ch'ing wu-shih-nien ching-chi ssu-hsiang-shih* [Economic Thought During the Last Fifty Years of the Ch'ing Period], Yenching Journal of Chinese Studies, Monograph Series no. 18 (Peiping, 1939).

24. Ch'en Kung-lu, *Chung-kuo ching-tai-shih* [Modern Chinese History] (Shanghai, 1946), II, 438. Pai Shou-i, *Chung-kuo chiao-t'ung-shih* [History of Chinese Communications] (Shanghai, 1937),

pp. 234–236. Chang Chih-tung was appointed Governor-General of Hukuang in 1891, a post he held until 1908. During those years be became a leading figure in China's railway politics, as the following pages will show. For Chang's life see *Ch'ing-shih kao,* "Biographies," ch. 224, and Arthur W. Hummel, *Eminent Chinese of the Ch'ing Period* (Washington, 1943), I, 27–31.

25. "Schools of modern learning," *North China Herald,* Feb. 23, 1906. *The Chinese Recorder and Missionary Journal,* Nov. 1910, p. 697, on the first industrial exposition in Nanking.

26. Sheng Hsüan-huai, *Yü-tsai ts'un-kao,* "Memorials," ch. 12, p. 1, Meml. of Sept. 1, 1905; see *Ch'ing-shih kao, loc. cit.,* ch. 258, for a brief sketch of Sheng's career.

27. Li Chien-nung, *Chung-kuo ching-pai-nien cheng-chih-shih* [Political History of China in the Past 100 Years] (Shanghai, 1947), I, 243–250.

28. For a view of the subjects included in the government's reform program, see Merebeth E. Cameron, *The Reform Movement in China 1898–1912* (Stanford, 1931).

29. Li, I, 221–234, 250–261. Rockhill Papers, Alfred Hippisley to Rockhill, Jan. 27, 1907.

30. Pai, pp. 244–245. Tseng, pp. 72–74, 76–77, 78–79, 80. *Tung-hua hsü-lu,* Kuang-hsü, ch. 207, pp. 14–15, Meml. of I-K'uang (Prince Ch'ing) et al. on the organization of the Board of Posts and Communications, Aug. 1, 1907.

31. Sheng, "Memorials," ch. 12, p. 5, Meml. of Sept. 1905.

32. THHL, KH, ch. 201, pp. 5–6, Meml. of Board of Commerce, July 14, 1906.

33. *Ibid.,* ch. 205, p. 18, Meml. of Board of Agriculture, Industry, and Commerce, May 8, 1907. *Ta-ch'ing li-ch'ao shih-lu,* Kuang-hsü, ch. 574, p. 7, Imperial decree, July 7, 1907.

34. THHL, KH, ch. 200, p. 10, Meml. of Board of Commerce, May 15, 1906.

35. TCLCSL, KH, ch. 572, p. 22, Meml. of Ch'ing Ch'un-hsüan, June, 1907. THHL, KH, ch. 208, p. 7, Meml. of Board of Posts and Communications, *re* Ch'ing's Meml., Aug. 21, 1907.

36. TCLCSL, Hsüan-tung, ch. 10, pp. 9–14, Meml. of Board of Posts and Communications, April 8, 1909. This was typical of the government's planning activities of the time. For example, it promulgated the Constitutional Principles in 1908, which consisted of a nine-year plan for the establishment of a constitutional government.

37. TCLCSL, KH, ch. 548, p. 12, Edict to Grand Councillors on

mining policy, Sept. 1905; ch. 554, p. 3, Meml. of Military Governor Ch'ung-shan of Foochow on shipbuilding, Feb. 1906. *British Parliamentary Papers*, no. 4015 Annual Series, "Report for the year 1907 on the Trade of Hankow," p. 6. *Chinese Recorder*, Jan. 1908, p. 35, Edict on the development of national resources, Aug. 2, 1907.

38. Fei Hsiao-t'ung, "Peasantry and Gentry: An interpretation of Chinese Social Structure," *American Journal of Sociology*, LII, no. 1, July 1946. Marion J. Levy and Shih Kuo-heng, *The Rise of the Modern Chinese Business Class* (New York, 1949), Part II, pp. 27–34, 40–44.

39. For instance, TCLCSL, KH, ch. 578, pp. 14–15, Imperial Decree on the establishment of Provincial Assemblies, Oct. 1907.

40. Overlach, p. ii. A. J. Sargent, *Anglo-Chinese Commerce and Diplomacy* (Oxford, 1908), pp. 294–295.

41. Overlach, pp. 50–60, 134–136. Some of the most vigorous writers on the evils of foreign debts at the turn of the century were the political reformers; see for example Liang Ch'i-ch'ao's articles on the subject, and reprints of current press opinion in China, in *Ch'ing-i-pao ch'üan-pien* (1898–1901) (Yokohama, n.d. [1900's]), vols. 4, 16.

42. P. H. Kent, *Railway Enterprise in China* (London, 1907), p. 126.

43. THHL, KH, ch. 195, p. 7, Meml. of Governor-General Ting of Yunnan, Aug. 22, 1905. TCLCSL, KH, ch. 591, p. 11, Meml. of the Censorate in behalf of non-metropolitan Yunnan officials, June 12, 1908. Mongton C. Hsu, *Railway Problem in China* (New York, 1915), pp. 92–99, 100–101.

44. *Parliamentary Debates*, 4th series, vol. 162, pp. 1424–1425, J. Walton, Aug. 2, 1906.

45. Rockhill Papers, Charles Denby to Rockhill, Sept. 12, 1905; also V. Chirol to Rockhill, Dec. 7, 1906. *North China Herald*, Feb. 26, 1906, p. 376.

46. H. B. Morse, *Trade and Administration of China* (Shanghai, 1908), pp. 80–85.

47. T'ang Ch'ing-tseng, "Ch'ing-tai t'ai-hsi shu-ju wo-kuo-chih ching-chi ssu-hsiang" [The introduction of economic thought into China during Ch'ing dynasty], *Chung-kuo ching-chi wen-t'i* [Economic Problems of China] (Shanghai, 1929), pp. 323–325.

48. Chao Yung-Seen, *Les Chemins de Fer Chinois* (Paris, 1938), p. 62.

49. Chang Chih-tung, *Chang Wen-hsiang-kung ch'üan-chi*, "Tele-

graphic Correspondence," ch. 76, p. 1, Chang to Governor-General Ch'ing of, Canton, Sept. 23, 1906.

50. *Ibid.*, "Memorials," ch. 66, pp. 23–25.

51. Sheng, "Board of Posts and Communications Memorials," Part II, Meml. on the bankruptcy of the Szechuan Railway Co., July–Aug., 1911.

52. Chang, "Memorials," ch. 68, p. 17, Meml. on the government purchase of one-half interest of all commercial railways after 30 years, Jan. 11, 1907. Tseng, pp. 100–107.

I: The Making of the Preliminary Agreements

1. *Ch'ing-chi wai-chiao shih-liao, Kuang-hsü*, ch. 116, pp. 6–7, Meml. of Secretary of the Imperial Granary Hsü Yin-k'uei, July 27, 1895.

2. *Ibid.*, pp. 35–37, Meml. of Chang Chih-tung, Aug. 8, 1895.

3. Ch'en Kung-lu, *Chung-kuo chin-tai shih* [Modern Chinese History], (Shanghai, 1946), I, 393.

4. *Ibid., loc. cit.* See also John K. Fairbank and S. Y. Teng, "Tributary Trade and China's Relations with the West," *Far Eastern Quarterly*, vol. I, no. 2, February 1942, pp. 129–149, for an interpretative analysis of the ideology underlying China's traditional relations with other parts of the world.

5. CCWCSL, KH, 118, pp. 1–2, 2–4, Memls. of Tsungli Yamen, Oct. 19, 1895, and Imperial rescript. THHL, KH, 136, pp. 8–9, complete Chinese text of the 1896 Russian Treaty. Nathan Pelcovits, *Old China Hands and the Foreign Office* (New York, 1948), pp. 195–201.

6. Pelcovits, pp. 148, 149.

7. *Ibid.*, pp. 202–204.

8. CCWCSL, KH, 118, pp. 8–9, telegram of Minister Kung Chao-yuan to Tsungli Yamen, October 27, 1895.

9. *Ibid.*, KH, 119, p. 3, Kung to Tsungli Yamen, December 23, 1895; pp. 4–5, Meml. of Tsungli Yamen, December 30, 1895; p. 9, telegram of Kung to Tsungli Yamen, January 14, 1896.

10. *Ibid.*, KH, 125, pp. 1–3, Meml. of Tsungli Yamen, with rescript, Feb. 4, 1897; pp. 4–6, text of agreement.

11. Pelcovits, pp. 210–214. *British Documents on the Origin of the War*, I, 11, no. 14, Salisbury to O'Conor (secret), Feb. 8, 1898. CCWCSL, KH, 129, pp. 22–23, Meml. of Prince Ch'ing et al. April 2, 1898.

12. Pelcovits, pp. 214–216.

13. CCWCSL, KH, 128, p. 6, telegram of Chang Chih-tung to Tsungli Yamen for Memorializing to the Throne, Feb. 3, 1898.

14. *Ibid.*, pp. 10–11, Meml. of Hu Yü-fen, Prefect of Shun-t'ien-fu, Feb. 5, 1898.

15. Pelcovits, pp. 211–212.

16. BDOW, I, 21, no. 31, MacDonald to Salisbury, March 18, 1898.

17. CCWCSL, KH, 128, p. 8–9, Chang Chih-tung to Tsungli Yamen, and Edict, Feb. 3, 1898.

18. *Ibid.*, pp. 19–20, confidential Meml. of Governor Ch'en Pao-chen and rescript, Feb. 17, 1898.

19. Pelcovits, pp. 214–215.

20. CCWCSL, KH, 128, p. 18, telegram of Chang Chih-tung to Tsungli Yamen, Feb. 17, 1898; KH, 129, pp. 2–3, telegram of Chang to Grand Council, Feb. 23, 1898; p. 4, Liu K'un-i to Grand Council, Feb. 24, 1898.

21. *China no. 1 (1899)*, p. 18, no. 20, enclosure 3, Tsungli Yamen to Sir C. MacDonald, Feb. 11, 1898.

22. CCWCSL, KH, 128, pp. 20–21, telegram of Chang Chih-tung to Tsungli Yamen, Feb. 17, 1898. His sources of information were said to be Western press and Japanese sources. Cf. Pelcovits, pp. 253–255, on China Association's advocacy of a Yangtse Protectorate.

23. *China no. 1 (1899)*, p. 29, no. 42, MacDonald to Salisbury, March 28, 1898.

24. *Ibid.*, p. 212, no. 314, MacDonald to Salisbury, Sept. 4, 1898; p. 344, no. 459, MacDonald to Lord Charles Beresford, Nov. 23, 1898.

25. Pelcovits, pp. 220–246.

26. W. W. Willoughby, *Foreign Rights and Interests in China* (Baltimore, 1920), pp. 526–527.

27. Ch'en Kung-lu, I, 427. BDOW, I, 36, no. 55, Salisbury to MacDonald, July 22, 1898; no. 56, MacDonald to Salisbury, July 25, 1898; p. 37, note to no. 56, Salisbury's minute, Aug. 8, 1898.

28. CCWCSL, KH, 135, pp. 18–20, Meml. of Hu Yü-fen, Nov. 13, 1898. J. V. A. MacMurray, *Treaties and Agreements with and Concerning China*, I, 174–175, articles IV and V.

29. William L. Langer, *Diplomacy of Imperialism*, II (New York, 1935), II, 679–683. BDOW, I, 8, note to no. 8, O'Conor to Salisbury (confidential), Jan. 30, 1898.

30. P. H. Kent, *Railway Enterprise in China* (London, 1907), pp. 3, 5–6; Pelcovits, pp. 224, 229, 258–259. Sheng, "Telegrams," ch. 8,

p. 77, Tsungli Yamen to Sheng, April 24, 1898. Daniel Thorner, *Investment in Empire* (Philadelphia, 1950), chapter 3.

31. CCWCSL, KH, 116, p. 8, telegram of Chang Chih-tung to Tsungli Yamen, July 31, 1895; KH, 118, p. 9, same to same, Oct. 29, 1895; KH, 119, pp. 1–2, same to same, Dec. 21, 1895; pp. 14–16, Meml. of Chang Chih-tung on surveying of the route, Jan. 17, 1896.

32. CCWCSL, KH, 129, p. 3, telegram of Chang Chih-tung to the Grand Council, Feb. 24, 1898; p. 4–5, same to same, Feb. 26, 1898.

33. *China no. 1 (1899)*, p. 4, no. 5, Ewen Cameron to the Foreign Office, April 4, 1898.

34. Sheng Hsüan-huai, *Yü-tsai ts'un-kao*, "Telegrams," ch. 8, p. 31, Chang to Sheng, April 30, 1898.

35. *Ibid.*, p. 31, same to same, April 29, 1898.

36. *Ibid.*, ch. 8, pp. 27–28, Sheng to Tsungli Yamen, April 25, 1898; p. 32, Sheng to Chang, May 1, 1898; ch. 9, p. 2, same to same, May 6, 1898.

37. Pelcovits, pp. 230–231. Sheng, "Telegrams," ch. 9, pp. 5–6, Sheng to Tsungli Yamen, May 12, 1898; p. 7, Sheng to Governors-General Liu, Wang, and Governor K'uei of Kiangsu, May 13, 1898. *China no. 1 (1899)*, p. 82, no. 92, p. 85, no. 101, show that the signature took place on the same day that Prince Henry reached Peking on his tour.

38. MacMurray, I, 404, Art. 25.

39. Sheng, "Telegraphic Memorials," ch. 1, pp. 9–11, joint Meml. of Sheng Hsüan-huai, Governors-General Wang of Chihli, Chang of Hukuang, on the draft loan agreement with the American company, March 28, 1898; p. 11, Meml. of Sheng, April 9, 1898.

40. *Tung-hua hsü-lu*, Kuang-hsü, ch. 146, pp. 6–8, Meml. of Sheng, July 28, 1898.

41. Pelcovits, p. 215. (Referring to British January demands *re* opening of Nanning, Yunnan Region, Yangtse non-alienation, *likin* exemption area: the dropping of English or Russian loan used as lever to pry loose commercial concessions vs. exclusive design of other powers.)

42. *China no. 1 (1899)*, p. 288, enclosure 2 in no. 383.

43. R. Stanley McCordock, *British Far Eastern Policy 1894–1900* (New York, 1931), p. 191.

44. Pelcovits, chaps. 7 and 8, *passim.*; *China no. 1 (1899)*, p. 281, no. 380.

45. The Tientsin-Chinkiang line was obtained by a joint Anglo-German effort, after the two banking groups had reached an understanding regarding the division of their interests. Then the con-

cession was pressed by both the British and German Ministers at Peking. *China no. 1 (1899)*, p. 258, no. 342; p. 164, no. 233; p. 168, no. 239; p. 169, no. 245.

46. Sheng, "Telegrams," ch. 8, p. 31, Chang Chih-tung to Sheng Hsüan-huai, April 30, 1898.

47. Sheng, "Telegrams," ch. 8, pp. 27–28, Sheng to Tsungli Yamen, April 23, 1898; ch. 9, p. 26, Li Hung-chang to Sheng, July 25, 1898; ch. 10, p. 4, Sheng to Bureau of Railways and Mines, Sept. 20, 1898.

48. CCWCSL, KH, 141, pp. 1–2, Meml. of Sheng Hsüan-huai, Nov. 19, 1899.

49. A good source for first-hand accounts of the conduct of foreign diplomats during the battle for concessions is Wong T'ung-ho, *Wong Wen-kung-kung jih-chi* [Diary of Wong T'ung-ho] (Shanghai, 1925), vol. 37 (1898), entries for first and second months, *passim*.

50. CCWCSL, KH, 136, p. 19, telegraphic Edict to Chang Chih-tung and Liu K'un-i, Dec. 29, 1898; cf. Lord Charles Beresford, *The Break Up of China* (London, 1899).

51. Ninety per cent was the lowest price for Chinese railway loan bonds contracted in this period. A comparison with the sale prices of loan bonds of various other countries shows that this seemed to be a safe mean price for the concessionaires to risk. As will be shown below, 90 was the figure retained in the final agreement on the Shanghai-Nanking Railway loan concluded in 1903. Over the twenty-year period 1885–1905, the sale price of various government loans of Argentina, Egypt, Mexico, Portugal, and Turkey, which were floated on the European market (including London), ranged on the whole between 78 and 99.5. Mexico rated two very low prices, 65 and 68, but her highest was 93.5, while Egypt did not go below 91. Turkey fluctuated between 78.5 and 96, and though the Bagdad Railway Convention of 1903 set the issuing price at 81.5, the loan bonds were sold at 86.4. See: Corporation of Foreign Bondholders, *Annual Reports*, no. 33 (1905–1906), London, 1907, pp. 50–58, 165–168, 252–256, 307–311, 383–389; and Edward Mead Earle, *Turkey, the Great Powers, and the Bagdad Railway* (New York, 1923), p. 91, note no. 48.

52. MacMurray, I, 402–404.

53. CCWCSL, KH, 139, pp. 9–13, Meml. of Governor-General Sung-fan of Yunnan, June 26, 1899; cf. Kent, pp. 177–180, *re* small commercial value of the Yunnan-Burma railway and small likeli-

hood of its being built, "unless political considerations render its construction desirable."

II: Railways of the Yangtse Delta

1. P. H. Kent, *Railway Enterprise in China* (London, 1907), p. 123. *Ch'ing-chi wai-chiao shih-liao*, Kuang-hsü, ch. 165, p. 10, Sheng to Foreign Ministry, Oct. 18, 1902.

2. London *Times*, April 8, 1903, p. 5; May 30, 1903, p. 7.

3. Sheng Hsüan-huai, *Yü-tsai ts'un-kao*, "Memorials," ch. 12, pp. 20–21, Meml. on the Management of the Shanghai-Nanking Railway, March, 1905.

4. *Ibid.;* also CCWCSL, KH, ch. 172, p. 2, Meml. of Foreign Ministry on the Shanghai-Nanking Railway Final Agreement, June 2, 1903.

5. Chang Chih-tung, *Chang wen-hsiang-kung ch'üan-chi*, "Telegraphic Correspondence," ch. 57, pp. 17, 18, Sheng to Chang, Feb. 13, 1902; Chang to Sheng, March 1, 1902.

6. *Ibid.*, p. 18, Sheng to Chang.

7. Sheng, "Memorials," ch. 12, pp. 20–22, Meml. on the Management of the Shanghai-Nanking Railway, March, 1906. CCWCSL, KH, ch. 172, p. 3, Meml. of Foreign Ministry on the Shanghai-Nanking Railway loan negotiations, June 9, 1903.

8. J. V. A. MacMurray, *Treaties and Agreements with and concerning China*, I, 401–402.

9. *Ibid.*, pp. 387–388, 402. Sheng, "Telegrams," ch. 42, p. 15, Sheng to Minister Chang in London, July 8, 1904.

10. MacMurray, I, 388.

11. *Ibid.*, p. 395, Art. IX; p. 389, Art. III; p. 396, Art. XII.

12. *Ibid.*, p. 389.

13. *Ibid.*, pp. 391–392, 403; cf. CCWCSL, KH, ch. 172, pp. 9–10.

14. For a while after the conclusion of the loan agreement there was an attempt by the British railway contractors, Pauling & Co., to obtain the contract for building this line. The British and Chinese Corporation acted as its agent and would not let the Chinese government negotiate directly with Pauling. Sheng was reluctant and finally refused the bid, because, as he stated in his official correspondence, it would lead to completely losing control of the railway to the contracting company, whereas the employment of a British chief engineer and chief accountant would at least nomi-

nally be placed under the control of the director-general and of the Board of Commissioners. That was the first instance of conflict regarding the power of control. See Sheng, "Telegrams," ch. 42, p. 4, Sheng to Governor-General Wei of Nanking and Governor-General Chang of Wuchang, June 18, 1904; pp. 8–9, Sheng to Foreign Ministry, June 27, 1904. George Pauling, *The Chronicles of A Contractor* (London, 1926), p. 223.

15. Sheng, "Telegrams," ch. 42, p. 14, Sheng to the Foreign Ministry, Board of Commerce, Governor-General Wei of Nanking, Chang of Wuchang, Commissioners Tuan-fang at Chinkiang and En-min at Soochow, July 6, 1904; p. 16, Sheng to Chang, July 14, 1904.

16. *Ibid.*, p. 16, Chang Chih-tung to Sheng, July 13, 1904.

17. *Ibid.*, ch. 45, pp. 25–28, Governor Lu of Kiangsu to Sheng, Sept. 22, 1905; Governor-General Chou Fu of Liangkiang to Sheng, Sept. 23, 1905; Sheng to Governor Lu, Sept. 24, 1905; Sheng to Governor-General Chou, Sept. 25, 1905.

18. *Ta-ch'ing li-ch'ao shih-lu,* Kuang-hsü, ch. 548, p. 14, Edict to the Grand Councillors, Sept. 18, 1905.

19. *Ibid., loc. cit.;* also ch. 550, p. 15, Edict to Grand Councillors, Nov. 17, 1905. *North China Herald,* Nov. 24, 1905, p. 428.

20. Kent, pp. 134–135, quoting an article in the London *Times*. For example, £250,000 were allotted to Sheng for the purchase of land, but that sum proved to be insufficient, and Sheng was reported to have requested more funds from the Corporation to cover the expenses. Cf. MacMurray, I, 393. Article VIII.

21. *North China Herald,* Dec. 1, 1905, pp. 513–514.

22. *Tung-hua hsü-lu,* Kuang-hsü, ch. 200, p. 18, Meml. of the Boards of Commerce and of Finance, June 3, 1906; ch. 203, p. 4, Meml. of the Board of Finance and T'ang Shao-i, Nov. 29, 1906.

23. *Ibid.*, ch. 200, p. 10, Meml. of Wu Yü-sheng, member of the Grand Secretariat and Councillor in the Board of Rites, May 21, 1906.

24. MacMurray, I, 391.

25. THHL, KH, ch. 200, p. 18, Meml. of the Boards of Commerce and of Finance, June 3, 1906.

26. *Ibid.*, ch. 203, p. 5, Meml. of Board of Finance and T'ang Shao-i, Nov. 29, 1906.

27. Kent, p. 136, note 1; he also records here that this issue of the bonds was successfully floated in London (January, 1907) at par.

28. Pelcovits, *Old China Hands and the Foreign Office* (New York, 1948), pp. 290, 291.

29. MacMurray, I, 391–392; cf. CCWCSL, KH, ch. 172, pp. 9–10, a Chinese text of the agreement.

30. Sheng, "Telegrams," ch. 42, p. 11, Foreign Ministry to Sheng, July 1, 1904.

31. *Ibid.*, pp. 11–12, Sheng to the Foreign Ministry, July 2, 1904.

32. THHL, KH, ch. 203, pp. 4–5, Meml. of the Board of Finance, Nov. 29, 1906.

33. Board of Posts and Communications, *Second Statistical Account of Communications* (1908), ch. 1, "Important facts on the Shanghai-Nanking Railway."

34. MacMurray, I, 392.

35. THHL, KH, ch. 203, p. 5.

36. Board of Posts, *op. cit.*, ch. 1. MacMurray, I, 405–408.

37. Board of Posts, *op. cit.*, ch. 4, "Railroad Administration, I: Chart showing staff organization of the Shanghai-Nanking Railway."

38. MacMurray, I, 405 ff.

39. *Ibid.*, pp. 405, 406.

40. *Ibid.*, p. 406.

41. For a detailed account of this controversy, see the author's study, "The Shanghai-Hangchow-Ningpo Railway Loan of 1908," *Far Eastern Quarterly*, X, no. 3, February, 1951.

42. Sheng, "Telegrams," ch. 43, p. 5, Board of Commerce to Sheng, Sept. 8, 1904. THHL, KH, ch. 200, pp. 12–13, Meml. of the Board of Commerce, May 25, 1906; ch. 201, p. 4, Meml. of same, July 4, 1906. TCLCSL, KH, ch. 547, p. 13.

43. CCWCSL, KH, ch. 196, Sheng's Meml. on the history of the Shanghai-Hangchow-Ningpo negotiations, March 20, 1906.

44. Sheng, "Telegrams," ch. 43, p. 6, Sheng to the Board of Commerce, Sept. 10, 1904.

45. THHL, KH, ch. 203, p. 19, Meml. of Governor Chang Tseng-yang of Chekiang, Jan. 10, 1907.

46. CCWCSL, KH, ch. 189, pp. 23–24, quoted in dispatch from Foreign Ministry to Governor of Chekiang, May 4, 1905.

47. TCLCSL, KH, ch. 548, p. 16.

48. CCWCSL, KH, ch. 196, pp. 6–8, Sheng's meml. of March 20, 1906.

49. The remonstrances of Sir Ernest Satow and later of Sir John Jordan are recounted in THHL, KH, ch. 210, pp. 4–5, Meml. of Foreign Ministry, Oct. 20, 1907.

50. *North China Herald*, March 2, 1906, The London *Times* quoted in the *North China Herald*, August 17, 1906. *Parliamentary*

Debates, 4th series, vol. 178, p. 321, Walter Runciman's reply to question, July 15, 1907.

51. THHL, KH, ch. 210, pp. 4–5, Meml. of Foreign Ministry, Oct. 20, 1907.

52. *Ibid.,* p. 5.

53. CCWCSL, KH, ch. 206, pp. 13–15, Letter of the Railway Companies of Kiangsu and Chekiang to Governor-General Tuan-fang, Oct. 24, 1907.

54. THHL, KH, ch. 211, pp. 4–5, Edict of Nov. 12, 1907.

55. *Ibid.,* p. 1, Edict of Nov. 7, 1907.

56. *Ibid.,* pp. 10–12, Meml. of Foreign Ministry, Nov. 29, 1907.

57. Sheng, "Telegrams," ch. 50, p. 4, Tuan-fang to Sheng, Jan. 10, 1908; p. 6, same to same, Jan. 16, 1908.

58. CCWCSL, KH, ch. 211, p. 4, Meml. of Foreign Ministry, March 6, 1908; p. 11, Signatures; cf. MacMurray, I, 707.

59. MacMurray, I, 704. Arthur G. Coons, *The Foreign Public Debt of China* (Philadelphia, 1930), p. 32.

60. MacMurray, I, 707.

61. *Ibid.,* p. 702.

62. Sheng, "Memorials," ch. 16, Meml. in conjunction with Vice-President Wu Yü-sheng of the Board of Posts, Feb. 1911. Also see MacMurray, I, 711–716, for final use of the loan funds in 1914.

63. Kent, pp. 129–130. *British Parliamentary Papers,* Annual series no. 4108, "Report on the Foreign Trade of Shanghai for 1907," p. 8.

64. Lord Charles Beresford, *The Break Up of China* (London, 1899), contains good examples of British mercantile opinion on China.

65. China Gazette, *The Threatened Decline of Great Britain in China* (Shanghai, 1903), pp. 1, 2, 10, 59–61. W. W. Rockhill, Rockhill Papers, Mss., Harvard University, Valentine Chirol's letter to a Mr. Smalley, May 9, 1902. Chang, "Telegraphic Correspondence," ch. 65, pp. 17–18, Chang to Grand Council and Governor-General Yuan of Chihli, March 5, 1903. William L. Langer, *Diplomacy of Imperialism,* (New York, 1935), II, 700–710.

66. *North China Herald,* Oct. 15, Oct. 22, and Oct. 29, 1902.

67. Sir Robert Hart, Letters, Mss., Harvard University, Hart to C. Hannen, June 3, 1903.

68. R. J. Dillon, "Foreign Affairs," *Contemporary Review,* Sept., 1902, pp. 444–445. J. O. P. Bland, *Recent Events and Present Policies in China* (Philadelphia, 1912), pp. 268–269; cf. Pelcovits, chap. IX, *passim.*

69. W. Henderson, *L'Exportation des Capitaux Anglais Avant et Après la Guerre* (Paris, 1924), p. 57. R. C. K. Ensor, *England 1870–1914* (Oxford, 1944), pp. 372–376, 504–505. For Britain's share in China's foreign trade between 1902 and 1908, see BPP, annual series nos. 3092, 4152, 4386; for traditional free-trade arguments given in opposition to Joseph Chamberlain's idea of imperial preference, see articles in *Fortnightly Review*, 1903; and in *Contemporary Review*, 1903.

70. W. W. Willoughby, *Foreign Rights and Interests in China* (Baltimore, 1920), pp. 534–535.

71. Li Chien-nung, *Political History of China in the Past 100 Years* (Shanghai, 1947), I, 265.

72. CCWCSL, KH, ch. 206, pp. 13–15, Letter from the Railway Companies of Kiangsu and Chekiang to Governor-General Tuan-fang, Oct. 24, 1907.

73. Sir John N. Jordan, "Some Chinese I Have Known," *The Nineteenth Century*, Dec., 1920, p. 947. Rockhill Papers, Rockhill to Alfred Hippisley, July 6, 1906.

III: The Southern Trunk: First Stage

1. Chao Yung-seen, *Les Chemins de Fer Chinois* (Paris, 1938), pp. 193–194. Barclay Parsons, *Report on the Survey and Prospects of a Railway Between Hankow and Canton* (New York, 1899), p. 33.

2. Sheng Hsüan-huai, *Yü-tsai ts'un-kao,* "Telegraphic Memorials," ch. 1, p. 11, Meml. of April 9, 1898.

3. *British Parliamentary Papers, China no. 1 (1899)*, p. 344, Enclosure 1 in no. 459; p. 347, Enclosure 3 in no. 459. P. H. Kent, *Railway Enterprise in China* (London, 1907), pp. 115–116.

4. W. W. Rockhill, *Treaties and Conventions with or Concerning China and Korea, 1894–1904* (Washington, 1904), p. 273.

5. Sheng, "Telegrams," ch. 34, p. 4, Minister Wu at Washington to Sheng, Jan. 11, 1902. Kent, pp. 114, 116–117.

6. Sheng, "Telegrams," ch. 34, pp. 9–10, Sheng to Chang Chih-tung, Feb. 12, 1902.

7. Kent, pp. 115, 120. Parsons, *passim*.

8. Chang Chih-tung, *Chang Wen-hsiang-kung ch'üan-chi,* "Memorials," ch. 65, pp. 21–22, on the redemption of the Canton-Hankow Railway, Jan. 21, 1906.

9. *Ch'ing-chi wai-chiao shih-liao,* Kuang-hsü, ch. 186, p. 4, Telegram from Chang Chih-tung and Sheng Hsüan-huai to the Foreign

Ministry, Dec. 22, 1904; Chang, "Telegraphic Correspondence," ch. 72, p. 1, Minister Liang Ch'eng at Washington to Chang Chih-tung, July 29, 1905.

10. Chang, "Memorials," ch. 65, pp. 21–22, in the memorial already cited.

11. *Ibid.,* "Telegraphic Correspondence," ch. 69, p. 14, Chang Chih-tung to Acting Hunan Grain Taotai Chang at Shanghai, Sept. 6, 1904.

12. *Ibid.,* ch. 74, pp. 2–3, Chang chih-tung to Ch'ü Hung-chi at Peking, Oct. 30, 1905.

13. *Ibid.,* "Official Correspondence," ch. 33, p. 2, Chang's reply to application for river steam navigation by Wang Hsien-ch'ien and others, April 28, 1894. In 1908 Wang received special commendation for four of his scholarly works and was promoted to the rank of a Grand Secretary: see *Tung-hua hsü-lu,* Kuang-hsü, ch. 217, p. 1, Edict of July 1, 1908.

14. *Foreign Relations of the United States,* 1902, pp. 209–221, 1905, pp. 204–234. *Ta-Ch'ing li-ch'ao shih-lu,* Kuang-hsü, ch. 548, p. 1, imperial decree to the Grand Secretariat *re* anti-American agitation, Aug. 31, 1905. London *Times,* May 1, 1903, p. 3, on the attack on American and Japanese engineers. Sheng, "Telegrams," ch. 42, pp. 32–33, Governor Chang of Kwangtung to Sheng, Aug. 14, 1904.

15. TCLCSL, KH, ch. 547, p. 5, Edict to Governor-General Ch'ing Ch'un-hsüan of Liangkwang.

16. Recounted in Chang, "Memorials," ch. 66, pp. 2–3, Meml. of Jan. 21, 1906.

17. Chang, "Official Correspondence," ch. 20, pp. 22–24, Chang to the Financial Commissioner, Aug. 6, 1904.

18. Sheng, "Telegrams," ch. 43, p. 6, The Foreign Ministry to Sheng, Sept. 9, 1904; p. 9, Sheng to Foreign Ministry, Sept. 1, 1904. Chang, "Memorials," ch. 65, pp. 22–23, Meml. of Jan. 21, 1906.

19. Chang, "Telegraphic Correspondence," ch. 70, p. 14, Chang to Governor-General Ch'ing at Kueilin, Governor Chang at Canton, etc., Dec. 10, 1904; their reply Dec. 13, 1904; pp. 15–16, Chang to Governor Lu etc. at Changsha, Dec. 12, 1904; their reply Dec. 22, 1904. Since the present chapter was written, the following study has appeared: William R. Braisted, "The United States and the American China Development Company," *Far Eastern Quarterly,* XI, no. 2 (February, 1952), in which the treatment of the seeming contradictions in the Chinese official stand regarding the redemption of the Hankow-Canton concession is hampered by the non-use

of Chinese source materials. The present paragraphs on the Sheng-Chang dispute should help to clear up the point.

20. Sheng, "Telegrams," ch. 43, pp. 17–18, Sheng to the Foreign Ministry, Oct. 17, 1904; ch. 44, p. 10, Chang Chih-tung to Sheng, Jan. 17, 1905; p. 11, Sheng to Chang, Jan. 18, 1905; p. 12, Chang to Sheng, The Foreign Ministry and the Ministry of Commerce, Jan. 19, 1905.

21. Gentry and student protests were reported in Chang, "Telegrams," ch. 13, p. 24, Chang Chih-tung to the Grand Council and the Foreign Ministry, Aug. 12, 1905.

22. TCLCSL, KH, ch. 548, p. 5, Imperial decree to the Grand Councillors for tele-transmission to Chang Chih-tung. Sept. 3, 1905.

23. Chang, "Memorials," ch. 65, pp. 24–25, Meml. of Jan. 21, 1906; ch. 66, pp. 4–5, Meml. in reply to the Censor Huang Ch'ang-nien, same date. FRUS, 1905, p. 134.

24. FRUS, 1905, p. 132, Acting Secretary of State Loomis to Minister Rockhill at Peking, June 8, 1905, and Rockhill to the Secretary of State, June 14, 1905, with enclosure.

25. Chang, "Telegraphic Correspondence," ch. 71, p. 33, to Governor Tuan-fang, et al., at Changsha, June 11, 1905.

26. *Ibid.*, p. 29, Chang to Governor-General Ch'ing and Governor Chang of Canton, June 2, 1905.

27. Quoted by Chang Chih-tung in *ibid.*, "Memorials," ch. 65, pp. 25–26, Meml. of Jan. 21, 1906.

28. *Ibid.*, "Telegraphic Correspondence," ch. 71, p. 29, cited in note 26.

29. J. V. A. MacMurray, *Treaties and Agreements with and Concerning China*, I, 520–521. FRUS, 1905, p. 135, Loomis to Liang Ch'eng, Aug. 29, 1905.

30. Chang, "Memorials," ch. 65, p. 25; those demands probably refer to the request for conclusion of the Canton-Kowloon Railway loan. See below.

31. Chang, "Telegrams," ch. 13, p. 26, Chang to Grand Council and Foreign Ministry, Aug. 12, 1905. CCWCSL, KH, ch. 190, pp. 19–21, Chang to Grand Council, Aug. 13, 1905.

32. Chang, "Memorials," ch. 65, pp. 25, 27, Meml. of Jan. 21, 1906.

33. Chang, "Memorials," ch. 65, p. 25, *op. cit.*

34. CCWCSL, KH, ch. 191, p. 7, Chang Chih-tung to Grand Council, Sept. 2, 1905.

35. CCWCSL, KH, ch. 191, pp. 10–11, Chang Chih-tung to Grand Council, Sept. 4, 1905. Chang, "Telegraphic Correspondence," ch.

72, p. 25, Chang to Liang Cheng, Sept. 4, 1905; p. 26, Chang to Foreign Ministry, Sept. 5, 1905.

36. Chang, "Memorials," ch. 65, pp. 27–28, Meml. of Jan. 21, 1906.

37. MacMurray, I, 529, Articles II and III.

38. *Ibid.*, p. 529–530, Article VII.

39. *Ibid.*, p. 529, Article V, VI. (Chinese text of the agreement in CCWCSL, KH, ch. 197, pp. 13 ff.)

40. MacMurray, I, 550, note to no. 1905/10.

41. *Ibid.*, pp. 530–531, *loc. cit.*; cf. Chinese text of letter in CCWCSL, KH, ch. 197, pp. 10–11.

42. Chang, "Letters," ch. 8, Chang Chih-tung to Consul-General Fraser, Aug. 19, 1905.

43. Chang, "Telegraphic Correspondence," ch. 72, p. 19, Chang to Ch'ing, Aug. 31, 1905; p. 20, Ch'ing to Chang, Aug. 31, 1905; p. 28, Chang to Ch'ing, Sept. 10, 1905.

44. *Ibid.*, ch. 73, p. 30, Chang Chih-tung to Minister Yang and Commissioner of Hupeh Student Affairs Li, at Tokyo, Oct. 25, 1905. CCWCSL, KH, ch. 197, pp. 10–11, Chang Chih-tung's meml. on Hankow-Canton Railway loan negotiations, June 6, 1906.

45. *British Parliamentary Papers*, no. 3578 Annual series, "Report for the Year 1905 on the Foreign Trade of Hankow," p. 3. W. W. Rockhill, The Rockhill Papers, Mss., Harvard University, Alfred Hippisley to Rockhill, Sept. 6, 1905.

46. CCWCSL, KH, ch. 192, p. 5, Chang to the Foreign Ministry, Oct. 25, 1905. Chang, "Memorials," ch. 66, pp. 8–9, Meml. in reply to Huang Ch'ang-nien, Jan. 21, 1906.

47. Chang Chia-ao, *China's Struggle for Railways* (New York, 1943), p. 43.

48. CCWCSL, KH, ch. 200, p. 5, Meml. of the Foreign Ministry on the Canton-Kowloon Railway Loan, Feb. 7, 1907, shows the provisions of the preliminary agreement.

49. Nathan Pelcovits, *Old China Hands and the Foreign Office* (New York, 1948), p. 291. As the agreement was finally concluded, the division of profits between the Chinese and British sections was not made according to the proportion of mileage, which would have given China 76 per cent and the British 24 per cent of the intake, but on a 65:35 ratio. This situation was changed in 1934 to a 72:28 division. See Cheng Lin, *Chinese Railways Past and Present* (Shanghai, 1937), p. 101.

50. CCWCSL, KH, ch. 141, pp. 1–2, Meml. from Sheng Hsüan-huai on the Canton-Kowloon Railway, Nov. 19, 1899.

51. Chang, "Telegraphic Correspondence," ch. 72, pp. 3–4, Chang Chih-tung to Governor-General Ch'ing and Governor Chang at Canton, July 8, 1905.

52. Sheng, "Telegrams," ch. 45, p. 17, Sheng to Ch'ing and Governor Chang, July 15, 1905.

53. Chang, "Telegraphic Correspondence," ch. 72, Governor-General Ch'ing and Governor Chang to Chang Chih-tung, July 10, 1905.

54. Sheng, "Telegrams," ch. 45, p. 17, Governor-General Ch'ing and Governor Chang to Sheng Hsüan-huai and the Foreign Ministry, July 19, 1905.

55. Chang, "Telegraphic Correspondence," ch. 72, pp. 7–8, 8–9, telegrams from Governor-General Ch'ing and Governor Chang to Chang Chih-tung, July 25, July 31, 1905, resp. CCWCSL, KH, ch. 190, p. 16, Foreign Ministry's telegram to Chang Chih-tung, July 31, 1905.

56. Chang, "Telegraphic Correspondence," ch. 72, p. 7, Chang Chih-tung to the Governor-General and Governor of Canton, July 27, 1905.

57. Sheng, "Telegrams," ch. 45, p. 19, Governor-General Ch'ing of Canton to Sheng Hsüan-huai, Aug. 8, 1905.

58. Chang, "Letters," ch. 8, p. 17, Chang Chih-tung to Fraser, Aug. 19, 1905. Kent, pp. 173–174.

59. Chang, "Telegraphic Correspondence," ch. 72, p. 9, Governor-General Ch'ing and Governor Chang to Chang Chih-tung, July 31, 1905. CCWCSL, KH, ch. 200, p. 5, Meml. from Foreign Ministry, Feb. 7, 1907.

60. MacMurray, I, 615, 625.

61. *Ibid.*, p. 616, Article I; pp. 620–621, 622, Art. VII, XI.

62. *Ibid.*, pp. 619–620, Art. VI. CCWCSL, KH, ch. 200, p. 11, Meml. of the Foreign Ministry on the Canton-Kowloon Railway loan, Feb. 7, 1907.

63. Chao, p. 196.

64. Chang, "Telegraphic Correspondence," ch. 74, pp. 2–3, Chang Chih-tung to Board President Ch'ü Hung-Chi and others, Oct. 29, 1905.

65. Rockhill Papers, Satow to Rockhill, Dec. 22, 1904.

IV: The Southern Trunk: Second Stage

1. *Ch'ing-chi wai-chiao shih-liao,* Kuang-hsü, ch. 173, pp. 4–5, Meml. of Hsi-liang, July 11, 1903.

2. F. V. Field, *American Participation in the China Consortium* (Chicago, 1931), p. 34.

3. *Ta-Ch'ing li-ch'ao shih-lu*, Kuang-hsü, ch. 550, p. 16, Edict to Grand Councillors, Nov., 1905.

4. *Tung-hua hsü-lu*, Kuang-hsü, ch. 194, p. 1.

5. *North China Herald*, Nov. 24, 1905.

6. Chang Chih-tung, *Chang Wen-hsiang-kung ch'uan-chi*, "Telegraphic Correspondence," ch. 72, p. 2, Chang to Governor-General Ch'ing and Governor Chang of Canton, July 6, 1905.

7. *Ibid.*, pp. 1–2, Chang to Governor-General Ch'ing, Sept. 29, 1905.

8. *Ibid.*, ch. 74, p. 24, Chang to Taotai Wang Pin-en of Canton, Jan 27, 1906.

9. Chang, "Memorials," ch. 66, p. 16, Meml. of Jan. 21, 1906.

10. *Ibid.*, pp. 18–19, item 6 in Meml. of Feb. 6, 1906. TCLCSL, KH, ch. 548, p. 6, Edict, Sept. 4, 1905.

11. Given in Chang, "Memorials," ch. 66, pp. 18–21.

12. Chang, "Telegraphic Correspondence," ch. 74, pp. 25–26, Chang to Governor-General Ch'ing of Canton, Jan. 28, 1906.

13. *Ibid.*, ch. 75, p. 5, Chang to Governor-General Ch'ing and others, March 15, 1906.

14. *Ibid.*, ch. 74, p. 29, Chang to the merchants Yang Jui-pin et al. at Hongkong, Feb. 4, 1906.

15. THHL, KH, ch. 205, p. 16, Meml. of the Board of Posts, July 6, 1907.

16. *Ibid.*, pp. 16–17.

17. *Ibid.*, *loc. cit.* Board of Posts and Communications, *Second Statistical Account of Communications* (*1908*), ch. 1, "Important Facts on the Hankow-Canton Railway"; cf. P. H. Kent, *Railway Enterprise in China* (London, 1907), p. 120.

18. THHL, KH, ch. 201, p. 17, Meml. of Board of Commerce, Aug. 9, 1906.

19. Chang, "Memorials," ch. 68, pp. 9–10, Meml. of January 11, 1907.

20. *Ibid.*, pp. 15–16, same Memorial.

21. TCLCSL, KH, ch. 592, p. 9, Meml. of Governor-General Ch'en K'uei-lung, June 27, 1908. Board of Posts and Communications, *op. cit.*, ch. 1.

22. Board of Posts and Communications, *op. cit.*, ch. 1.

23. THHL, KH, ch. 192, p. 10, Meml. of Governor Hsi-liang, April 15, 1905.

24. Chang, "Memorials," ch. 67, p. 12, Meml. of Aug. 21, 1906.

25. Chang, "Telegraphic Correspondence," ch. 72, pp. 30–31, Commissioner Yü to President Ch'ü, Sept. 25, 1905.

26. CCWCSL, KH, ch. 192, pp. 25–26, telegram, Chang Chih-tung to the Foreign Ministry, Oct. 25, 1905. Chang, "Telegraphic Correspondence," ch. 74, p. 7, Chang to Hsi-liang, Nov. 3, 1905.

27. Chang, "Telegraphic Correspondence," ch. 76, p. 13, Chang to Governor-General Ch'ing at Canton and Governor P'ang at Changsha, Oct. 31, 1906.

28. CCWCSL, KH, ch. 174, pp. 18–19, note from French Consul to Hsi-liang, Sept. 20, 1903; *ibid.*, ch. 184, p. 16, note from Sir Ernest Satow to the Foreign Ministry, Sept. 21, 1904. *Foreign Relations of the United States,* 1909, p. 147, enclosure 2 in Huntington Wilson to Ambassador Reid, June 3, 1909.

29. FRUS, 1909, p. 146, enclosure 1 in *loc. cit.*

30. Chang, "Telegraphic Correspondence," ch. 77, pp. 3–4, Chang to the Board of Posts and Communications, April 1, 1907; ch. 79, p. 9, Chang to Yuan Shih-k'ai, Aug. 2, 1907; p. 10, Yuan to Chang, Aug. 5, 1907.

31. *Ibid.*, ch. 77, p. 4, *op. cit.*

32. Recounted in *ibid.*, ch. 80, p. 8, Chang to Fraser, Oct. 3, 1908.

33. *Ch'ing-shih kao,* "Biographies," ch. 224.

34. FRUS, 1908, p. 208. Chang, "Memorials," ch. 70, p. 27, Draft Meml. no. 1, 1909.

35. Chang, "Telegraphic Correspondence," ch. 80, p. 6, Chang to Governor-General Ch'en at Wuchang and the Taotais of the (Hunan) Railway Co., Aug. 6, 1908.

36. John G. Reid, *Manchu Abdication and the Powers* (Berkeley, 1935), p. 24; cf. Herbert Croly, *Willard Straight* (New York, 1924), pp. 288–289.

37. Chang, "Telegraphic Correspondence," ch. 78, pp. 3–4, to Liang Tun-yen (of the Foreign Ministry), June 24, 1907.

38. *Ibid., loc. cit.*

39. *Ibid.*, ch. 80, pp. 7–8, Chang's telegram to Governor-General Ch'en at Changsha, Sept. 21, 1908; pp. 32–33, Chang's telegram to Governor Ch'ing and the Hunan Railway Co., May 19, 1909.

40. *Ibid.*, p. 8, Chang to Fraser, Oct. 3, 1908; pp. 8–9, same to same, Oct. 10, 1908.

41. *Ibid.*, p. 8, telegram of Oct. 3, 1908.

42. TCLCSL, Hsüan-t'ung, ch. 3, p. 1, Meml. of Chang Chih-tung with Imperial Rescript, Nov. 24, 1908. Chang, "Telegraphic Correspondence," ch. 80, p. 11, Chang to Governor-General Ch'en, Nov. 27, 1908.

43. Sheng, "Telegrams," ch. 51, p. 12, Sheng to Chang, Dec. 18, 1908.

44. Chang, "Memorials," ch. 70, p. 28, Draft Meml. no. 1, 1909.

45. *Ibid.*, p. 34, Draft Meml. no. 1, 1909.

46. Willard D. Straight, *China's Loan Negotiations* (Worcester, 1912), pp. 16–17.

47. Chang, "Memorials," ch. 70, p. 33, Draft Meml. no. 2, 1909; "Telegraphic Correspondence," ch. 80, p. 21, Chang to Fraser, Feb. 14, 1909.

48. Chang, "Telegraphic Correspondence," ch. 80, pp. 20–21, Chang to Fraser, Feb. 14, 1909.

49. German Minister Rex's report from Peking, March 12, 1909, cited in Reid, p. 24.

50. Chang, "Memorials," ch. 70, pp. 28–29, Draft Meml. no. 1; pp. 33–35, Draft Meml. no. 2.

51. Chang, "Letters," ch. 8, pp. 23–24, Chang to Liang Tun-yen, Feb. 20, 1909.

52. J. O. P. Bland, *Recent Events and Present Policies in China* (Philadelphia, 1912), p. 275.

53. Chang, "Letters," ch. 8, pp. 25–26, Chang to Liang Tun-yen, March 8, 1909.

54. Chang, "Memorials," ch. 70, pp. 34–35, Draft Meml. no. 2, 1909.

55. *Ibid.*, p. 29, Draft Meml. no. 1, 1909; cf. Reid, p. 25.

56. *Die Grosse Politik Der Europaïsche Kabinette*, XXXII, 5, Bülow to William II, May 14, 1909; p. 20, enclosure in no. 11622.

57. CCWCSL, HT, ch. 3, p. 50.

58. Chang, "Memorials," ch. 70, pp. 29–30, Draft Meml. no. 1, 1909; "Telegraphic Correspondence," ch. 80, pp. 29–30, Chang to Hukuang Governor-General Chen and Hunan Governor Ch'ing, May 19, 1909; cf. J. V. A. MacMurray, ed., *Treaties and Agreements with and Concerning China*, I, 880 ff., note 1 to no. 1911/5, for text of the preliminary agreement.

59. GP, XXXII, 6, Rex to Bülow, May 21, 1909.

60. *Ibid.*, p. 5, Bülow to William II, May 15, 1909.

61. *Ibid.*, pp. 6–7, Rex to Bülow, May 21, 1909.

62. G. P. Gooch and H. Temperley, *British Documents on the Origins of the War*, VII, 133, enclosure in no. 148.

63. *Ibid., loc. cit.*

64. MacMurray, I, 832; cf. Reid, p. 25, *re* "Charles Addis." Chang Chia-ao, *China's Struggle for Railway Development* (New York,

1943), pp. 13–14, 93, show that "Sir Charles Addis" in 1936 was a representative of British interests *re* Chinese railway loans.

65. *Parliamentary Debates,* new series, vol. 2, pp. 752, 1201.

66. *Ibid.,* vol. 3, p. 1505; vol. 4, p. 11.

67. *Ibid.,* vol. 4, pp. 395–396; vol. 10, pp. 6–7.

68. *Ibid.,* vol. 8, p. 724.

69. *Ibid.,* vol. 10, p. 550.

70. *Ibid.,* 5th series, vol. 16, pp. 1221–1222.

71. Chang, "Memorials," ch. 70, p. 35, Draft Meml. no. 2, 1909.

72. Bland, pp. 271–276, 280–281, 289–290.

73. Croly, pp. 290–292. Reid, pp. 37, 38–39.

74. W. W. Rockhill, Diary of 1909, Mss, Harvard University, entry for May 25, 1909. Chang, "Letters," ch. 8, pp. 6–7, Chang to the Foreign Ministry, June 6, 1909.

75. Cf. texts of the 1903 and 1904 notes, FRUS, 1909, pp. 155–156.

76. *Ibid.,* p. 154. Reid, p. 38.

77. Croly, pp. 281–284, 286, 290.

78. FRUS, 1909, p. 165, Ambassador Bryce to Secretary Knox, June 24, 1909; Reid, pp. 42–46, 47–49, 52–53. Chang, "Letters," ch. 8, pp. 8–9, Chang to Foreign Ministry, July 13, 1909; pp. 10–11, same to same, July 30, 1909; p. 26, Chang to Liang Tun-yen, Aug. 26, 1909.

79. Rockhill Papers, J. S. Pearson (of the International Banking Corp., New York) to Rockhill, Feb. 25, 1909.

80. FRUS, 1909, pp. 147–148, encls. 3 and 5 in H. Wilson to Reid, June 6, 1909; pp. 149–150, memorandum of Grey to Reid, June 8, 1909; p. 160, Bryce to Knox, June 14, 1909; p. 165, Bryce to Knox, June 24, 1909; p. 167, Grey to Reid, June 23, 1909; cf. Rockhill Papers, J. R. Carter (of the U.S. Embassy in London) to Rockhill, Dec. 8, 1905.

81. FRUS, 1909, pp. 169–170, instruction from Acting Secretary H. Wilson to Ambassador Reid for information of the American group, July 9, 1909; cf. Willard Straight, *The Politics of Chinese Finance* (Boston, 1913), p. 6.

82. FRUS, 1910, p. 279. Reid, p. 232.

83. *Ibid.,* pp. 208–209, Grey's memorandum to Reid, Oct. 20, 1909; cf. GP, XXXII, 29–30.

84. FRUS 1909 and 1910 contain detailed information on this mileage controversy.

85. FRUS, 1910, p. 270, Grey to Reid, Jan. 3, 1910; cf. pp. 277–278, Grey to Reid, April 11, 1910.

86. *Ibid.*, pp. 280–281, memorandum of agreement between bankers on May 23, 1910; pp. 285–286, Grey to Reid, June 7, 1910.

87. Reid, pp. 78, 133.

88. Field, pp. 44–45; 48–49. The text of the Quadruple Agreement is in MacMurray, I, 828–832, 833–835, note to no. 1910/5.

89. THHL, KH, ch. 216, pp. 19–20, Edict of June 25, 1908.

90. Chang, "Telegraphic Correspondence," ch. 80, p. 3, Chang to Railway Manager Liang Chen-tung in Hongkong, Aug. 6, 1908; pp. 4–6, Chang to Governor-General Ch'en and railway officials (of Hunan and Hupeh), same day.

91. Chang, "Memorials," ch. 70, p. 26, Meml. of Oct. 4, 1909. FRUS, 1909, p. 154, Fletcher to Knox, June 9, 1909.

92. Chang, "Telegraphic Correspondence," ch. 80, pp. 12–13, Chang to Governor Ch'ing at Changsha, and Wang of the Railway Co., Dec. 3, 1908.

93. TCLCSL, HT, ch. 24, pp. 7–8, Meml. of Censor Huang Jui-lin, Oct. 1909; ch. 25, pp. 24–25, Meml. of Hunan Governor Ch'ing Ch'un-hsüan, Nov. 23, 1909.

94. *Ibid.*, HT, ch. 8, pp. 8–9, Meml. of Board of Posts, Feb. 27, 1909. FRUS, 1909, pp. 157–158, Fletcher to Knox, June 10, 1909.

95. CCWCSL, HT, ch. 13, pp. 1–3, 3–4, identical notes from Ministers of Great Britain, France, and Germany, to Foreign Ministry, Feb. 12 and April 22, 1910; p. 3, note from the U.S. Minister to Foreign Ministry, April 22, 1910. *Parl. Deb.*, 5th series, vol. 19, p. 816, Sir Edward Grey, June 28, 1910.

96. Texts of these notes are in FRUS, 1910, pp. 288–291. CCWCSL, HT, ch. 15, pp. 45–47; ch. 16, pp. 38–42; ch. 17, pp. 38–40; ch. 18, pp. 9–10; ch. 20, p. 22.

97. CCWCSL, HT, ch. 3, p. 50, text of Hukuang Preliminary Agreement.

98. *Ibid.*, ch. 17, pp. 38–40, identical notes to the Foreign Ministry from Ministers of Britain, France, Germany, and the U.S., Oct. 22, 1910.

99. FRUS, 1910, p. 290, U.S. Minister Calhoun to Secretary Knox, Oct. 5, 1910 (paraphrase).

100. CCWCSL, HT, ch. 20, p. 27, Meml. of Board of Posts, May 9, 1911.

101. *Ibid.*, pp. 27 ff., *op. cit.*, pp. 36 ff., joint Meml. of Board of Posts and of Foreign Ministry, May 20, 1911; cf. FRUS, 1912, pp. 87–88.

102. MacMurray, I, 868–877, text of the agreement.

103. *Ibid.*, pp. 873–874, Art. XV; p. 876, Art. XIX.

104. *Ibid.*, pp. 874–875, Art. XVII.

105. Sheng, "Telegrams," ch. 54, pp. 28, 29, 30, 34.

106. *Ibid.*, "Memorials," ch. 17, pp. 1–3, Meml. on railway policy, May, 1911. TCLCSL, HT, ch. 52, pp. 28–30, Edict of May 10, 1911.

107. TCLCSL, HT, ch. 53, pp. 7–8, Edict to the Grand Secretariat, May 22, 1911.

108. Sheng, "Memorials," ch. 17, pp. 31–32, Meml. on the nationalization of Hankow-Canton-Szechuan Railways, June, 1911.

109. It was estimated that in Kwangtung where some construction had taken place, the total mileage built was only 128 *li* (43 miles) in 1910; the average cost per *li* was $57,000. See TCLCSL, HT, ch. 24, pp. 23–24. Sheng, "Memorials," ch. 17, p. 32.

110. Sheng, "Memorials," ch. 17, p. 27; "Telegrams," ch. 54, p. 7, Governor Yang of Hunan to Sheng, May 15, 1911; p. 23, Sheng to Governor-General Jui-cheng of Wuchang, Governor Yang of Hunan, Governor-General Wang of Szechuan, Governor-General Chang of Canton, May 31, 1911; p. 27, Governor-General Wang to Sheng, June 3, 1911; ch. 55, p. 5, Sheng to Governor-General Chang, June 18, 1911. TCLCSL, HT, ch. 54, p. 21, Edict to Grand Secretariat, June 14, 1911.

111. Tseng K'un-hua, *Chung-kuo t'ieh-lu shih* [History of Chinese Railways], (Peking, 1924), pp. 114–115.

112. *Ibid.*, pp. 115–116.

113. Mougton C. Hsu, *Railway Problem in China* (New York, 1915), pp. 117–118.

V: Projects and Conflicts in North China

1. P. H. Kent, *Railway Enterprise in China* (London, 1907), pp. 61–64.

2. J. V. A. MacMurray, *Treaties and Agreements with or Concerning China*, I, 331.

3. *Ibid.*, p. 332.

4. *Ch'ing-chi wai-chiao shih-liao*, Kuang-hsü, ch. 155, p. 17, Meml. from the Foreign Ministry for reconsideration of the agreement on the North China Railway with England, May 17, 1902.

5. MacMurray, I, 335, dispatch of Prince Ch'ing to M. Lessar, June 23, 1902.

6. MacMurray, I, 334.

7. *Ibid.*, *loc. cit.*

8. CCWCSL, KH, ch. 155, pp. 17–18, Meml. from the Foreign Ministry, May 17, 1902.

9. MacMurray, I, 207–208, note to no. 1899/5; p. 330, in note 1 to no. 1902/3; cf. *Documents Diplomatiques Français, 2e* ser., I, 167–168, 202–203. G. P. Gooch and H. Temperly, *British Documents on the Origins of the War,* II, 38–39.

10. Li Hung-chang, *Li Wen-chung-kung ch'üan-chi,* "Telegrams," ch. 33, p. 29, Li to the Field Grand Council at Sian, March 19, 1901.

11. MacMurray, I, 335–336, note 1 to no. 1902/4.

12. Kent, pp. 70–73. *Tung-hua hsü-lu,* Kuang-hsü, ch. 196, pp. 12–13, Meml. of Yuan Shih-k'ai and others, Oct. 23, 1905. *Ta-Ch'ing li-ch'ao shih-lu,* Hsuan-t'ung, ch. 19, p. 22, Meml. of Board of Posts, Sept. 7, 1909.

13. CCWCSL, KH, ch. 155, pp. 2–4, telegram of the Chargé of the Chinese Legation at Brussels to the Foreign Ministry, May 9, 1902; pp. 4–5, Meml. of the Foreign Ministry, May 10, 1902; ch. 157, p. 9, telegram from Sheng Hsüan-huai to Foreign Ministry, June 9, 1902.

14. Chao Yung-seen, *Les Chemins de Fer Chinois* (Paris, 1938), pp. 76–77; cf. CCWCSL, KH, ch. 189, p. 1, Meml. of Sheng Hsüan-huai, April 23, 1905.

15. A comparison of the English and Chinese texts of the agreement points to the above conclusion. W. W. Rockhill, *Treaties,* p. 309. MacMurray, I, 134. CCWCSL, KH, ch. 132, p. 5, Honan Mining Agreement.

16. *British Parliamentary Papers, China no. 1 (1899),* pp. 216, 241. CCWCSL, KH, ch. 189, p. 1, Sheng's Meml., *op. cit.*

17. CCWCSL, KH, ch. 152, p. 14, Sheng's telegram to Foreign Ministry, Feb. 27, 1902.

18. Sheng Hsüan-huai, *Yü-tsai ts'un-kao,* "Telegrams," ch. 34, p. 12, Sheng to Chang Chih-tung, March 2, 1902. Chang Chih-tung, *Chang Wen-hsiang-kung ch'uan-chi,* "Telegraphic Correspondence," ch. 57, pp. 16–17, Chang to Sheng, March 1, 1902. CCWCSL, KH, ch. 189, p. 2, Sheng's Meml. of April 23, 1905.

19. CCWCSL, KH, ch. 172, p. 33, Telegram, Sheng to the Foreign Ministry, June 7, 1903.

20. London *Times,* April 8, 1903, p. 5; cf. Sheng, "Telegrams," ch. 34, p. 12, Sheng to Chang Chih-tung, March 2, 1902.

21. CCWCSL, KH, ch. 172, p. 33, Telegram, Sheng to Foreign Ministry, June 8, 1903.

22. T. W. Overlach, *Foreign Financial Control in China* (New York, 1919), p. 67.

23. CCWCSL, KH, ch. 155, p. 3, telegram of Governor Hsi-liang to Foreign Ministry, May 9, 1902; p. 4, telegram of Foreign Ministry to Hsi-liang, May 10, 1902. Cheng Lin, *Chinese Railways Past and Present* (Shanghai, 1937), p. 111.

24. CCWCSL, KH, ch. 157, p. 16, Foreign Ministry to Hsi-liang, June 13, 1902.

25. *Ibid.*, ch. 172, p. 32, telegram of Sheng to Foreign Ministry, June 7, 1903.

26. *Ibid., loc. cit.;* ch. 181, p. 14, telegram of same to same, Jan. 28, 1904.

27. Pai Shou-yi, *Chung-kuo chiao-t'ung shih* [History of Chinese Communications], (Shanghai, 1937), pp. 173, 175–176.

28. Sheng, "Telegrams," ch. 42, p. 2, Sheng to the Foreign Ministry and Board of Commerce, and to Governor Chang at Taiyuan, June 15, 1904; ch. 43, p. 14, Sheng to Foreign Ministry, Oct. 7, 1904. CCWCSL, KH, ch. 189, pp. 2–3, Meml. of Sheng, April 23, 1905.

29. Cheng, p. 111. Sheng, "Telegrams," ch. 44, p. 12, Sheng to Foreign Ministry, Jan. 26, 1905.

30. See Sheng's Meml. of April 23, 1905. Kent, pp. 126–127.

31. Texts of the agreements in MacMurray, I, 506–511, 512–515.

32. *Ibid.*, p. 515–516, note 1 to no. 1905/5; pp. 698–700. Board of Posts and Communications, *Second Statistical Account of Communications,* 1908, ch. 1, "The Toakou-Chinghua Railway."

33. See preceding chapter.

34. The southern terminus of the line was eventually changed from Chinkiang to Pukou, in order the better to connect with the Shanghai-Nanking Railway across the Yangtse River. Kent, p. 148.

35. Sheng, "Memorials," ch. 12, p. 9, joint Meml. of Sheng, Yuan Shih-k'ai, and Chang Chih-tung, Oct. 14, 1905; pp. 10–11, joint Meml. of Sheng and T'ang Shao-i, November, 1905.

36. CCWCSL, KH, ch. 173, p. 3, telegram of Von Mumm to Foreign Ministry, July 7, 1903. THHL, ch. 213, p. 4, Meml. of Chang Chih-tung et al., Jan. 13, 1908. Kent, p. 152.

37. THHL, KH, ch. 186, p. 12, Meml. of Yuan Shih-kai et al., May 4, 1904; ch. 187, pp. 1–2, Meml. of Foreign Ministry, May 15, 1904. Kent, p. 144.

38. Kent, p. 152. By this time the Chinese Central Railways Co.

had replaced the British and Chinese Corporation as the British concessionaire.

39. Chang, "Telegraphic Correspondence," ch. 77, p. 2, Chang to President Lu Ch'uan-lin (of the Board of Works) et al., March 12, 1907; p. 6, Chang to Lu, April 14, 1907.

40. TCLCSL, KH, ch. 570, p. 9, Edict to Grand Councillors, March 29, 1907.

41. See Kent, pp. 141–144.

42. Chang, "Telegraphic Correspondence," ch. 77, pp. 10–11, Yuan Shih-kai to Chang Chih-tung, May 3, 1907.

43. *Ibid.*, p. 12, Chang to President Lu, April 30, 1907.

44. *Ibid.*, p. 15, Chang to Yuan, May 13, 1907.

45. *Ibid.*, pp. 15–16, Yuan to Chang, May 15, 1907.

46. *Ibid.*, p. 17, Chang to Yuan, May 20, 1907.

47. *Ibid.*, pp. 23–24, Chang to Secretary Li Tz'u-hsiang and members of the Three Provinces Association, May 24, 1907.

48. *Ibid.*, pp. 15–16, Chang to Yuan, May 13, 1907; Yuan to Chang, May 15, 1907; pp. 19, 21–22, Chang to Yuan, May 20, 1907. This was a year before Chang and Bland broke up their relations over the Hukuang Railways loan.

49. *Ibid.*, ch. 78, pp. 6–7, Chang to Yuan and Liang Tun-yen, July 6, 1907.

50. *Ibid.*, ch. 79, p. 12, same to same, Aug. 4, 1907. THHL, ch. 213, p. 4, Meml. of Chang Chih-tung et al., Jan. 14, 1908.

51. Kent, p. 152.

52. Chang, "Telegraphic Correspondence," ch. 78, pp. 16–17, Chang to President Lu and Kao Tse-yu, July 19, 1907. THHL, KH, ch. 123, p. 4, Meml. of Chang Chih-tung et al., Jan. 14, 1908.

53. MacMurray, I, 690, Art. XVII; cf. pp. 695–696, Arts. 18 and 19, note to no. 1908/1.

54. *Foreign Relations of the United States*, 1908, p. 200, Chargé H. P. Fletcher to Secretary of State, Jan. 17, 1908.

55. MacMurray, I, 688, Art. XXII; p. 691, Art. XX; cf. p. 695, Art. 14; p. 697, Art. 30, note to no. 1908/1.

56. *Ibid.*, p. 686, Art. IX; pp. 694–695, Art. 9, note to no. 1908/1.

57. Overlach, pp. 154–155.

58. Chang, "Telegraphic Correspondence," ch. 77, p. 19, Chang to Yuan, May 20, 1907.

59. *Ibid.*, ch. 78, p. 7, Chang to Yuan and Liang Tun-yen, July 6, 1907.

60. *Ibid.*, ch. 77, pp. 20–21, Chang to Yuan, May 20, 1907.

61. THHL, KH, ch. 213, pp. 15–16, Meml. of Chang Chih-tung et al., Jan. 26, 1908.

62. *Ibid.*, ch. 215, pp. 8–9, Meml. of Lü Hai-huan, Chang Chih-tung, and Yuan Shih-kai, April 9, 1908.

63. London *Times*, July 1, 1909, p. 7.

64. CCWCSL, Hsuan-t'ung, ch. 17, pp. 1, 14, Memls. of Hsü Shih-ch'ang (new Director of the Tientsin-Pukou Railway), Sept. 22, Sept. 28, 1910. MacMurray, I, 814 ff. The last loan transactions for this railway took place in 1912. See MacMurray, I, 824, 825, 826–827.

65. The length of the line was 1,319 kilometers (about 824 miles); see Cheng, p. 107.

66. Sheng, "Memorials," ch. 12, p. 11, joint Meml. of Sheng and T'ang, Nov., 1905.

67. *Ibid.*, ch. 11, pp. 17–18, confidential Meml. on the reorganization of the Peking-Hankow Railway, June, 1905.

68. *Ibid.*, ch. 12, pp. 24–27, Meml. on the redemption of railway loan, March, 1906. THHL, ch. 205, p. 12, Meml. of Board of Posts. April 30, 1907.

69. Sheng, "Memorials," ch. 18, p. 27.

70. Board of Posts and Communications, *Second Statistical Account of Communications* (Peking, 1911), ch. 1, "Important Facts on the Peking-Hankow Railway."

71. THHL, ch. 220, pp. 12–13, Meml. of the Board of Posts, Oct. 8, 1908.

72. *Ibid.*, p. 13; cf. FRUS, 1908, p. 203, Edict of Oct. 8, 1908.

73. For the text of the agreement see MacMurray, I, 747–751.

74. FRUS, 1908, p. 204.

75. MacMurray, I, 748.

76. FRUS, 1908, p. 204.

77. CCWCSL, KH, ch. 218, pp. 25–26, Meml. of Board of Posts, Jan. 6, 1909.

78. W. W. Rockhill, Rockhill Papers, Mss., Harvard University, J. R. Carter to Rockhill, Dec. 8, 1905.

79. Cheng, pp. 39–40, 43, 83.

80. MacMurray, I, 752.

81. *Ibid.*, p. 756, note to no. 1908/13. The terms of this loan were satisfactory to the Chinese authorities, and it was reported they were endeavoring to contract other similar loans, creating keen competition among foreign bankers; see FRUS, 1910, p. 291.

82. MacMurray, I, 758.

VI: Plans for the Northeastern Provinces

1. For proposals of development plans, see Chang Chih-tung, *Chang Wen-hsiang-kung Ch'uan-chi,* "Telegrams," ch. 13, p. 21, Chang to Grand Council, April 28, 1905; "Telegraphic Correspondence," ch. 71, pp. 41–42, Yuan Shih-kai to Chang, July 1, 1905. *Ch'ing-chi wai-chiao shih-liao,* Kuang-hsü, ch. 195, p. 20, General Ch'eng Te-ch'üan of Heilungkiang's Meml., Jan. 10, 1906. For a general view of Chinese policy in this period see Hsü Shu-hsi, *China's Political Entity* (New York, 1926), chapter 6, "The Reconstruction of Manchuria."

2. *North China Herald,* April 12, 1906, p. 93.

3. W. W. Rockhill, Rockhill Papers, Mss., Harvard University, Rockhill to Theodore Roosevelt, July 7, 1905.

4. *Ibid.,* W. D. Straight to Rockhill, Mukden, April 1, 1907. CCWCSL, KH, ch. 207, *passim.*

5. H. B. Morse, Letterbooks, V, Mss., Harvard University, p. 416, Morse to Sir Robert Hart, Feb. 5, 1907.

6. *Tung-hua hsü-lu,* Kuang-hsü, ch. 205, pp. 10–11, Meml. of the Board of Posts, April 30, 1907; p. 17, Imperial decree, May 8, 1907. CCWCSL, KH, ch. 188, p. 4, Imperial rescript to Ch'eng Te-ch'üan's Meml., April 5, 1905.

7. Herbert Croly, *Willard Straight* (New York, 1924), pp. 242–243.

8. CCWCSL, KH, ch. 207, pp. 10–11, letter from Hsü Shih-ch'ang and T'ang Shao-i to the Foreign Ministry, Nov. 20, 1907. The other two sections of the projected railway were Fakumen-Taonan, and Taonan-Tsitsihar.

9. CCWCSL, KH, ch. 207, pp. 9–10.

10. *Ibid.,* p. 11.

11. CCWCSL, KH, ch. 205, p. 1, paraphrased in the dispatch from the Foreign Ministry to the Japanese Chargé d'Affaires, Sept. 10, 1907.

12. Seiji Hishida, *Japan Among the Great Powers* (New York, 1940), pp. 181–184.

13. CCWCSL, KH, ch. 205, p. 1, Foreign Ministry to the Japanese Chargé, Sept. 10, 1907.

14. *Ibid.,* ch. 205, p. 3, Foreign Ministry's note to Japanese Chargé, Oct. 17, 1907; ch. 208, pp. 8–9, Hsü Shih-ch'ang to Foreign Ministry, Dec. 12, 1907; ch. 214, pp. 1–2, Foreign Ministry to Japanese Ministry, May 6, 1908. C. Walter Young, *Japan's Special*

Position in Manchuria (Baltimore, 1931), pp. 110–114, 115–119.

15. CCWCSL, KH, ch. 207, pp. 19–20, telegram of Hsü and T'ang to Foreign Ministry, Nov. 30, 1907; ch. 208, pp. 8–9, Hsü, *op. cit.*

16. *Ibid.*, ch. 214, pp. 2–3, telegram of Foreign Ministry to Minister Li Ching-fang at London, May 7, 1908.

17. Young, pp. 119–121. P. H. Kent, *Railway Enterprise in China* (London, 1907), pp. 74–75.

18. CCWCSL, KH, ch. 214, pp. 20–22, Japanese Chargé to Chinese Foreign Ministry, June 27, 1908.

19. *Ibid.*, Hsuan-t'ung, ch. 1, p. 5, Foreign Ministry's telegram to Hsü, Jan. 28, 1909; pp. 5–6, Hsü's telegram to Foreign Ministry, Jan. 30, 1909.

20. *Ta-Ch'ing li-ch'ao shih-lu*, Hsuan-t'ung, ch. 10, p. 59, Meml. of Hsü shih-ch'ang, April 19, 1909.

21. Young, pp. 114–115, note 11. Croly, p. 252.

22. *Parliamentary Debates*, new series, II, 1045–1046, McKinnon Wood, March 17, 1909; pp. 1444–1445, Sir William Bull and McKinnon Wood, March 22, 1909.

23. G. P. Gooch and H. Temperley, *British Documents on the Origin of the War*, VIII, 467, MacDonald to Grey, May 13, 1909.

24. Young, p. 109, note 5.

25. *American Journal of International Law*, Supplement (New York, 1910), IV, 130.

26. When prospects for the Fakumen Railway were dim, Hsü suggested that a line might be planned from Chinchow or some other point to Taonan and Tsitsihar: CCWCSL, HT, ch. 1, p. 6, Hsü to Foreign Ministry, Jan. 30, 1909.

27. *Ch'ing-shih kao*, "Biographies," ch. 236, p. 2.

28. *British Parliamentary Papers, China no. 2 (1940)*, pp. 55 ff. A. L. P. Dennis, *Adventures in American Diplomacy 1896–1906* (New York, 1928), p. 376, App. B.

29. Dennis, p. 365.

30. Rockhill Papers, Minister Griscom to Secretary of State, July 29, 1905; Griscom to Rockhill, November 6, 1905. *Foreign Relations of the United States*, 1905, I, 171–172, 174, Chargé Wilson at Tokyo to Secretary of State, March 15 and 28, 1906.

31. Croly, pp. 169–170, 200, 204–207, 226, 232 ff. Rockhill Papers, Straight to Rockhill, May 2 and May 24, 1907.

32. George Kennan, *E. H. Harriman* (Boston, 1922) II, 24–25.

33. *Ibid.*, pp. 1–3, 13–15, 21. Croly, p. 297.

34. Maurice Paléologue, *Un Tournant de la Politique Mon-*

diale, 1904–1906 (Paris, 1934), pp. 419, 435–436. Chang Chung-fu, *The Anglo-Japanese Alliance* (Baltimore, 1931), p. 212.

35. W. W. Rockhill, Diary of 1908, Mss., Harvard University, April 28, 1908.

36. Croly, pp. 263–266.

37. *Ibid.*, pp. 271–272, 275–276, 278, 296–297, 301.

38. See trade returns in *British Parliamentary Papers, Diplomatic and Consular Report*, no. 4108, Annual series, "Report for the year 1907 on the Trade of Shanghai"; no. 4191, ". . . 1908 . . . Newchuang"; no. 4366, ". . . 1908 . . . China"; no. 4556, ". . . 1909 . . . China"; no. 4751, ". . . 1910 . . . China."

39. Rockhill, Diary of 1908, April 29, 1909; May 2, 3, 4, 1909.

40. CCWCSL, HT, ch. 9, pp. 4–5, 6, Minister Li Ching-fang at London to Foreign Ministry, Sept. 16, 1909, and enclosing Pauling's letter to Counsellor Yamasa of the Japanese Embassy, Aug. 18, 1909.

41. *Ibid.*, pp. 5, 6–7, Pauling to Li Ching-fang, Aug. 19, 1909, and Précis of Pauling's article in the London *Times*.

42. *Ibid.*, ch. 7, pp. 47–48, Foreign Ministry to the Board of Posts, Aug. 25, 1909.

43. *Ibid.*, ch. 10, pp. 4–5, Hsi-liang to Foreign Ministry, Oct. 28, 1909.

44. *Ibid.*, ch. 6, pp. 3–4, Gov. Chou Shu-mo to Foreign Ministry, Aug. 1, 1909.

45. *Ibid.*, ch. 9, p. 33, Hsi-liang and Ch'eng Te-ch'üan to the Grand Council, Oct. 2, 1909.

46. *Ibid.*, pp. 33–34. Croly, p. 302.

47. FRUS, 1910, pp. 231–232.

48. J. V. A. MacMurray, *Treaties and Agreements with and Concerning China*, I, 801.

49. *Ibid.*, p. 801, Art. IV.

50. *Ibid.*, Arts. I, V.

51. FRUS, 1910, pp. 233–234, enclosure in Fletcher to Knox, Oct. 7, 1909.

52. CCWCSL, HT, ch. 10, p. 4, Foreign Ministry's letter to Korostovetz, Oct. 24, 1909.

53. *Ibid.*, pp. 42–44, Meml. of the Foreign Ministry, Board of Finance, and Board of Posts and Communications, Nov. 24, 1909.

54. TCLCSL, HT, ch. 23, pp. 20–21, Meml. of Hsi-liang, December 23, 1909, with rescript.

55. FRUS, 1910, p. 234, Knox's memorandum for transmission to the British Foreign Office, Nov. 6, 1909.

56. *Ibid., loc. cit.*

57. *Ibid.*, pp. 234–235.

58. Croly, pp. 306–308. H. F. Wright, "Philander C. Knox," *American Secretaries of State and Their Policies*, S. F. Bemis, ed. (New York, 1929), IX, 303–304, 318; Knox was greatly influenced by his own long experience as railway legislator.

59. FRUS, 1910, pp. 235–236, Grey to Reid, Nov. 25, 1909.

60. Rockhill Papers, Knox to Rockhill, Nov. 10, 1909.

61. FRUS, 1910, pp. 236, 237.

62. John Gilbert Reid, *The Manchu Abdication and the Powers* (Berkeley, 1935), pp. 67, 71. Rockhill papers, Rockhill to Knox, Nov. 13, 1910. B. de Siebert, *Entente Diplomacy and the World (1909–1914)* (New York, 1921), p. 14, Izvolsky to the Ambassador at London, Jan. 13, 1910.

63. Reid, pp. 93–94; *Die Grosse Politik der Europaïsche Kabinette*, XXXII, 84, App. to no. 11682.

64. FRUS, 1910, p. 241, enclosure in Fletcher to Knox, Dec. 28, 1909. TCLCSL, HT, ch. 11, pp. 10–11, Fletcher's note to the Foreign Ministry, Jan. 1, 1910.

65. FRUS, 1910, pp. 237, 242. Reid, pp. 74–75.

66. FRUS, 1910, p. 242. G. P. XXXII, 71.

67. GP, XXXII, 87–88, Mumm to Bethmann-Hollweg, Jan. 2, 1910.

68. *Ibid.*, p. 66, Bethmann-Hollweg to William II, Dec. 23, 1909; p. 79, Mumm to Bethmann-Hollweg, Jan. 8, 1910; p. 91, Radolin to Bethmann-Hollweg, Jan. 15, 1910. Reid, p. 98.

69. GP, XXXII, 88, Mumm to Bethmann-Hollweg, Jan. 2, 1910, reporting a conversation with Sir Claude MacDonald.

70. FRUS, 1910, p. 245, Fletcher to Knox, and Knox to Fletcher, Jan. 7, 1910.

71. CCWCSL, HT, ch. 12, pp. 19–21, Foreign Ministry's confidential letter to the Boards of Finance and of Posts, Jan. 12, 1910.

72. *Ibid.*, p. 24, Board of Posts to Foreign Ministry, Jan. 16, 1910.

73. *Ibid.*, pp. 35–37, joint Meml. of the Foreign Ministry, Boards of Finance and of Posts, Jan. 20, 1910.

74. FRUS, 1910, pp. 252–253, Fletcher to Knox, Jan. 24, 1910; p. 255, Prince Ch'ing to Fletcher, Jan. 27, 1910.

75. Reid, p. 102.

76. CCWCSL, HT, ch. 12, p. 47, note from Ijuin to Foreign Ministry, Jan. 31, 1910.

77. *Ibid.*, Korostovetz to Foreign Ministry, Feb. 2, 1910; pp. 47–48, same to same, Feb. 4, 1910, and Feb. 8, 1910, transmitting Rus-

sian notes to the U.S. government. FRUS, 1910, p. 225, Memorandum from Russian Embassy, Feb. 2, 1910; pp. 225–226, same to same, Feb. 4, 1910.

78. FRUS, 1910, p. 257, Fletcher to Knox, Feb. 7, 1910.

79. Reid, p. 104. GP, XXXII, 96 Bernstorff to German Foreign Office, received Feb. 18, 1910; p. 99, Mumm's telegram, Feb. 12, 1910; pp. 103–104, Mumm to Bethmann-Hollweg, Feb. 16, 1910. CCWCSL, HT, ch. 12, p. 49, note from French Minister to the Foreign Ministry, Feb. 18, 1910. T. F. Millard, *Our Eastern Question* (New York, 1916), p. 20.

80. GP, XXXII, 101, Rex to Bethmann-Hollweg, Feb. 14, 1910. Croly, pp. 307, 310–311.

81. FRUS, 1910, pp. 261–262, Memorandum from Russian Embassy to State Department, Feb. 24, 1910. CCWCSL, HT, ch. 12, pp. 49–50, note from Russian Minister to Foreign Ministry, March 6, 1910.

82. FRUS, 1910, pp. 264–265, Memorandum from State Department to Russian Embassy, April 18, 1910.

83. CCWCSL, HT, ch. 12, pp. 48–49, note from Ijuin to Foreign Ministry, Feb. 14, 1910. Cf. GP, XXXII, 101, Rex to Bethmann-Hollweg, Feb. 14, 1910.

84. CCWCSL, HT, ch. 13, p. 34, Hsi-liang et al. to Foreign Ministry, March 12, 1910; p. 35, Foreign Ministry to Hsi-liang et al., March 14, 1910; Hsi-liang and Ch'eng Te-ch'üan to Foreign Ministry, March 15, 1910.

85. Reid, p. 133. Edward H. Zabriskie, *American-Russian Rivalry in the Far East* (Philadelphia, 1946), pp. 161–168.

86. CCWCSL, HT, ch. 15, pp. 16–17, telegram of Hsi-liang to the Grand Council, the Foreign Ministry, the Boards of Finance and of Posts, June 22, 1910; p. 17, letter from Foreign Ministry to Hsi-liang, June 26, 1910.

87. E. B. Price, *The Russo-Japanese Treaties of 1907–1916 Concerning Manchuria and Mongolia* (Baltimore, 1933), pp. 42–43. Zabriskie, pp. 169–171.

88. Price, pp. 44–45.

89. G. P. Gooch and H. Temperley, ed., *British Documents on the Origins of the War,* VIII, 483–485, MacDonald to Grey, July 2, 1910.

90. CCWCSL, HT, ch. 15, p. 18, Hsi-liang to Grand Council, July 7, 1910.

91. Sh'eng Hsüan-huai, *Yü-tsai ts'un-kao,* "Telegrams," ch. 53,

p. 6, Sheng to Yao Fu-tung for transmission to Prince Tsai-hsun, July 30, 1910; p. 7, Sheng to Hsi-liang, August 1, 1910.

92. CCWCSL, HT, ch. 16, p. 7, letter of Governor Chou Shu-mo of Heilungkiang to Foreign Ministry, Aug. 12, 1910; p. 16, telegram of Minister Chang Yin-t'ang at Washington to Foreign Ministry, Aug. 21, 1910.

93. Rockhill Papers, Straight's letter to Rockhill, Dec. 11, 1910; Memorandum by Lord ffrench, Feb. 1, 1911.

Conclusion

1. *North China Herald,* Aug. 24, 1906.

2. Sheng Hsüan-huai, *Yü-tsai ts'un-kao,* "Telegrams," ch. 53, p. 7, Sheng to Hsi-liang, Aug. 1, 1910.

3. Li Chien-nung, *Chung-kuo Ching-pai-nien cheng-chih shih* [Political History of China in the Past 100 Years] (Shanghai, 1947), I, 235–241, 269.

4. G. P. Gooch and Harold Temperley, *British Documents on the Origins of the War,* III, 407, App. to no. 445, Memorandum of Eyre Crowe, Jan. 1, 1907. This lengthy document (pp. 397–431) with endorsements and minutes from members of the Foreign Office gives a good summary of England's contemporary relations with France and Germany.

5. Sir Edward Grey, *Speeches on Foreign Affairs 1904–1914* (London, 1931), pp. 26–32, 38.

6. From an article in *Osaka Mainichi,* March, 1916, quoted in A. M. Pooley, *Japan's Foreign Policies* (London, 1920), p. 29.

7. *Parliamentary Debates,* 5th series, vol. 17, pp. 1376–1390, Grey, June 16, 1910.

8. Lionel M. Gelber, *The Rise of Anglo-American Friendship* (New York, 1938), pp. 167–168. T. F. Millard, *Our Eastern Question* (New York, 1916), pp. 6–11. Herbert Croly, *Willard Straight* (New York, 1924), pp. 333–334. Edward H. Zabriskie, *American-Russian Rivalry in the Far East* (Philadelphia, 1946), chapter 6.

9. Chang Chia-ao, *China's Struggle for Railway Development* (New York, 1943), pp. 39, 86–88.

Glossary of Chinese Names*

Board of Posts and Communications 郵傳部

Bureau of Railways and Mines 路鑛總局

Chang Chih-tung 張之洞

Chang Tseng-yang 張曾敭

Chang Wen-hsiang-kung ch'üan-chi 張文襄公全集

Ch'en Kung-lu 陳恭祿

Ch'en Pao-chen 陳寶琛

Ch'eng Te-ch'üan 程德全

Chiao-t'ung Bank 交通銀行

Ch'ing-chi wai-chiao shih-liao 清季外交史料

Ch'ing Ch'un-hsüan 岑春煊

Ch'ing-i-pao ch'üan-pien 清議報全編

Ch'ing-shih-kao 清史稿

* This list contains the more important Chinese names, terms, and authors and titles of works written in Chinese. It does not include geographical names.

Ch'ing-tai t'ai-hsi shu-ju wo-kuo chih ching-chi ssu-hsiang 清代泰西輸入我國之經濟思想

Chou Fu 周馥

Chou Fu-hsien 周福銑

Chou Shu-mo 周樹模

Ch'ü Hung-chi 瞿鴻璣

Chung-kuo chiao-t'ung shih 中國交通史

Chung-kuo chin-pai-nien cheng-chih shih 中國近百年政治史

Chung-kuo chin-tai shih 中國近代史

Chung-kuo fen-sheng hsin-t'u 中國分省新圖

Chung-kuo li-tai chiang-yü-t'u 中國歷代疆域圖

Chung-kuo mien-yeh chih fa-chan 中國棉業之發展

Chung-kuo t'ieh-lu shih 中國鉄路史

Director-General of the (Imperial Chinese) Railway Administration 督辦鉄路大臣

Field Grand Council 行在軍機處

Governor-General of Hukuang 湖廣總督

Governor-General of Liangkiang 兩江總督

Governor-General of Liangkwang 兩廣總督

Hsi-liang 錫良

Hsü Shih-ch'ang 徐世昌

Hsü Yin-k'uei 許應騤

ho-k'ou **(a term in the 1898 Peking Syndicate mining and railway agreement.)** 河口

Hu Yü-fen 胡燏棻

I-k'uang (Prince Ch'ing) 奕劻

Kung Chao-yuan 龔照瑗

Li Chien-nung 李劍農

Li Ching-fang 李經芳

Li Hung-chang 李鴻章

Li Wen-chung-kung ch'üan-chi 李文忠公全集

Liang Ch'eng 梁誠

Liang Tun-yen 梁敦彥

Liu K'un-i 劉坤一

Lu Ch'uan-lin 鹿傳霖

Lü Hai-huan 呂海寰

Pai Shou-i 白壽彝

Prince Ch'ing (see I-k'uang) 慶親王

Sheng Hsüan-huai 盛宣懷

Ta-Ch'ing Bank 大清銀行

Ta-Ch'ing li-ch'ao shih-lu 大清歷朝實錄

T'ang Ch'ing-tseng 唐慶增

T'ang Shao-i 唐紹儀

T'ang Shou-ch'ien 湯壽潛

Ting, V. K. (Ting Wen-chiang) 丁文江

Tseng K'un-hua 曾鯤化

Tseng Shih-ying 曾世英

Tsungli (ko-kuo shih-wu) yamen 總理各國事務衙門

Tuan-fang 端方

Tung-hua hsü-lu 東華續錄

T'ung Shih-heng 童世亨

Wang Hsien-ch'ien 王先謙

Wong T'ung-ho 翁同龢

Wong Wen-kung-kung jih-chi 翁文恭公日記

Wu Yü-sheng 吳郁生

Yen Chung-p'ing 嚴中平

Yü Shao-k'ang 余肇康

Yü-tsai ts'un-kao 愚齋存稿

Yuan Shih-k'ai 袁世凱

Yuan Shu-hsün 袁樹勛

Bibliography

I. Primary Sources

A. Documents in Chinese

Board of Posts and Communications. *Ti-erh-tz'u chiao-t'ung t'ung-chi-piao* [Second Statistical Account of Communications] 1908. Compiled by the Statistical Office of the Board of Posts and Communications, Peking, 1911.
This publication consists of official data on the work of the Board in 1908. A section is devoted to railways, including their brief history. Useful for information on the general state of existing railways.

Chang Chih-tung. *Chang Wen-hsiang-kung ch'üan-chi* [The Complete Works of Chang Chih-tung], Wang Shu-t'ung, ed. Pub. by Wen-hua-tsai Book Store, Peiping, 1928.
This collection of Chang's papers contains much important information on Chinese history during the decades when Chang was active. Particularly useful are letters and telegrams that he exchanged with other officials. The following categories in the collection have been used in the present study: "Memorials," "Telegraphic Memorials," "Telegraphic Correspondence," "Letters," and "Official Correspondence."

Ch'ing-chi wai-chiao shih-liao [Documents on the History of Foreign Relations in Late Ch'ing Dynasty], with index. Wang T'ao-fu and Wang Liang, editors and compilers. Peiping, 1932–1933.
Included are official correspondence, notes, memorials, decrees, and texts of agreements, arranged chronologically, on subjects that involved relations with foreign powers during the reigns of Kuang-hsü and Hsüan-t'ung. Railway affairs are treated as a part of diplomatic relations.

Li Hung-chang. *Li Wen-chung-kung ch'üan-chi* [The Complete Works of Li Hung-chang], Wu Ju-lun, ed. Commercial Press, Shanghai, 1921.
The collection also contains memorials and correspondence of this leading official. Useful source material for the years before 1902.

Sheng Hsüan-huai. *Yü-tsai ts'un-kao* [Collected Papers of Sheng Hsüan-huai]. Pub. by Sau-pu-lou [name of Sheng family studio?], n.p., 1930[?].

Valuable for material regarding the introduction of new industrial undertakings into China. Include much information on railway negotiations. These categories of the papers have been used in this study: "Memorials," "Telegraphic Memorials," "Telegrams," and "Board of Posts and Communications Memorials."

Ta-ch'ing li-ch'ao shih-lu [Records of the Reigns of Ch'ing Dynasty], compiled by the Department of State of "Manchokuo." Pub. in Tokyo, 1937.

A large compilation of official documents and records of the Manchu dynasty, beginning with the pre-conquest reigns down to the Republican Revolution. Used for the present study are volumes for the reigns of Kuang-hsü and Hsuan-t'ung; many of the documents have been abridged and are printed in digest form but are reliable on the whole. Contains some material not found in other collections.

Tung-hua hsü-lu [Tung-hua Documents, Continued], compiled by Chu Shou-p'eng. T'u-shu chi-ch'eng Publishing Co., Shanghai, 1909.

Government documents in the reign of Kuang-hsü. Still useful, although part of the contents of this collection can be found also in later compilations.

B. WORKS IN ENGLISH AND OTHER LANGUAGES

American Society of International Law. *American Journal of International Law*, Supplement IV, 1910, "Official Documents," New York, 1910.

This supplement contains texts of legalistically significant international agreements concluded in 1909.

Beresford, Lord Charles. *The Break Up of China*. Harper, New York, 1899.

Beresford's report to the Associated Chambers of Commerce of Great Britain, in whose behalf he went to China in 1898–1899. The account is notable for its vivid reflection of contemporary British opinion regarding international rivalry in China.

Bishop, J. B. *Theodore Roosevelt and His Times Shown in His Own Letters*, I. Scribner's, New York, 1920.

British Parliamentary Papers, Diplomatic and Consular Reports Annual Series, China.

These consular reports contain commercial statistics drawn from data furnished by the local Imperial Maritime Customs stations, and are helpful sources of information on the conditions of China's foreign trade. The particular numbers cited in the text are shown in the following list.

Number	*Subject*	*Year*
Cd. 3092	China	1902
3578	Hankow	1905
3641	Newchuang	1905
3801	Hankow	1906
3817	Chinkiang	1906
3837	Newchuang	1906
3898	Canton	1906
3916	Tientsin	1906
3943	China	1906
3992	Antung	1907
4000	Newchuang	1907
4011	Chinkiang	1907
4015	Hankow	1907
4108	Shanghai	1907
4152	China	1907
4191	Newchuang	1908
4386	China	1908
4556	China	1909
4751	China	1910

British Parliamentary Papers, State Papers.

China No. 2 (1898), "Despatch from Her Majesty's Minister at Peking, forwarding Copies of Notes Exchanged with the Chinese Government respecting the Nonalienation of the Yangtse Region."

China No. 1 (1899), "Correspondence respecting the Affairs of China."

China No. 2 (1904), "Correspondence respecting the Russian Occupation of Manchuria and Newchuang."

Material on the battle for concessions is contained in *China No. 1 (1899)*; the other items do not include documents that bear directly on the railway question.

Corporation of Foreign Bondholders, *Annual Reports*, No. 33 (1905–1906). Council House, London, 1907.

Documents Diplomatiques Français, Relatifs aux Origines de la

Guerre de 1914 (1871–1914), 2e série (1901–1911), T. VIII, Imprimerie Nationale, Paris, 1938.
This volume is of slight direct use to the study of Chinese railway loans. The second series of these documents stopped in 1906.

Eckardstein, Hermann von. *Ten Years at the Court of St. James's.* T. Butterworth, London, 1921.
Of little use to the present study.

Foreign Relations of the United States, Government Printing Office, Washington, D.C.
Use for this study are volumes for 1905 (I), 1906, 1907, 1908, 1909, 1910, 1912. A substantial supplement to the other documentary material, especially in cases of railways that involved the United States.

Gérard, Auguste. *Mémoires: La Vie d'un Diplomat sous la Troisième République.* Libraire Plon, Paris, 1928.
Gives some background to the railway problem.

Gooch, G. P., and H. Temperley, editors. *British Documents on the Origins of the War.* H. M. Stationery Office, London, 1927 ff.
Vol. III, "The Testing of the Entente, 1904–1906."
IV, "The Anglo-Russian Rapprochement, 1903–1907."
VII, "The Agadir Crisis."
VIII, "Arbitration, Neutrality, and Security."
IX, "Balkan Wars, Part I, Prelude to War."
These documents give much help in clarifying the diplomatic issues that were involved in the railway loans.

Grey, Sir Edward. *Speeches on Foreign Affairs 1904–1914,* Paul Knaplund, ed. Allen and Unwin, London, 1931.

Hayashi, Count Tadasu. *The Secret Memoirs of Count Tadasu Hayashi,* Andrew M. Pooley, ed. Putnam, New York, 1915.
The evolution of Hayashi's policies are explained and justified in these memoirs.

Lepsius, J., A. M. Bartholdy, and F. Thimme, editors. *Die Grosse Politik der Europaïsche Kabinette, 1871–1914.* Berlin, 1924 ff.
Band XIV, I, "Weltpolitische Rivalitäten," Part I. Band XXXII, "Die Mächte und Ostasien 1909–1914."
Volume 32 is especially useful respecting Chinese railway politics in those years.

MacMurray, John V. A., ed. *Treaties and Agreements with and concerning China,* I, "Manchu Period, 1894–1911." Oxford University Press, New York, 1921.
Included here are most of the important documents, both offi-

cial and non-official, that touch on China's relations with foreign powers. A good collection.

Paleologue, Maurice. *Un Grand Tournant de la Politique Mondiale, 1904–1906*. Libraire Plon, Paris, 1934.

The French diplomat's journal of three years to the eve of the Anglo-Russian Entente. Preoccupied with indictment of the Kaiser's policy.

The Parliamentary Debates, H. M. Stationery Office, London.

4th series, vols. 167, 178, 185.

5th series, vols. 14, 15, 16, 17, 19.

New series, vols. 2, 3, 4, 8, 10.

Material on Chinese railways is scanty, but some of the questions and speeches throw light on British policy.

Parsons, W. Barclay. *Report on the Survey and Prospects of a Railway Between Hankow and Canton.* Privately published, New York. 1899.

A first-hand report by the head of the engineering group that surveyed the route for the American China Development Company.

Pauling, George. *The Chronicles of a Contractor: Being the Autobiography of the late George Pauling,* David Buchan, ed. Constable, London, 1926.

Contains only one chapter on the company's China ventures; material on the Manchurian projects very thin.

Rockhill, William Woodville, compiler. *Treaties and Conventions with or concerning China and Korea, 1894–1904.* Government Printing Office, Washington, D.C., 1904.

Contains some documents not included in MacMurray.

Siebert, Benno de. *Entente Diplomacy and the World (1909–1914).* Edited, arranged and annotated by George de Schreiner. Knickerbocker, New York, 1921.

These documents are useful for a comprehensive view of Entente diplomacy. Chapter I points to the importance of the Far East in that diplomatic system.

Straight, Willard D. *China's Loan Negotiations,* Address at Clark University, Worcester, November, 1912.

—— *The Politics of Chinese Finance,* Address at East Asiatic Society of Boston, May, 1913.

These addresses were made with a view to popularizing American loans to the Chinese government.

C. MANUSCRIPTS

Hart, Sir Robert. Letters and Papers of Sir Robert Hart (in two folio envelopes), donated by H. B. Morse, 1931. Houghton Library, Harvard University.
These letters cover the years from the 1860's to 1912, dealing chiefly with the Imperial Maritimes Customs and with then current problems in China. Morse had used the most important parts in vols. II and III of his *International Relations of the Chinese Empire*.

Morse, Hosea Ballou. Letterbooks of H. B. Morse while Commissioner of Customs, 1886–1907. Houghton Library, Harvard University.
A collection of letters that give insight into the conditions of the Imperial Maritime Customs, and the contemporary situation in China as seen through foreign eyes.

Rockhill, William Woodville. The Papers of William Woodville Rockhill, presented by Courtland Hoppin, 1947. Houghton Library, Harvard University.

—— Diary, January 1 to December 31, 1908; Diary, January 1 to December 31, 1909.
Rockhill was U.S. Minister at Peking 1905–1909, and Ambassador to Russia, 1909–1911. These diaries are brief notations that record his personal opinions, contain little important new factual information.

—— Rockhill Papers.
An interesting collection of personal and official papers, manuscripts of articles, etc., numbering 3,082 items. Of these 3,007 are letters to and from Rockhill, ca. 1882 to 1914. Many of the items are valuable for the study of Far Eastern affairs.

II. Secondary Sources

A. WORKS IN CHINESE

Chao Feng-t'ien. *Wan-Ch'ing wu-shih-nien ching-chi ssu-hsiang shih* [Economic Thought during the Last Fifty Years of the Ch'ing Period]. Yenching Journal of Chinese Studies, monograph series no. 18, Peiping, 1933.

Ch'en Kung-lu. *Chung-kuo chin-tai shih* [Modern Chinese History]. 2 vols. Commercial Press, Shanghai, 1946 ed.

Cheng Ho-sheng. *Chin-shih Chung-hsi shih-jih tui-chao piao* [Comparative Calendars for Modern Chinese and Western History]. National Institute of Compilation and Translation, Nanking, 1934.

Ch'ing-shih-kao [Draft History of Ch'ing Dynasty]. Pub. by Bureau of Ch'ing History, Chao Erh-hsün, director. Peking, 1927.

Li Chien-nung. *Chung-kuo chin-pai-nien cheng-chih shih* [The Political History of China in the Past 100 Years]. 2 vols. Commercial Press, Shanghai, 1947.

Liu Hsiung-hsiang. *Ch'ing-chi shih-nien chih lien-O cheng-ts'e* [A Decade of Pro-Russian Policy in the Late Ch'ing Dynasty]. San-yu Book Co., Chungking, 1943.

Pai Shou-i *Chung-kuo chiao-t'ung shih* [History of Chinese Communications]. Commercial Press, Shanghai, 1937.

T'ang Ch'ing-tseng. "Ch'ing-tai T'ai-hsi shu-ju wo-kuo chih ching-chi ssu-hsiang" [The Introduction of Western Economic Thought into China during Ch'ing Dynasty], *Chung-kuo ching-chi wen-t'i* [Economic Problems of China]. Review of the Chinese Economic Society, no. 1, Commercial Press, Shanghai, 1929.

Ting, V. K., Wong Wen-hao and Tseng Shih-ying. *Chung-kuo fen-sheng hsin-t'u* [New Atlas of China], 6th ad revised ed. Pub. by Shen-pao, Shanghai, 1948.

Tseng K'un-hua. *Chung-kuo t'ieh-lu shih* [History of Chinese Railways]. Yenching Publishing Co., Peking, 1924.

T'ung Shih-heng. *Chung-kuo li-tai chiang-yü t'u* [Historical Atlas of China]. Commercial Press, Shanghai, 1926 ed.

Yen Chung-p'ing. *Chung-kuo mien-yeh chih fa-chan* [The Development of the Chinese Cotton Industry]. Commercial Press, Chungking, 1943.

B. WORKS IN ENGLISH AND OTHER LANGUAGES

Bailey, Thomas A. *Theodore Roosevelt and the Japanese-American Crisis*. Stanford University Press, Stanford, 1934.

Bau, Joshua M. C. *The Foreign Relations of China*. Revell, New York, 1922.

Bemis, Samuel Flagg, ed. *American Secretaries of State and Their Policies,* IX. Knopf, New York, 1929.

Used for this study is H. F. Wright's account of Philander C. Knox which is a favorable portrait of the man.

Bland, J. O. P., and E. Backhouse. *China under the Empress Dowager*. Lippincott, Philadelphia, 1910.

Deeply prejudiced in favor of the Empress Dowager's regime.

Bland, J. O. P. *Recent Events and Present Policies in China.* Lippincott, Philadelphia, 1912.
Interesting as an example of the dissatisfaction of an "old China hand" with the British policy in China.

Brandenburg, Erich. *From Bismarck to the World War.* Translated by Annie Elizabeth Adams. Oxford University Press, 1927.

Brunnert, H. S., and V. V. Hagelstrom. *Present Day Political Organization of China.* Revised by N. Th. Kolessoff; translated from the Russian by A. Beltchenko and E. E. Moran. Kelly and Walsh, Shanghai, 1912.

Cameron, Meribeth. *The Reform Movement in China 1898–1912.* Stanford University Publications, University Series, History, Economics, and Political Science, Vol. III, No. 1, Stanford, 1931.

Chang Chia-ao (Chang Kia-ngau). *China's Struggle for Railroad Development.* Day, New York, 1943.
The major portion of this book deals with Chinese railway problems from the 1930's to 1942.

Chang Chung-fu. *The Anglo-Japanese Alliance.* Johns Hopkins Press, Baltimore, 1933.

Chao Yung-seen. *Les Chemins de Fer Chinois.* University of Paris, Paris, 1938.

Cheng Lin. *The Chinese Railways Past and Present.* China United Press, Shanghai, 1937.

Clyde, Paul Herbert. *International Rivalries in Manchuria.* Ohio State University Press, Columbus, 1926.

Coons, Arthur Gardiner. *The Foreign Public Debt of China.* University of Pennsylvania Thesis in Economics, Philadelphia, 1930.

Croly, Herbert. *Willard Straight.* MacMillan, New York, 1924.
A substantial biography containing much information and analysis of U.S. interests in the Far East.

Dennis, A. L. P. *Adventures in American Diplomacy.* Dutton, New York, 1928.

—— *The Anglo-Japanese Alliance.* University of California Press, Berkeley, 1923.

Earle, Edward Mead. *Turkey, the Great Powers, and the Bagdad Railway.* MacMillan, New York, 1923.

Ensor, R. C. K. *England 1870–1914.* Clarendon Press, Oxford, 1944.

Fairbank, John K. *The United States and China.* Harvard University Press, Cambridge, 1948.

Fei Hsiao-t'ung. "Peasantry and Gentry, An Interpretation of Chinese Social Structure," *American Journal of Sociology,* LII, No. 1, July, 1946.

Feis, Herbert. *Europe, the World's Banker 1870–1914.* Yale University Press, New Haven, 1931.

Field, F. V. *American Participation in the China Consortium.* University of Chicago, for the Institute of Pacific Relations, Chicago, 1931.

Gelber, Lionel M. *The Rise of Anglo-American Friendship: A Study in World Politics 1898–1906.* Oxford University Press, New York, 1938.

Gulley, Elsie E. *Joseph Chamberlain and English Social Politics.* Columbia University Press, New York, 1926.

Hart, Sir Robert. *These from the Land of Sinim: Essay on the Chinese Question.* Chapman and Hall, London, 1901.

Henderson, W. *L'Exportation des Capitaux Anglais Avant et Après la Guerre.* University of Paris, Paris, 1924.

Hishida, Seiji. *Japan Among the Great Powers.* Longmans, Green, New York, 1940.

Hobson, C. K. *The Export of Capital.* Macmillan, New York, 1914.

Hsu, Mongton C. *Railway Problems in China.* Columbia University Studies in History, Economics, and Public Law, Vol. 66, No. 2, Columbia University, New York, 1915.

Hsu Shuhsi. *China and Her Political Entity.* Oxford University Press, New York, 1926.

Hummel, Arthur W. *Eminent Chinese of the Ch'ing Period.* 2 vols. Government Printing Office, Washington, D.C., 1943.

Jordan, Sir John N. "Some Chinese I Have Known," *Nineteenth Century,* December, 1920 (Vol. 88[2]).

Kennan, George. *E. H. Harriman.* 2 vols. Houghton Mifflin, Boston, 1920.

Kent, Percy Horace. *Railway Enterprise in China.* Edward Arnold, London, 1907.

Langer, William L. *The Diplomacy of Imperialism 1890–1902.* 2 vols., II. Knopf, New York, 1935.

Lee, Sir Sidney. *King Edward VII.* 2 vols., II, "The Reign." Macmillan, New York, 1927.

Levy, Marion J., and Shih Kuo-heng. *The Rise of the Modern Chinese Business Class.* Institute of Pacific Relations, New York, 1949.

McCordock, R. Stanley. *British Far Eastern Policy 1894–1900.* Columbia University Press, New York, 1931.

Millard, Thomas F. *Our Eastern Question*. Century, New York, 1916.

Morse, Hosea Ballou. *The Trade and Administration of China*. Kelly and Walsh, Shanghai, 1921.

Overlach, T. W. *Foreign Financial Control in China*. MacMillan, New York, 1919.

Pelcovits, Nathan. *Old China Hands and the Foreign Office*. King's Crown Press, for the Institute of Pacific Relations, New York, 1948.

Pooley, Andrew M. *Japan's Foreign Policies*. Allen and Unwin, London, 1920.

Price, Ernest Batson. *The Russo-Japanese Treaties of 1907–1916 Concerning Manchuria and Mongolia*. Johns Hopkins Press, Baltimore, 1933.

Reid, John Gilbert. *The Manchu Abdication and the Powers*. California University Press, Berkeley, 1935.

Remer, C. F. *Foreign Investments in China*. *MacMillan*, New York, 1933.

—— *The Foreign Trade of China*. Commercial Press, Shanghai, 1926.

Sargent, A. J. *Anglo-Chinese Commerce and Diplomacy*. Clarendon Press, Oxford, 1907.

Smith, C. A. Middleton. *The British in China and Far Eastern Trade*. Constable, London, 1920.

Thorner, Daniel. *Investment in Empire*. University of Pennsylvania Press, Philadelphia, 1950.

Willoughby, Westel W. *Foreign Rights and Interests in China*. Johns Hopkins Press, Baltimore, 1920.

Wright, Stanley F. *The Collection and Disposal of the Maritime and Native Customs Revenue Since the Revolution of 1911*. China: Maritime Customs, II, special series no. 41, Shanghai, 1927.

Young, C. Walter. *The International Relations of Manchuria*. University of Chicago Press, for the Institute of Pacific Relations, Chicago, 1929.

—— *Japan's Special Position in Manchuria*. Johns Hopkins Press, Baltimore, 1931.

Zabriskie, Edward H. *American-Russian Rivalry in the Far East: A Study in Diplomacy and Politics, 1895–1914*. University of Pennsylvania Press, Philadelphia, 1946.

C. NEWSPAPERS AND PERIODICALS

The China Gazette
The Threatened Decline of Great Britain in China, reprinted from the China Gazette, March, 1903.

The *Chinese Recorder and Missionary Journal,* published monthly by the American Presbyterian Press, Shanghai.

Ch'ing-i-pao ch'üan-pien (Complete Collection of the *Ch'ing-i-pao*), Yokohama, undated [1900's].

Contemporary Review

Fortnightly Review

The *North China Herald* (weekly edition of the *North China Daily News*), Shanghai.

The *Times* of London

Index

Bei Fragen zur Produktsicherheit wenden Sie sich bitte an:
If you have any questions regarding product safety,
please contact:

Walter de Gruyter GmbH
Genthiner Straße 13
10785 Berlin
productsafety@degruyterbrill.com